EXPORTING RECONSTRUCTION

RECONSTRUCTION RECONSIDERED

Series Editors
J. Brent Morris and Hilary N. Green

EXPORTING RECONSTRUCTION

ULYSSES S. GRANT AND A NEW EMPIRE OF LIBERTY

RYAN P. SEMMES

© 2024 University of South Carolina

Published by the University of South Carolina Press
Columbia, South Carolina 29208

uscpress.com

Printed in the United States of America

Library of Congress Cataloging-in-Publication Data can be found
at http://catalog.loc.gov/

ISBN: 978-1-64336-517-6 (hardcover)
ISBN: 978-1-64336-518-3 (ebook)

For Alisa

*Thank you for everything you do
and have done for me.*

CONTENTS

Acknowledgments ix

Introduction 1

Part I
RECONSTRUCTION ON THE GLOBAL STAGE

Chapter 1. Exporting Republicanism beyond the South 25

Chapter 2. Challenges to Annexation 47

Chapter 3. Annexation's Failure 69

Part II
RECONSTRUCTION IN THE AMERICAN WEST

Chapter 4. Reconstructing the "Uncivilized" 101

Chapter 5. Native Americans, Chinese Immigrants, and Civilization 121

Conclusion 147

Notes 155

Bibliography 185

Index 207

ACKNOWLEDGMENTS

This book represents nearly ten years of work discovering what Allan Nevins called the "Inner Workings of the Grant Administration." As the Director of Research for the Ulysses S. Grant Presidential Library, my job is to organize and preserve the documents and artifacts in our collection for use by researchers, but part of that job is to know what is "IN" the manuscripts to better help researchers find the materials they need. As such, I became fascinated by the foreign policy of Grant's presidency upon the discovery of Orville E. Babcock's diaries in our collections. His Santo Domingo diaries led me to discover more about Grant's presidency and the connections between his foreign policy and Reconstruction and, as I entered the doctoral program as a part-time graduate student at Mississippi State University, I felt that the historiography was missing a significant connection between Grant's foreign and domestic policies. After a false start involving Grant's famous World Tour, I began studying Grant's secretary of state, Hamilton Fish, and convinced myself that Nevins's biography needed updating. Thankfully, my dissertation committee steered me away from the mistake of writing what, at the time, would have been a traditional biography of Fish into an examination of citizenship through foreign and domestic policy.

As there was no historian of Civil War–era foreign policy at MSU, I was fortunate to have a committee that met all the needs of my dissertation topic through foreign policy, Reconstruction, and nineteenth-century Europe. My advisor, Professor Richard V. Damms, provided excellent advice not only on how to restructure problematic chapters, but also on basic grammatical issues. Professor Andrew F. Lang was always willing to meet to discuss the broader themes and to help me out of the weeds and to look at the bigger picture. Professor Anne E. Marshall provided the kick start I needed during the proposal defense when she stated, "This is a dissertation about Reconstruction, not a biography," and made me rethink everything I had proposed. And Professor Alexandra Hui provided much needed international perspectives on global change in the mid-nineteenth century, helping me to understand the revolutionary changes taking place in Europe during the 1870s.

My research took me to several archival repositories where I consulted fabulous archival collections and interacted with some excellent fellow archivists and librarians. At the Library of Congress's Manuscripts Reading Room, I utilized the papers of Hamilton Fish, Nathaniel Banks, Frederick Douglass, and many others. (There I received excellent assistance from my former University of South Carolina classmates Lewis Wyman and Ashley Greek. I also interacted with Dr. Michelle Krowl, fellow New Orleans Saints sufferer Neely Tucker who located a difficult-to-find congressional committee investigation transcript for me, and I received much needed research assistance from MSU alum Dr. Alyssa Warrick.) I was fortunate to visit the British Library in London and consult the papers of Prime Minister William E. Gladstone as well as the papers of Lord Ripon. I enjoyed one short but fruitful day of research at the beautiful Huntington Library in Pasadena where Dr. Ronald White was kind enough to host me for lunch and I was able to view the papers of Francis Lieber. Finally, thanks to modern technology, I was able to request items from the Ely S. Parker papers from the University of Rochester with the kind assistance of librarian Melinda Wallington. All these institutions, organizations, and individuals helped me along the way to producing this work and I am forever grateful for their kindness.

As a full-time professor and archivist at the Mississippi State University Libraries, I could not have completed this degree program without the support and encouragement of the administration, namely former deans of libraries, Frances Coleman and Tommy Anderson, and current dean, Lis Pankl. They supported my taking classes, taking research trips, study and writing days, all with the goal of completing this book. I am grateful for their support. My colleagues in the MSU Libraries and the U. S. Grant Presidential Library have also been extremely helpful in my reaching this goal. The late Dr. Michael B. Ballard, Civil War historian, archivist, and devoted mentor, guided me in my early career. Dr. John F. Marszalek, Amanda Carlock, Professor Kate Gregory, Professor David Nolen, Louie Gallo, Eddie Rangel, and all my colleagues at the MSU Libraries have supported my time and efforts in so many ways and I could not have accomplished this goal without them. I also want to thank the historians I have met through conferences, research, and online who have provided kind words, research tips, and support, including, Drs. Charles W. Calhoun, Joan Waugh, Heather

Cox Richardson, Joanne Freeman, and numerous others following along on Twitter with the hashtag: #twitterstorians. I thank them all. Also, I cannot express how thankful I am to my Series editor, Dr. Hilary Green, and her kindness and hard work, as well as the University of South Carolina Press Acquisitions Editor, Dr. Ehren Foley, who made this such an easy process. Thank you!

Finally, I want to thank my family who have been so supportive throughout this process. I began researching Grant's presidency in January 2012 and since then we have gone through numerous bouts of cancer, surgeries, marriages, births, and we lost my stepmother, Janice. But through it all my family has remained supportive of me as I continued to "write my paper." My mother Barbara, my father Bill, my late stepfather Charlie, my late stepmother Janice, my sisters Dana, Miranda, Kristen, Kate, and Tiffany, all my brothers-in-law, my numerous nieces, nephews, and grandnieces are all in my heart and I love them for their support. My mother-in-law, Kathy Whittle, and my late father-in-law, Dr. Douglas Whittle, were both so supportive and kind during this process and I could not be luckier to have had two such wonderful individuals as my in-laws. They are the reason that my favorite, my Alisa, exists. She and I met when I was a graduate student at the University of South Carolina, though neither of us remembers it. We reconnected when I lived in Washington, DC, and stayed connected through social media. In 2015, we jumped off a cliff together and she has been my source of strength and support ever since. I cannot express how hard this entire process would have been without her by my side. All the research trips out of town, the vacations that were just conferences, and the hours spent locked in my home office writing have kept us from living a "normal" life these first eight years of our marriage. At the same time, we traveled to Ireland, saw the sights in LA, watched our favorite shows, and enjoyed life as newlyweds. Alisa is my everything and she is the reason I can accomplish anything.

INTRODUCTION

The assassination of Abraham Lincoln in April 1865 forced the presidency of Andrew Johnson upon the United States and a change in leadership at American missions around the globe. Charles Francis Adams, United States minister to Great Britain, was replaced by Reverdy Johnson of Maryland, the former attorney general and senator who famously defended Mary Surratt in the Lincoln assassination conspiracy trial. Reverdy Johnson was boastful and partial to drink, and American legation secretary Benjamin Moran immediately disliked him. The President tasked the new minister with addressing the outstanding issues between the United States and Great Britain that arose from the American Civil War, chiefly the *Alabama* claims: the settlement of the destruction of American merchant ships by the British-built Confederate cruiser *Alabama*. Reverdy Johnson negotiated with the British foreign secretary, the Earl of Clarendon, to settle the *Alabama* claims without the British having to admit wrongdoing in supplying the ship to the Confederates. Republican party members in the United States, led by famed abolitionist Senator Charles Sumner of Massachusetts, were incensed both that the British refused to acknowledge their role in the building of the Confederate fleet and with Reverdy Johnson for not including indirect claims—those not directly attributable to the ships but attributable to the prolonging of the war. As Ulysses S. Grant took the office of the presidency in March 1869, he inherited a diplomatic stalemate between the United States and Great Britain. He turned to his new secretary of state, Hamilton Fish, to focus on foreign policy while Grant sought to implement constitutional changes domestically in the South and the West. He also sought American expansion into the Caribbean as means of divesting the United States from importing goods produced through Cuban slave labor, and for strategic bases in the event of war with Great Britain. In the end, these policies developed into a coherent administration strategy for handling all the issues of rebuilding the social, political, diplomatic, bureaucratic, and economic foundation of the United States.[1]

This book examines the period of the nineteenth century commonly known as the Reconstruction era. It examines the decision-making of the Grant administration during this era and the responses of leaders in the Republican Party (both elected officials and advocates). It focuses, generally, on the eight years of the Grant Administration (1869–1877) as it looks at the ways in which President Grant and his cabinet enacted a strategy that sought the inclusion of millions of people of color into the body politic, and the racial litmus test of western civilization that Grant required for admittance to the citizenry. It examines two areas of imperial expansion—the Caribbean and the American West—as well as the international threats to such expansion during the period. In particular, this book studies the proposed annexation of the Dominican Republic as a development of a policy of expanding citizenship throughout the Western Hemisphere, and how a similar policy in the American West represented the Grant administration's Peace Policy. Through the lens of citizenship, we can view a single foreign and domestic policy that welcomes immigrants, migrants, African Americans, and individuals in expanded territories as candidates for American citizenship. In short, establishing a new empire that exported republican liberty.

American republicanism developed from the political thinking of the Founding Fathers, thinking that evolved as the nation evolved. Historian Andrew F. Lang notes that republicanism "defined white Americans' citizenship, individual liberty, and protection of natural rights by government, while limiting the coercive scope of governing institutions." This republican tradition was in stark contrast to the monarchy and oligarchy of Europe; "the citizen was supreme ruler" in American society where he was expected to govern his own actions. This book uses Lang's definition of republicanism as a basis for its analysis of Grant's political ideology. Grant embraced this American republicanism, particularly the belief in the citizen-soldier; men "guided by the culture of civic virtue." For Grant, any men who expressed their liberty through free labor, who aspired to own property, and who answered the call of military service, were worthy of the rights of citizenship. The oligarchic society of the American South denied enslaved African Americans the rights to their own free labor. With the passing of the Reconstruction Amendments, Grant envisioned expanding the reach of republicanism beyond just white and Black American citizens, but to other marginalized groups he deemed civilized or, at least, capable of civilization.[2]

The concept of civilization was based on notions of white superiority and the superiority of western culture. African Americans embraced the cultural trappings of western civilization in this era, and as such in the post–Civil War era, many white Americans saw Black Americans as worthy of citizenship, if not equality. Whites saw most Native Americans, according to historian Kathleen DuVal, as living "in an earlier stage of development than themselves." Therefore, white Americans like Grant believed that Native Americans needed to embrace the building blocks of civilization to become citizens of the United States, rather than wards of the nation. As DuVal notes, whites wanted Native Americans to become more like whites by training "in white ways of farming, domestic production, and worship." Lang argues that "a civilized nation allegedly conquered the barbaric state of nature to obviate retrograde, deteriorating savagery." To prevent such a regression, Americans needed to bring all who lived within the nation to the same level of civilization. Grant, thus, embraced this civilizing force for Native Americans. When *Exporting Reconstruction* analyzes the administration's Peace Policy and Grant's civilizing pathway to citizenship, it is a policy established through the "white ways" of farming, production, and religion.[3]

Prior to the Civil War, the concept of citizenship was almost exclusively connected to discussions of white men. Free African Americans moved through their daily lives in a nebulous state of being, free Americans with little to no political rights. As Martha S. Jones notes, citizenship in the antebellum period was "a claim to place, to enter and remain within the nation's borders." It was not, however, a signifier of political rights. After the Civil War, though, citizenship rights changed. Not only was citizenship a "claim to place," but it was also a signifier of political rights found not only in the Civil Rights Acts of 1866, but also the Fourteenth Amendment. The establishment of birthright citizenship automatically guaranteed the millions of African Americans in the United States legal rights under the constitution. Native Americans' position as citizens were complicated by the Fourteenth Amendment's clause excluding "Indians not taxed," thus Grant sought to develop a policy that created a pathway to citizenship. These Native Americans would have to establish western political structures in their territories and reservations, embrace farming, production, and religion, and leave their culture behind. Doing so, though, would mean guaranteeing their rights under the Constitution of the United States and eventual participation in the body politic, which included paying taxes. Citizenship, then, was the reward for embracing a civilized, republican ideology.[4]

On a gloomy, rainy morning in Washington, DC, in March 1869, soldiers, citizens, and pickpockets alike traversed the crowded streets in the cool rain, hoping to catch a glimpse of the procession as it made its way to the Capitol. By midmorning, the clouds had parted, throngs of umbrellas snapped shut, and a starter gun was fired, signaling the beginning of the parade. Windows, rooftops, and balconies along Pennsylvania Avenue teemed with onlookers hoping to catch a glimpse of the victorious general and President-elect, Ulysses S. Grant. The general and his predecessor, President Andrew Johnson, could barely stand one another, and the inaugural committee had secured separate carriages for the two men. At the last minute, Johnson took his leave, foregoing the procession and the inaugural ceremony altogether, one last affront to political convention. Grant, instead, traveled with his military staff, accompanied along the route by over a dozen military regiments, companies of firemen, the Supreme Court, members of the US House and Senate, veterans of the Mexican American War, and thirty veterans of the War of 1812. When the procession reached the Capitol, the members of the Senate, the House, the cabinet, and the Supreme Court entered the Senate chamber and took their seats. General Grant's father, Jesse Grant, sat next to Senator James Nye of Nevada waiting for his son to enter the chamber. Vice President-elect Schuyler Colfax took his oath of office, made a short speech, administered the oath to the newly elected senators, and adjourned those gathered to the platform outside the Capitol.[5]

Ulysses S. Grant was born Hiram Ulysses Grant on April 27, 1822, in Point Pleasant, Ohio. His father, Jesse Root Grant, was a tanner and an outspoken abolitionist; his mother, Hannah Simpson Grant, was stern and quiet. Hiram entered the United States Military Academy at West Point, New York in 1839 where a clerical error listed him as Ulysses S. Grant. After a few years he begrudgingly accepted the moniker as his new name. Grant was a middling student who racked up demerits, but he was also honest, loyal, and a skilled horseman. After graduation he was assigned to the Fourth Infantry Regiment and sent to Mexico during the Mexican American War. There he showed bravery during battle, modeling himself after the old "Rough and Ready" general, Zachary Taylor. Grant later was sent to the Pacific Northwest, a voyage that required him to cross the Isthmus of Panama where his Regiment lost nearly 150 men and their families to cholera. This experience later informed his desire to establish a canal in Central America enabling for safe passage across the isthmus. While on the West Coast, Grant took to drinking to mask his depression, leading to his resignation from the army. He next moved to St. Louis, Missouri, where he worked on his father-in-law's plantation and where he enslaved workers on his farm, much to the chagrin of his father. He attempted several business ventures which all failed and, in 1860, Grant moved his family to the bustling town of Galena, Illinois, to work with his father and brothers in their leather goods store. In Galena he made friends with local political heavyweights such as Elihu B. Washburne and John Rawlins, and he became acquainted with Ely S. Parker, an engineer for the federal government and a chief of the Seneca tribe of New York.

It was in Galena that Grant learned of secession and offered himself for a commission as an officer in the US Army. Grant quickly rose through the ranks and soon he was collecting victories at Fort Donelson, Shiloh, and the watershed siege of Vicksburg. Following another great victory in Chattanooga, President Abraham Lincoln tasked General Grant with defeating Robert E. Lee in Virginia. Grant and Lee traded blows for over a year, with Grant finally accepting Lee's surrender on April 9, 1865. For the victorious Union, Grant became the most celebrated warrior of the American Civil War. He maintained his role as General of the Army during the presidency of Andrew Johnson, with whom Grant clashed. In 1868 the Republican Party nominated Grant as its candidate for the presidency, a nomination which he claimed to accept reluctantly. On November 3, 1868, Grant was elected President of the United States, defeating Democrat Horatio Seymour. At forty-six years old, Grant became the youngest person elected to the presidency at that time.[6]

Grant took the oath of office upon a platform adorned with flags and bunting; his appearance led to multiple rounds of cheers from the crowd gathered on the lawn. After Chief Justice Salmon P. Chase administered the oath, President Grant began his inaugural address in "a clear but not very loud tone." The address focused mostly on the enormous cost of the Civil War, both in men and treasure. Grant promised the American people he would be honest about his policies, conveying them to Congress and the people, and that he understood the enormity of the position. "The young men of the country . . . have a peculiar interest in maintaining the national honor," Grant noted to the crowd, "a moment's reflection as to what will be our commanding influence among the nations of the earth in their day . . . should inspire them with national pride." At this moment, Grant recognized that the United States was entering into a new era, one in which the promises of liberty and national honor put the United States on an equal footing with the rest of the world. This new era meant the coming together of all citizens, old and new, into a "common sentiment" that would cross "all divisions, geographical, political, and religious." Grant's plain language and directness pleased one editor of the local *National Republican,* who told his readers: "How wonderfully he possesses the faculty of reaching the popular heart through brief but pungent appeal to its judgment and sense of right and wrong!"[7]

Towards the end of his address, Grant appealed to Americans to consider the rights of all citizens, whether natural-born, newly freed, or naturalized, and their place in the world. "In regard to foreign policy," President Grant noted, "I would deal with nations as equitable law requires individuals to deal with each other, and I would protect the law-abiding citizen, whether native or of foreign birth, where ever his rights are jeopardised [sic] or the flag of our country floats. I would respect the rights of all nations demanding equal respect for our own; but if others depart from this rule, in their dealings with us, we may be compelled to follow their precedet [sic]." As he spoke, Britain and Spain held under arrest American citizens, both native-born and naturalized, for their political activities in the Caribbean, Canada, and Ireland. The new administration thus would pursue international agreements that would protect citizenship and its attendant rights on behalf of these citizens. Foreign powers, Grant argued, were required to respect the sovereignty of the United States and respect its citizens no matter where they roamed. Yet many American citizens were aiding rebellions against sovereign nations, violating not only the laws of those nations but also the laws of the United States. The actions of certain naturalized citizens forced the Grant administration to redefine exactly how the United States would respond to its citizens inciting rebellion in the name of liberty in foreign lands. The question of exactly how to respond would dominate the new administration's foreign policy.[8]

Grant used the occasion of his first inaugural address to promote his ideas about who should be included in the republican experiment. Toward the end of his address, he mentioned the plight of Native Americans and, for the first time in history for an American president, outlined a path to citizenship for them. "The proper treatment of the original occupants of the land, the Indian, is one deserving of careful study," he told the crowd. "I will favor any course towards them which tends to their civilization, Christianization and ultimate citizenship." Grant's short statement encapsulated his republican ideology: a faith that men, regardless of race, once civilized and faithful Christians, accepting of Western civilization and assimilating into republican society, were welcomed into the body politic of the United States. A republican society was one that embraced freedom and equality, and a civilized society was one that embraced progress and prosperity through modernity. Native Americans would be welcomed into the body politic when they accepted both republicanism and civilization and became American citizens. That Indigenous populations constituted sovereign nations mattered little to Grant, as he believed all civilized people who dwelled within US territories were American and subject to the blessings bestowed by the Constitution. Grant's inaugural address prefigured the themes of the Grant administration's foreign and domestic policy. Until that time, Native American tribes had dealt with the United States as independent and sovereign nations, even if the United States Supreme Court viewed them as domestic dependent nations. Such nations agreed to treaties with the federal government, negotiating for land, hunting, and water rights in territories occupied by white settlers. Often, however, white settlers had violently defied these treaties, with the support of the US Army, provoking reprisals from Indian nations. The army then sent troops to quell the defiant Indigenous population, perpetuating the cycle of violence.

Grant claimed that he sought to end violence toward Native Americans, first by reforming the Indian Agency by placing military officers in charge of securing the peace, and then having religious groups nominate suitable local agents. He also sought to reform the way the federal government negotiated with Native American nations. By placing his friend Ely S. Parker, a member of the Seneca tribe in New York, as Head of the Bureau of Indian Affairs, Grant sought to show that "civilized" Native Americans could accept the republican institutions of the United States. The United States, then, would no longer treat Native American tribes as sovereign nations. Instead, they would become wards of the government, neither foreigners nor citizens, bowing to the national bureaucracy and the ever-expanding powers of the central government. Such an approach destroyed the autonomy of Native Americans and threatened many Indian Nations with annihilation; however, Grant believed his prescribed path to citizenship for Native Americans comported with his republican ideology. For Grant, once all Native Americans had fully embraced the trappings of civilization and assimilated into the republican culture of the United States, their citizenship would be guaranteed as would be their prosperity.[9] Grant saw the Reconstruction era as a time when people, long left out of the republican experiment, could finally enjoy the blessings of liberty. Nevertheless, Grant still held to nineteenth-century concepts of Western civilization that considered Native American culture to be uncivilized and Indigenous sovereignty anathema to American supremacy in the Western Hemisphere. Once Native Americans accepted republican norms and assimilated into western culture, Grant believed that the United States should count Indigenous Americans as equal citizens of the republic. This plan failed, as the violence that had proliferated in the West for decades prior to Grant's presidency transitioned into a series of increasingly bloody reprisals and attacks that approached eradication.[10]

Grant's ideas protecting the rights of American citizens abroad and a pathway to citizenship for Native Americans aligned with his larger vision for the United States during the Reconstruction era. He believed that the American Civil War had fundamentally transformed the United States into a nation that was finally living up to the ideals of its founders. "There has been no event since the close of the war in which I have felt so deep an interest as that of the ratification of the fifteenth amendment," Grant told the assembled reporters and Republicans gathered outside of the Executive Mansion. "I have felt the greatest anxiety ever since I have been in this house to know that that was to be secured. It looked to me as the realization of the Declaration of Independence." Such an opinion differed from notable Republicans such as Charles Sumner who, along with several fellow radicals, were unhappy with the amendment. African Americans, though, were enjoying freedom and citizenship through the ratification of the Thirteenth and Fourteenth Amendments to the Constitution. Grant hoped to export these tenets of republicanism throughout the Western Hemisphere as a doctrine of liberty. During his administration he would articulate a policy for the Caribbean that envisioned an exceptional United States as the arbiter of freedom and democracy in the World, exporting this ideology through expansion and reorganization of territories. This policy, which I call "The Grant Doctrine," spurred Grant's attempt to annex the Dominican Republic to the United States as a territory with a path to statehood, guaranteeing citizenship rights for the Dominicans and offering the island as a haven for African Americans fleeing the onslaught of racist whites in the former

Confederacy. Grant's "Peace Policy" for Native Americans would take a similar approach; he relied on the assistance of his former military aide, Ely S. Parker, to implement his plan to assimilate Native Americans with a view to organizing the Indian Territory in Oklahoma into a state. Grant hoped that Native Americans would self-remove from their land to populate this territory, as full citizens, entering the Union as equals. If the Oklahoma Territory could join the Union as a state, perhaps the Dakota Territory might follow? These actions, he hoped, would occur at the same time as the reorganization of the former Confederate states, territories that would develop around republican principles and the acceptance of a multi-racial political body.[11]

The Grant Doctrine envisioned massive political and social change throughout the Western Hemisphere. Grant saw the United States as a leader of emancipation, civilization, and republicanism. The United States would strangle slavery out of the region, exporting republican ideology and economics to do so. He believed that indigenous populations and people of color in the Caribbean were ready to become citizens of the United States, alongside the millions of newly freed African Americans and naturalized citizens. The Grant Doctrine envisioned an expansion of US territory in the Caribbean to accompany an expansion of the republican values of free labor and economic stability. Grant's vision failed for a variety of reasons, not the least of which was racial prejudice within his own party, but also because many Americans viewed Reconstruction as a completed process once national reunification had been achieved. What it was not, to these Americans, was a policy by which marginalized groups other than African Americans became citizens. Apathy and white supremacist violence towards non-whites ultimately doomed any chance of expanding the reach of American democracy throughout the Western Hemisphere.[12]

Grant ended his first inaugural address with a plea to the American people to support the newest citizens of the nation, African Americans. "The question of suffrage is one which is likely to agitate the public so long as a portion of the citizens of the nation are excluded from its privileges in any state," he intoned. "It seems to me very desirable that the question should be settled now, and I entertain the hope and express the desire that it may be by the ratification of the fifteenth article of amendment to the Constitution."[13] The Fifteenth Amendment to the Constitution stated that "The right of citizens of the United States to vote shall not be denied or abridged by the United States or by any State on account of race, color, or previous condition of servitude."[14] For Grant, the Fifteenth Amendment was the epitome of the administration's core values of liberty and freedom and individual rights. Alongside the Thirteenth and Fourteenth Amendments, the Fifteenth Amendment fulfilled the promise of the nation's founding. Grant wrote that the ratification of the Fifteenth Amendment "completes the greatest civil change and constitutes the most important event since the nation came into life."[15]

For Grant the promise of Reconstruction was the promise of equal rights, and the violence of Reconstruction was the contestation of that promise. Grant's policies rested on the acceptance of equality by the American public. Grant's presidency represented a unique moment in its history for the United States to realize the promises of the Declaration of Independence that "all men are created equal" through enactment of the Reconstruction amendments. The Grant Doctrine advocated exporting these Reconstruction ideals beyond the traditional boundaries of the United States into the Caribbean, and eventually, throughout the Western Hemisphere; likewise the Peace Policy sought to bring citizenship to Native Americans in territories of the American West. Grant also hoped to utilize the expanding concept of citizenship inherent in the Reconstruction amendments to redefine naturalization laws both nationally and internationally, thus solidifying the United States' position on the world stage as a champion of republican values. Reconstruction, to Grant, meant much more than merely the political rehabilitation of formerly rebellious states. To Grant, who knew better than anyone what the purchase price of Reconstruction had been, the sacrifices of the Civil War would only be valid if it meant a broader political revision of rights and freedoms not merely within the established borders of the US, but beyond as well—and for that to occur, it would mean revising prevailing American notions of race.

African American political leaders held varying views not only toward the administration but with one another. These leaders argued about what was best for African Americans as a whole and for the cause of liberty in the Western Hemisphere. While African Americans supported the Republican Party, they did not wholly support the Grant administration's foreign policy initiatives towards the Caribbean. In fact, many African American leaders openly challenged President Grant for his decision-making in matters of foreign policy. African American leaders criticized the president's Caribbean policy, yet they were conflicted about issues such as Chinese immigration; they both supported free labor for Chinese workers but prioritized Black employment over Chinese workers when labor conflicts arose. The various points of view of leading African Americans, including Frederick Douglass, John Lynch, Hiram Revels, Sojourner Truth, and P. B. S. Pinchback, expressed through their correspondence, speeches, and in the pages of their Black-owned newspapers, show disjointed support for Grant's policies but an unwavering support for the Republican Party. Grant failed to marshal support from African American leaders for his Caribbean policy, thus depriving him of a significant voting bloc which propped up the Republican Party.[16] Grant's support for African American equality in the United States waned towards the end of his second term, through the loss of Republican-controlled legislatures, and through a lack of support from white Americans. Grant himself noted that he grew tired of the constant violence directed at African Americans in the South, yet towards the end of his presidency he was less inclined to do anything to stop said violence. In the end, Grant allowed Reconstruction to fail because he was unwilling to continue to fight for African American equality. How could the Grant Doctrine succeed abroad if Grant allowed domestic Reconstruction in the South to fail?[17]

This book examines Grant's Reconstruction domestic and foreign policies as an integrated whole. It builds on existing scholarship of Reconstruction and studies that examine the development of citizenship rights and equality for African Americans in the period following the Civil War, and views the ways in which the Grant administration pursued its vision of who should be counted as a citizen, against those who saw it otherwise. This book demonstrates that Grant's Reconstruction policy focused on the broad application of citizenship rights, not only for African Americans in the South, but for many different people in the larger American sphere of influence. Part I of this book shows how Grant hoped to apply the ideals of Reconstruction, the rights of citizenship, and the republican values of the Reconstruction amendments to people never previously considered for membership in the body politic of the United States. Covering the period from Grant's inauguration in March 1869 to his reelection in 1872, Part I examines the development of Grant's Caribbean policy and the various foreign policy initiatives that hindered American expansion there. Grant attempted to export the rights of citizenship through expansion, both in the Caribbean and the American West. His proposal to annex the Dominican Republic and grant the Dominicans citizenship, and his pursuit of new treaties to define how and when an immigrant became a citizen, reflected a new interpretation of the Constitution and the responsibilities of the president in enforcing equal rights both for the people of the nation and those seeking to join it.

In Part I, *Exporting Reconstruction* analyzes the policies of the Grant administration surrounding expansion in the Caribbean. It does so through examining the policy documents and policy makers within the administration. These policies coalesced into a distinct foreign and domestic agenda revolving around citizenship. The Caribbean policy, which I call the Grant Doctrine, develops through the lens of three men and two policy documents. President Grant, Secretary of State Hamilton Fish, and personal aide to the president, Orville E. Babcock, contribute to the annexation of the Dominican Republic scheme and the development of Grant's "Reasons why San Domingo should be annexed to the United States" memorandum, as well as his official letter to the United States Senate on the same subject. These documents reflect Grant's and his policy advisors' ideas about the United States' role in the world, as well as his vision for exporting citizenship rights and American republican values to the people of the Dominican Republic. Though Fish did not support Grant's expansionist goals, he did, though, support the president's foreign policy aims, particularly strengthening the nation's position in the world. By examining these documents that make up the Grant Doctrine, we can see that Grant and his administration had a vision of the United States' place in the international system in the Reconstruction-era and a view of using expansion to answer some of the questions of Reconstruction.

Part II of *Exporting Reconstruction* examines the Grant administration's Peace Policy and the policy makers who influenced Grant's attempt to lay out a "civilizing" pathway to citizenship for Native Americans. Grant's personal relationship with Native American Ely S. Parker influenced his decision-making on Indian Affairs, most notably his belief in the idea of the civilized native man. Parker's embrace of western civilization and his military service played into Grant's beliefs about citizen-soldiers and their role in a civilized society. Parker's work with the "Civilized Tribes" in Oklahoma to organize their territory and adopt a constitution led Grant to believe that a homogenous Indian state in the Union was possible. When political enemies attacked Parker's credibility, Grant continued to support his friend's policies, even after the former Seneca chief's resignation from the administration. Grant then turned to his Secretary of the Interior, Columbus Delano and his report on Native American citizenship as a basis for his Peace Policy. For Grant, becoming citizens of the United States should be the ultimate goal for all who lived within its borders. Through Parker's policies and Delano's report, Grant envisioned a clear path toward civilization that led to the bestowing of citizenship upon the many Native Americans.

Part II examines Grant's desire to provide a path to citizenship for Native Americans (whether they wanted it or not): his definition of who was worthy of that. This section returns to March 1869 with Grant's inaugural address and concludes with the nation at war with Native Americans in the West by the end of his second term in 1877. Grant's contradictory plan to expand white settlements in the West while undermining the individual rights of Native Americans led the nation into a protracted war against the indigenous populations in these territories. Grant's Reconstruction policy also extended to his desire to help Chinese immigrants break the bonds of forced labor, which led unwittingly to their eventual exclusion. At the same time, Grant continued to court the support of African American leaders, individuals who questioned his decision-making and argued against his policies, even as they continued their electoral support of him and his party.[18]

Grant's political enemies, and even many of his supposed political allies, resisted his attempts to bring new citizens—particularly non-whites—into the republican experiment, eventually fracturing the Republican Party and strengthening the Democratic Party. White Americans engaged in violent uprisings across the South and West to protect white supremacy and to undermine equality. Whites directed this same violence against non-white immigrants, particularly Chinese immigrants in the West, to protect white laborers' position of supremacy. Historian Stacey L. Smith notes that, "Reconstruction, in short, was a thoroughly national, continental political struggle over the federal government's power to make citizens." The centralization of this power in the hands of the federal government threatened the pre-war political structure to which so many whites clung, so much so that Democrats in New York naturalized thousands of Irish and German immigrants in the days before the 1868 election to undermine Reconstruction policies. Conversely, Mark Wahlgren Summers contends that the main goal of Reconstruction "was to bring the nation back together and this time for good, to banish the prospect of future war, to break the power of the former slave states . . . to end slavery . . . and all this without sacrificing the political framework that had made the Union special." These two perspectives on Reconstruction are not mutually exclusive. Rather, many Americans, both white and Black, sought to achieve both objectives following the Civil War. The contrasting narratives of how Americans defined Reconstruction is prevalent throughout the literature. Historians often define the meaning of Reconstruction as either national reunification or the restructuring of society in the American South. The idea of a greater Reconstruction, however, shifts prevailing narratives beyond the confines of the South and enables us to see how Grant's expansion attempts in the Caribbean and his Indian Peace Policy in the West were both part of a broader vision of what, precisely, needed to be reconstructed. These differing narratives of Reconstruction reflect the Grant administration's struggle to develop a coherent foreign and domestic policy that would advance its Reconstruction goals in the post–Civil War era. Success to the Grant administration entailed the reunification of the states, the integration of African Americans into the body politic of the United States, and the introduction of republican ideals of freedom and equality and the civilized ideals of progress and prosperity into US foreign policy initiatives toward the Western Hemisphere.[19]

While historians studying broader aspects of Reconstruction embrace the idea of a "Greater Reconstruction," other historians have questioned whether the term "Reconstruction" remains pertinent. Gregory P. Downs and Kate Masur argue that the term Reconstruction is lacking in usefulness for describing the frameworks of historical analysis that look beyond the traditional definition of "a dynamic period of political debate and social upheaval in the South that followed the Civil War." They look to Elliot West's "Greater Reconstruction" argument as proof that the term is no longer viable. They argue that framing post–Civil War works around Reconstruction precludes researchers "from considering postwar history from different angles." As such, they consider the period as "The World the War Made," viewing it as the growth and reaction to the impact of the massive Civil War the nation had endured. This view of the postwar era, removing Reconstruction from the center of the framework, helps to explain the seemingly dichotomous understanding of a stronger centralized government operating, as they argue, as a "Stockade State," run through a series of territorial outposts. However, I argue that removing Reconstruction from the framework does a disservice to the complexity of the time. The people of the United States understood they were living through Reconstruction and saw, for themselves, the connections between the policies that governed the Reconstruction of the South and those that affected the lives of non-whites throughout the West and in potential new territories.[20]

Exporting Reconstruction examines both the foreign and domestic policies of the Grant administration as a unified effort to include previously excluded civilized peoples in the national experiment. It shows the myriad ways the Grant administration sought to convey citizenship upon people of color who previously were denied citizenship, examines the people who Grant believed were not worthy of citizenship, and explains the diplomatic and political roadblocks that undermined his efforts. This book builds on many of the same themes as West's "Greater Reconstruction" by examining the Grant administration's attempted expansion into new territories and the cultural and political impact of potentially including hundreds of thousands of new non-white citizens into the polity of the United States in the West and in the Caribbean. It also follows in the trajectory of Heather Cox Richardson's *West from Appomattox* which examined the development of the American West as a region distinct from the North and South, built by the development of an emerging American middle class. Richardson argues that the new nation, buoyed by western expansion, created a national government that propped up the rights of the middle class and the industrial class at the expense of marginalized groups. This book examines the early days of this Reconstruction process, when the Administration attempted to use the force of the federal system on behalf of the marginalized, often to the detriment of those very same groups, to increase the prosperity and progress of the nation. Although Grant and many of his Republican allies supported equal rights for African Americans, many did so to an end, to strengthen the Union through the reunification of the states and to create a sense of national identity that helped build economic growth in the South and in the expanding territories in the West. For the Grant administration, though, Reconstruction was an attempt to make reunification and equality succeed in both domestic and foreign policy. Grant argued that some people deserved citizenship more than others. Those who were civilized, such as African Americans, Dominicans, and Cubans, and who embraced modernity and progress, were worthy of immediate citizenship. Those who were not civilized, such as Native Americans and Chinese immigrants, were deemed "heathens" and "barbarians" who could only join as citizens if they accepted the tenets of civilization. Grant considered these various groups as part of the new world wrought by the Civil War during Reconstruction. This book, then, will examine the successes and failures of the administration's Reconstruction policy writ large.[21]

The centerpiece of Grant's Reconstruction Caribbean policy is "The Grant Doctrine," articulated in a memorandum that Grant wrote in late 1869 while considering whether to annex the Dominican Republic to the United

States and a letter to the Senate articulating the same. Titled "Reasons why San Domingo should be annexed to the United States," the memorandum encapsulates Grant's policy of exporting his republican ideology abroad. Grant hoped that the annexation of the Dominican Republic (or San Domingo as he often referred to the nation) would allow the United States finally to divest itself from the slave society of Cuba, which was the main supplier of tropical goods to the country. The Grant Doctrine differed from the Monroe Doctrine in that previous presidents had utilized Monroe's doctrine during a period when the United States was still a slave-holding republic. Though Grant espoused the same belief as Monroe that the United States should be the arbiter of disputes in the Western Hemisphere and that Old World imperialism was unwanted in the region, the Monroe Doctrine's implicit vision was of an expanding slave-holding republic. The Monroe Doctrine, then, was worthy of reexamination in the post–Civil War United States. Grant's secretary of state, Hamilton Fish, reasserted the Monroe Doctrine's "no transfer principle," which stated that Cuba was "no longer regarded as subject to transfer from one European power to another." After Monroe, each new president interpreted the Monroe Doctrine to fit his own political vision. As historian Jay Sexton notes, "There would be as many Monroe Doctrines as foreign policy perspectives." The Grant Doctrine, however, represented a new philosophy toward the Western Hemisphere. The United States would act not as the purveyor of slavery in the region but as the exemplar of how to emancipate the enslaved. Grant intended to assert American influence in the region by acquiring bases in the Caribbean that would put the United States in a position of naval dominance, asserting control over important shipping lanes, and exercising influence over the remaining European colonies. However, the Grant Doctrine also sought to incorporate the people of the Dominican Republic into the electorate of the United States, and to welcome the people of the neighboring slave-holding islands of Cuba and Puerto Rico to come of their own accord to the beacon of American freedom. Grant's doctrine took its cues from the Reconstruction amendments. His plan for the Dominican Republic was to export citizenship rights to the Dominican people, build up its economy with free labor, and, in doing so, gradually strangle the slave economy of Cuba.[22]

Citizenship was a key tenet of the Grant Doctrine. Grant hoped that, through annexation, the Dominican Republic could become a state, allowing American citizens the chance to make their fortunes in the fertile lands of the island nation and providing the Dominican people the right to live and work throughout the United States as equal citizens. But he took note to focus on African Americans as the citizens best suited for the territory. Drawing on the race-based biology of his day, Grant believed they would find the climate congenial, but he also believed they would want to leave the South to escape the oppressive white supremacy of the former Confederate states, which he believed was inevitable. "[The Dominican Republic] is capable of supporting the entire colored population of the United States, should it choose to emigrate," Grant wrote. He understood that the hostility of former Confederates toward African Americans might last many years, but economic realities in the South could mitigate conditions. "The colored man cannot be spared until his place is supplied," he wrote, "but with a refuge like San Domingo his worth here [in the US South] would soon be discovered, and he would soon receive such recognition as to induce him to stay: or if Providence designed that the two races should not live to-gether [sic] he would find a home in the Antillas [sic]." Emigrating from the South seemed to be a logical move for African Americans there and Grant considered the Dominican Republic to be an ideal location. In fact, Grant's idea was a few decades early, as millions of African Americans would eventually leave the South during the Great Migration of the early twentieth century.[23]

This notion of individual freedom of movement was a key component to citizenship in the nineteenth century. Prior to the Civil War, African Americans had been limited in their movements, whether slave or free, unlike white Americans. Historian Martha Jones notes that the loss of locomotion, or the ability to move about the nation freely, was at the heart of denying Black people the right of citizenship. This "right indispensable to citizenship" was central to Grant's Reconstruction policy. He understood that the nation was expanding into the West, and he sought ways to incorporate African Americans into the body politic and the pool of free laborers. Both white and Black Americans crossed the Mississippi River to settle the West, pushing Native Americans off land that the United States was bound by Grant's Peace Policy and by treaty to protect. Grant initially sent the US Army to the West to protect Native lands and to enforce these treaties. At the same time, the federal government actively underwrote western expansion and the eradication of Native peoples. The acquisition of the Dominican Republic, then, potentially provided another venue for the United States to extend republicanism and territory to other benighted peoples.[24]

The Grant Doctrine, though, was novel in its notion of expanding American influence and republican values, not just for economic or political gain, but also as an effort to promote freedom throughout the Western Hemisphere. Conversely, it was also a naïve concept that proved to be impossible to implement due to the fear of undercutting vital diplomatic negotiations, and the racist beliefs of whites in the Republican Party. When faced with the opportunity to support democratic efforts for freedom in Cuba and when faced with violence that undercut racial equality, Grant proved unwilling to act upon his stated beliefs. Doing so would undermine the administration's efforts to settle the *Alabama* claims with Great Britain. Grant's attempts to negotiate with the Spanish, rather than get directly involved in the Cuban rebellion, failed to end the threat there. Ultimately, the capture and execution of the passengers and crew onboard the filibustering ship *Virginius* drew the United States directly into the rebellion. His desire to end the practice of sexual slavery committed upon Chinese women ultimately led to Chinese exclusion. Finally, a meddlesome House of Representatives committee undermined his Peace Policy's plan to create a path to citizenship for Native Americans and led to the escalation of the genocide against the indigenous in the West. The Grant administration's Reconstruction-era policies were an exercise in which the president laid out a strategy of combining the international, political, and economic power of the United States with the domestic reconstruction of its political institutions. It was an effort to redefine the role of the nation in the Western Hemisphere and to expand the American republican system through the annexation of territory in the Caribbean. His failure to implement his ideas, however, should not detract from their intent, particularly the quest to dismantle slavery, bolster trade, and supersede European influence in the region.

The Grant administration's foreign policy is often overlooked given the intense scholarly focus on its domestic Reconstruction policies. The foreign and domestic concerns of the Reconstruction era cannot be divorced from one another. Heather Cox Richardson argues that "what we now know as 'Reconstruction' is being redefined as the Era of Citizenship, when Americans defined who would be citizens and what citizenship meant." This is precisely what the Grant administration tackled during Reconstruction, not merely as a function of foreign policy, but as part of an overall policy of Reconstruction that brought both the foreign and domestic policies into one course of action, seeking to determine who deserved to be counted among the citizenry of the United States. The Grant Doctrine attempted to redefine the place of the United States in the world and how American citizens functioned within that world. While many of Grant's initiatives failed, it is important to remember that the Reconstruction amendments lived on and forever altered the Constitution. Grant's attempts to incorporate new peoples into the American citizenry did not die with his failed policies. African Americans, Chinese immigrants, and Native Americans all continued to fight for their equal rights throughout the nineteenth and twentieth centuries. Though Grant's policies were detrimental to some of these ethnic groups (such as his support for the Page Act, the first of many Chinese exclusion acts), the ideas behind the Grant Doctrine (free labor, eradicating slavery in the Western Hemisphere, and expanding citizenship to non-whites in territories outside of the South) lived on in American political consciousness.[25]

For Grant, Reconstruction was about exporting ideas and having people accept those ideas within the confines of the international system. While the Grant Doctrine was a nationalist project designed to preserve free labor, protect and stabilize the Union, and establish citizenship rights within the United States, the administration confronted a host of transnational issues along the way. Grant was hopeful that enslaved persons would flee slavery in Cuba, but American citizens could not foment rebellion there and violate international norms to free them. With the Peace Policy, it was acceptable for Native Americans to hold onto traditional leadership systems if they assimilated and incorporated their traditions into republican structures. Republican citizens accepted their place in a republican society, assimilating the American political, economic, and social ideals into their daily existence. Accepting republican ideals was imperative to any immigrant hoping to join the citizenry of the United States. It was the duty of the United States to offer these ideals within the acceptable existing international norms, by not defying existing treaties, not violating neutrality in international conflicts, and seeking arbitration of international disputes. For Grant, it was the duty of the United States to export republican ideals to new peoples, without sacrificing the country's position and security as a world power.

Grant's foreign and domestic policies grew from the Reconstruction amendments, which revolutionized the Constitution, forever changing the meaning of the document. The amendments changed the nation itself fundamentally, as millions of formerly enslaved persons became citizens and hundreds of thousands of Black men became voters. The later addition of millions of immigrants from Europe, the Caribbean, South America, and Asia changed the complexion of what an American citizen could look like and how the body politic should define citizenship. However, to many

Americans long enjoying the benefits of citizenship, Reconstruction redefined the nature of their relationship with the federal government, and not, as they saw it, always to the good, as they came to perceive government intervention in the political sphere of the nation on behalf of the freedmen as problematic. Because of this, many white Americans wished to view Reconstruction as a process by which the government reunited the southern states into the Union and nothing more. Equal rights were not the main goal. Therefore, even if it took well over one hundred years to realize, it was through the implementation of the Reconstruction amendments, the redefinition of citizenship, the realization and reinterpretation of who could be a citizen, and the struggle of non-white Americans to force whites to accept them as equal citizens, that the nation eventually implemented civil rights for all.[26]

Grant's attempts at exporting Reconstruction are often viewed as nothing more than imperialism, but his attempts are significantly different from the imperialism of the late nineteenth century. Presidents William McKinley and Theodore Roosevelt, famous for their imperial expansion, looked to exploit the peoples of foreign lands for their natural resources in the name of American values, but did not intend to incorporate those people into the body politic of the United States as equals. In fact, the race and culture of these people were detriments to these colonial ventures as Americans saw their possible incorporation into the United States as having a deleterious effect on American society and morals. The Grant administration maintained a different vision. Grant saw the people of the Dominican Republic as republican, civilized individuals who were welcome as citizens of the United States. He intended for these people to become citizens, not wards, of the United States—laborers, taxpayers, voters, and more than likely, members of the Republican Party.

Grant saw the strategic location of the Dominican Republic as beneficial to the United States, but he also saw the republican ideals of the United States as something worth exporting to neighboring countries. He believed in a domino theory of republicanism in the Caribbean, assuming that exhibiting republican ideals in one place would mean that neighboring polities would soon adopt similar republican systems. He believed slaveholding in the Western Hemisphere societies of Cuba, Puerto Rico, and Brazil would crumble under the weight of an American economic system no longer dependent upon them for tropical goods, and he believed laborers and formerly enslaved persons would travel to the shores of an annexed Dominican

Republic to taste the freedom of the United States. As for his Peace Policy, he believed that the only way to incorporate Native Americans into the American system was to make them assimilate to western values and join with their neighbors to become American citizens, rather than remain separate nations within the North American continent. Finally, he believed in celebrating the labor of immigrants from China, but he supported policies that undermined their ability to become citizens of the United States due to their supposed "uncivilized nature." These policies laid the groundwork for the Chinese Exclusion Acts that remained salient well into the twentieth century. Grant's policies toward the Caribbean and toward Native Americans, though, represented a change in American foreign and domestic policy that was defined in the Reconstruction era. Exporting Reconstruction beyond the borders of the South and opening up citizenship to non-white people, which had never been considered before, defined the Grant administration's Caribbean and Native American policies as the president hoped to establish a new empire of liberty in the Western Hemisphere.[27]

Part I

RECONSTRUCTION ON THE GLOBAL STAGE

Chapter 1

EXPORTING REPUBLICANISM BEYOND THE SOUTH

In early April 1869, President Grant summoned the new secretary of state, Hamilton Fish, to the White House. The President wished to discuss the readmission of Virginia into the Union and whether he should submit a letter to Congress approving that state's new Constitution, as well as other matters relating to public education for African Americans. Fish and Secretary of the Treasury George S. Boutwell recommended that there was not enough time in the current session of Congress to address the matter, to which Grant concurred. The president then inquired whether Fish had received the resignation of Reverdy Johnson, minister to Britain, as well as the resignation of John P. Hale, the minister to Spain. Fish returned to his office to prepare telegrams to the US diplomats abroad, when the Spanish minister, Señor Don M. Lopez Roberts, entered complaining bitterly that pro-Cuban independence groups planned to pass his home that evening singing songs of liberty. Fish dismissed it as idle gossip but promised to take up the matter with the chief of police in Washington, whom he summoned right away. Next to arrive at his office was Sir Edward Thornton, minister from Great Britain, who presented Fish with an affidavit on the recent capture of the *Mary Lowell*, an American ship accused of providing military aid to the Cuban rebellion. Fish thanked the minister for the affidavit, promising to forward it on to Reverdy Johnson (along with his request for the man's resignation). An otherwise busy, but normal morning was then interrupted by a visit from an unfamiliar guest, a man named Joseph W. Fabens.[1]

Fabens arrived in Fish's office with a proposal that would change the trajectory of the Grant administration's foreign policy. The American adventurer "brought a memorandum purporting to be from . . . the Dominican Republic, proposing annexation to the U. S." Using the admission of Texas as the blueprint for his plan, Fabens, on behalf of the Dominican Republic, proposed entering the American Union as a state. Fish questioned by whose authority Fabens was made to propose such an enormous question, to which Fabens replied that he was a "confidential agent" of the Dominican Republic. Fish balked at the proposal, noting that he was against the idea and that it would never pass Congress. "If it were possible," Fish told the filibusterer Fabens, he "had not the time or inclination to take part in its consideration, or in urging it." Fabens provided the secretary with a statistical report of the nation's economy, which Fish promised to read when he had the time. At that, the chief of police arrived, and Fish returned to the threat of a serenade against the Spanish minister. The next morning, at the meeting of Grant's cabinet, following a discussion of the recognition of Cuban independence, Fish "informally presented" Fabens' proposal to the president, with the caveat that he was against the whole scheme. The cabinet members all agreed that it was not the right time to bring such a proposal to Congress and the secretary of state assumed the matter was closed. Unfortunately for Fish, this was just the beginning, as President Grant embarked on a quixotic attempt to bring the Dominican Republic into the national union, and to export American republicanism to the Dominican people, a brand of republicanism that Grant deemed superior to the Dominican brand.[2] These entries in the diary of Hamilton Fish encapsulated the issues that defined Grant's Reconstruction domestic and foreign policy. From issues related to reestablishing the Union, educating freedmen, recognizing Cuban independence, settling grievances with Britain and Spain, supporting American citizens abroad, and exporting the ideals of the newly freed nation, the first year of the Grant administration forced the president and secretary of state to confront a host of important questions. Among these were who deserved to be citizens of the United States and what was the responsibility of the nation to those who yearned to join the Union. The attempted annexation of the Dominican Republic shaped Grant's policies into a doctrine that defined liberty and republicanism in the Western Hemisphere and ultimately failed.

Grant's annexation of the Dominican Republic envisioned an American expansion that signaled a renewed effort of imperialism, in which the United States sought to establish itself as an economic world power. At the close of the Civil War, Abraham Lincoln's secretary of state, William Henry Seward, had envisioned an ever-expanding United States that would rival European economic influence in the Western Hemisphere through the annexation of Alaska as well as other territories in the Caribbean. Grant's scheme for the

Dominican Republic, though, represented a significant shift in the arc of American imperialism. Grant intended that the people of the Dominican Republic would enjoy citizenship rights and the protections guaranteed by the United States Constitution. Annexation was, to Grant, the answer to numerous problems affecting the United States during Reconstruction. For Grant, the annexation of the Dominican Republic to the United States was the first step toward the fulfillment of his hemispheric strategy. His Caribbean policy placed the United States at the forefront of hemispheric abolitionism, economic development, and military superiority. Acquiring the Dominican Republic would lead to a strengthening of the Union, the expansion of American influence over North America, South America, and the Caribbean, and positive social and political gains in the United States— including full political participation, economic opportunities, and social equality for African Americans. The influx of over one hundred thousand new citizens of Hispanic, African, and indigenous origin into the United States would, Grant hoped, encourage racial reconciliation in the South or, failing that, provide an American territory where non-white citizens could enjoy the fruits of their own labor and the blessings of republican liberty. But the Administration's policy was about more than race, it was about the role of the government in crafting policies both foreign and domestic and about stabilizing the Union through the efforts of Reconstruction.[3]

Grant was not alone in this line of thinking, as Republican members of Congress were also looking to the Caribbean as an example of American progress. Both US Representatives Nathaniel Banks and Godlove Orth introduced resolutions or floor statements in favor of annexing the Dominican Republic as a territory or protectorate. As early as eight days after the inauguration, Banks introduced a joint resolution "concerning the annexation of the republic of Santo Domingo to the United States." The resolution (H. R. No. 3) was referred to the Committee on Foreign Affairs and never heard from again. On that same day, Orth introduced a similar resolution stating that "the people of [the Dominican Republic] shall adopt a republican form of territorial government," the petition for annexation shall be approved by the government and submitted to the US Congress for approval, and "the admission of said Territory shall be with the view to the ultimate establishment of a State government republican in form." At the end of the first session in April, Orth went to the House floor and had the March resolution read by the clerk. Orth then delivered a lengthy floor statement that reflected what would become the Grant Doctrine.[4]

Orth intended his resolution to start a conversation on American expansion. He noted to the House chamber that the subject of Dominican annexation was one that the American people must resolve. "The friends of this measure do not shrink from such consideration," he argued, "feeling satisfied that the practical sense of our people will easily comprehend and appreciate the national importance of so valuable an acquisition." Orth reminded the assembly that the late Civil War had settled the question of Union and dispelled the subject of dissolution. More importantly, however, the war "eradicated from our system that 'relic of barbarism' so long our bane and our shame," freeing millions of enslaved persons, conferring upon them "those 'natural and inalienable rights' so long and so wickedly withheld." Orth, a former Whig and Know-Nothing, held fast to the free soil and free labor beliefs of the Republican Party. However, these were not the only results of the war. Orth argued that the struggle had been between "republican and monarchical institutions of government," in which men of the Western Hemisphere were "capable of self-government" and this form of government was the only form that would last. Orth was extolling an American exceptionalism that had existed from the nation's founding. Of German ancestry, Orth argued that monarchial machinations from Europe, such as Napoleon III's occupation of Mexico after the American Civil War, were linked with the former slave-holding Confederacy. Yet it was the republicans of Mexico who won the day, pushing against French intervention. Such European influence in the western hemisphere, expressed in the British to the north, the Russians to the northwest, and the Spanish Caribbean to the south, continued to conflict with American republican institutions. Therefore, he argued, it was the duty of the United States to intervene in the rebellion in Cuba and to annex the Dominican Republic. The Cuban struggle "if successful, will result in the emancipation of her slaves, the adoption of a republican form of government, and will enable her to enter upon a career of unexampled prosperity."[5]

Orth understood that the United States, after the Civil War, was hoping to become a world economic power. "It has long been our settled policy to cultivate the most intimate and friendly relations with all the nations of the American continent," Orth acknowledged to his fellow Congressmen. It was a responsibility for the United States to use its "kindly offices in creating, fostering, and protecting sentiments and interests which are exclusively and peculiarly American." These relationships grew from the soil of commerce. "We are rapidly becoming a commercial people," Orth noted, "and we should avail ourselves of all just means which tend to foster and protect commercial interests." Annexing the Dominican Republic and supporting Cuban independence did just that, as it would "establish peace and quiet within its borders, to give protection to the industry and enterprise of man." American influence in the Caribbean was a stabilizing force, preventing incursions from other island nations and monarchial European powers. Orth quoted Joseph Fabens' description of the *Vega Real,* or the Royal Valley, a land where the "productive resources of this famous valley . . . equal those of the Island of Barbadoes [sic] . . . it would of itself support a population of four millons [sic]." Orth quoted Fabens' report on the minerals, products, and history of the Dominican Republic, alluding to Christopher Columbus and Toussaint L'Ouverture. Noting the history of the entire island, as it evolved from French slavery into two viable republics, Orth argued that the people of the Dominican Republic were ready to join the American Union, "to place themselves and their territory under the control of our laws; in a word, to share our destinies." Orth argued that the acquisition of Haiti was an inevitability once the Dominican Republic joined the Union. Senator Charles Sumner would charge Grant with a similar scheme towards Haiti, though the President was adamant that he was not interested in the Haitian republic.[6]

Orth ended his address by examining objections to the proposed acquisition of the Dominican Republic. A major objection concerned the acquisition of the new territory itself. Some members of Congress, he noted, believed that the United States possessed more territories than it could possibly handle. This was a common refrain from anti-expansionists in the nineteenth century. To that objection Orth asked if any member would be willing to sell or transfer those territories to other powers. Another objection was the assumption of Dominican debts. To this Orth argued that previous territorial acquisitions came with the stipulation that those territories manage their debt before being allowed to organize as an American state. Finally, Orth examined the most prominent objection: race. "I refer to the peculiar color, and probably also the peculiar odor of a very large portion of the inhabitants of the island," Orth noted with cruel racism. "It is true they are black, very black, much blacker I am told than our Americans of African descent," Orth stated, "[b]ut they are free, and they fought for and achieved their own freedom, and for nearly three fourths of a century have maintained their freedom by organizing and successfully maintain[ing] their own Government." Orth's own racial prejudice clouded his view of the

Dominicans, yet his belief in republican institutions superseded his own racism. "This objection on the score of color is founded upon prejudice," Orth noted, "for prejudice is blind and listens not to reason." Following the Civil War, so-called Radical Republicans such as Orth embraced the pillars of the Republican Party over their own prejudice regarding racial differences. Orth, who later became a vocal proponent for racial equality, argued that the Dominican Republic could hold every Black American comfortably should they choose to emigrate there. Fabens, in an 1862 paper read before the American Geographical and Statistical Society of New York, argued that the Dominican Republic could support a population exceeding four million people. This point would influence an important part of the Grant Doctrine as Grant would argue that every African American in the United States, should they choose, could safely emigrate to the Dominican Republic.[7]

Questions of race and citizenship dominated the discussion following Orth's speech. His colleague from Indiana, Democrat William Ellis Niblack, asked if Orth considered "an increase of our colored population desirable under existing circumstance." Orth asked if Niblack considered losing laborers in the US desirable. Niblack responded that Orth was not answering the question, and that if he proposed increasing the Black population in the country, he "should at once propose an amendment to our naturalization laws so that colored people may immigrate . . . and become citizens by naturalization. . . . As is well known, none but white people can be naturalized under existing laws." Orth agreed to support such a bill if Niblack would introduce it. A staunch Democrat, Niblack stated that he would not, "under no circumstances in the present condition of the country." Niblack wanted clarification to Orth's point: Was the fact that the Dominicans were "very black" an "objection in his mind to their being incorporated among the people of the United States?" Orth shot back that if Niblack did not know his position on equality after serving with him in Congress since the Civil War, he did not "think he ever will." At this point Banks entered the debate, asking Niblack if any Democrats would object to acquiring new territories "simply because a few colored laborers happen to live there?" Niblack responded that he would not reject a territory for that reason alone, but that "the character of the population ought always to be considered under such circumstances." "I consider the gentleman a convert," Banks quipped. With that the discussion of annexation ended, put before the Congress and the people as Orth intended. Many of Orth's statements mirror those that Grant would offer to promote annexation. The salient point of the fitness of the

Dominicans as citizens of the United States became the most important factor of Grant's decision to support annexation.[8]

Grant's attitudes toward citizenship were part of a long American tradition regarding republicanism. Most Americans cleaved to the idea that the people of the United States were the sovereign voice, and that voice represented the best of American idealism. To Grant, African Americans were citizens because they had worked hard, accepted the cultural norms of civilized society, and, most importantly, had served and fought for their freedoms. African Americans had proven their worth as citizen-soldiers and, because of the Fourteenth and Fifteenth Amendments, now had the constitutional right to participate in the body politic. The idea of the citizen-soldier in the United States was born out of a republicanism that dated back to the nation's founding. Though this ideology would change drastically after the Civil War, as many Americans increasingly accepted the role of a strong coercive government, Grant continued to believe that African Americans had proven to the nation, through their labor and their service, their ability to make good American citizens. While many Republicans viewed the civil rights amendments as measures to bring about an end to Reconstruction and to restore the Union, Black Americans and their white allies understood the revolutionary nature of their entrance into the body politic, possibly none more so than Black veterans.[9]

Grant based his definition of citizenship upon his notions of what constituted a civilized citizen. Civilization, to Grant, was contingent upon the acceptance of western social and religious norms, free labor, and modernity. A civilized republican citizen eschewed barbarism and aristocracy, while embracing progress and liberty. African Americans had fully assimilated into Western civilization, in Grant's eyes, as had the Dominican people, both groups therefore obviously worthy of the rights of citizenship afforded by the US Constitution. Several prominent Republicans, though, disagreed that Dominicans were civilized. They claimed that the Dominicans had proven they were incapable of self-government due to their innate laziness and their inability to maintain a cohesive political system and were therefore not fit to be Americans. They also argued that the environment in the Caribbean, the heat, humidity, and disease, caused Dominican laziness and an inability to successfully implement republican systems. Due to his emphasis on equality and citizenship, Grant's ideas did not represent the beliefs of the entire Republican Party, as many members of his party opposed legislation that provided equality for African Americans. These Republicans were fearful of a strong federal government, and they did not support "uses of federal power that they admitted could be seen as tyrannical." These "Liberal Republicans" were a small group consisting primarily of Charles Francis Adams, Lyman Trumbull, and Carl Schurz and a few dozen more politicians, writers, editors, and businessmen. All vocally criticized President Grant's annexation scheme, but they conditionally supported his plans for Reconstruction in the American South. This support, though, did not equate to believing in the equality of Black Americans. They feared the centralized power of the federal government, believing it akin to the slave power that Grant's army had overthrown in the war, and a body politic diluted by an unfit electorate. They also feared corruption, as they saw federal support of Blacks as akin to socialism, and they suspected corruption of being behind the Dominican Republic scheme as well as within majority Black Southern legislatures. Traditional republicanism did not allow for the federal government to craft legislation providing equal rights to the freedmen and it certainly did not permit the president to annex a nation which they saw as unassimilable.[10]

Grant's attempt to annex the Dominican Republic was not the first overture by the United States toward expansion in the Caribbean. Many prior administrations had argued that a strong presence there was vital for strengthening American commerce and military security. Previous administrations had sought coaling stations on the island, and some had considered territorial acquisitions in the area. These earlier expansionist schemes, however, ran counter to Grant's logic regarding the annexation of the Dominican Republic. In the early days of the nineteenth century, Southern slave-owners had sought to strengthen slavery by annexing Cuba. Indeed, United States interest in acquiring Cuba was one of the reasons that President James Monroe had originally issued the Monroe Doctrine. These early Cuban annexation schemes would have provided citizenship not to the vast majority of those inhabiting the island—enslaved persons—but only to the select planters who maintained the profitable sugar plantations. This would specifically have averted the "Haitianiziation" of the island by forestalling a slave insurrection against a weakening colonial power. Grant, in contrast, intended for the entire Dominican population to become full US citizens and he supported, in theory, the democratic aims of the Cuban rebellion. The freedoms and citizenship that Grant intended for Black Americans would also be available to the Dominicans, regardless of their racial background, but would have to be won by the Cubans. Citizenship for the

Dominicans was a revolutionary idea. At no other time before, nor for many years after, would an American president suggest full citizenship to people whom many white Americans viewed as an unworthy "other."[11]

Before he would support annexation, the president dispatched a fact-finding mission to ascertain the Dominicans' desire for union and their ability to maintain economic and political stability. Although Secretary of State Fish did not personally support annexation, he agreed to send one of his staff members to the Dominican Republic to report on the situation on the ground. The first two men he selected were unable to begin their missions (one due to illness, the other due to shipwreck). At the last minute, Grant sent his personal assistant and former aide-de-camp, Orville E. Babcock, in their stead. Fish was not keen to send a non-diplomat to perform such work, but with such little notice and Grant's impatience to obtain information on the Caribbean nation, Fish relented. He provided the young officer with a passport and instructions, sending him on his way in mid-July 1869.[12] The president and the secretary of state instructed Babcock to report on "[the] population in principal towns, cities, and country. Total, North and South or any other order of distribution." Fish requested information on "Revenue for last fiscal year and the half of present year, How obtained; Expense for last fiscal year and the half of present year; Tonnage and flag under which the business was done last fiscal year and half of the present year; National debt, foreign and domestic, how issued, where held, rate of interest, how to be paid, what guarantee." Of importance to the secretary of state was whether any foreign power held grants in the Dominican Republic, asking Babcock to provide a "List and character of grants and concessions to private individuals and to companies; List of public property, in general terms; Size of Army and Navy; Copy of the Constitution."[13]

Fish also requested information on the "number of whites, pure Africans, of mulattoes, and of other mixtures of the African and Caucasian races; of Indians, and of the crosses between them and whites, and Africans, respectively." Both Grant and Fish understood that the racial makeup of the island would be just as important to Congressional leaders as the economic and foreign entanglements of the Dominican government. While racial equality was an important aspect of Reconstruction, racist politicians argued that it was an impediment to progress and national unity, as many Republicans and all Democrats believed African Americans were not members of the body politic. The racial makeup of the Dominicans was a necessary factor for many members of Congress, such as Congressman Niblack, who would eventually lead the charge against annexation. Fish often expressed displeasure at the idea of bringing in hundreds of thousands of people of color into the United States, yet Grant supported including these people, preferably as members of the Republican Party, and he believed that having this information would better enable him to make his argument to Congress on behalf of annexation and would prepare him for any challenges to the acquisition of the nation by European powers.[14]

As Grant's private secretary, Babcock did not question the appropriateness of his selection to visit the Dominican Republic. The last-minute nature of Babcock's selection undermined all the charges later levied against Grant and his personal secretary that they had been in collusion with Dominican speculators for months prior to Babcock's departure. In fact, the choice of two diplomats prior to Babcock, made by annexation skeptic Hamilton Fish, further undermined such charges. Babcock took his mission as a direct order from his commander-in-chief, and he left with the understanding that his was a fact-finding mission and that he had no other authority or treaty making powers. Babcock returned bearing samples of natural resources, economic data, and a report of his visit. However, he also provided Grant and Fish with a memorandum, drawn up by the Dominican president Buenaventura Baez, expressing his administration's desire for annexation, which embarrassingly referred to Babcock as President Grant's "Aide-de-camp."[15] Some historians have maintained that Babcock went beyond his mandate to report about the island's economy, industry, and resources and instead assisted the Dominican president in creating a protocol stipulating terms for annexation. While Babcock's official commission from Hamilton Fish limited him to inquiry only, it is clear from Babcock's own journal entries and from subsequent correspondence with Grant himself, that the president intended Babcock to obtain written requests from the Dominican government. Though researchers should read Babcock's accounts with caution, much of his diary matches up with the Senate testimony of his colleagues and many of the central figures in the annexation discussion. In fact, his diaries reveal him as a naïve diplomat instead of the shrewd conspirator so often depicted by his critics. Historian Allan Nevins argued that Grant gave Babcock instructions to work out Baez's desires on annexation "without Fish's knowledge." This is highly unlikely. Nevins pointed to Babcock's testimony in the subsequent House of Representatives investigation as evidence of this subterfuge by Fish. Babcock testified that he handed Baez a memorandum containing his instructions that matched the instructions that Fish gave to him. He then signed a memorandum stating Baez's wishes and requirements toward annexation. According to Babcock, "it was signed without any official capacity" but merely as proof that the two parties had discussed its contents. Nevins provides no evidence of Fish being "disturbed and indignant" at Babcock's memorandum save for a quote in Jacob Cox's 1890s account of the scheme, an account that Nevins describes as "manifestly inaccurate" and "full of error." The lack of any documentation in Fish's diaries or correspondence showing indignancy toward Babcock undercuts an argument that historians have since buoyed as fact. Eric Foner made the same claim about Babcock and Fish, but his source is Nevins's book, while others use Eric Foner as their source to make the same claim. Several historians and popular authors continue to echo the Nevins claim that Babcock angered Fish by returning with a signed memorandum.[16]

Babcock's diaries also provide insight into what the potential annexation of the Dominican Republic would mean to the educated elite class of Republican men who controlled Reconstruction politics and policy. Babcock observed a strange and foreign "other" through his own personal prism of republicanism and civilization. Post-war republicanism viewed civilized men through the lens of individual liberty, while at the same time viewing the uncivilized as a monolithic group. A young officer like Babcock would have found it difficult to separate the actions and potentials of individual Dominicans from the whole of their society. Seeing them as people of color first and civilized people second would have colored his views of the Dominicans on his tour. That Grant and Fish had tasked Babcock to report on the economic, political, and social conditions is evident throughout the journals, yet what also comes across are Babcock's distinct ideas about what republican political tradition and civilized society meant to him. Babcock's experiences in the Dominican Republic ultimately informed Grant's opinion on the annexation scheme, and, as a result, lay the groundwork for the Grant Doctrine. Grant developed a policy of not only economic advancement but also for the broader expansion of republicanism. This ideology was central to the tenets of the Republican Party (and the Whigs before them). Babcock's mission, then, provided the first analysis of the Dominican people as potential republican beneficiaries of Grant's hemispheric Reconstruction.[17]

In 1869, the Dominican Republic was a nation attempting to emerge from decades of turmoil and strife resulting from both internal clashes and external conflicts. Following its separation from Haiti in 1844, the Dominican Republic suffered civil rebellion and a constant threat of Haitian domination. The Dominicans established a republican form of government, but internal tensions undermined the efforts to establish democracy. Regional leaders fought for position and influence in the newly independent nation, hoping to exert their will over the populace. Buenaventura Baez and Pedro Santana headed opposing factions, and each led the nation respectively and attempted to consolidate power. This included courting the support of foreign powers. While Baez turned to the United States in 1855, offering a lease of Samaná Bay, Santana sought the assistance of the British and the Spanish. The Europeans and the Haitians looked warily upon any US military presence in the Caribbean.[18] As Santana and Baez traded the presidency back and forth, fighting between their two factions left the nation in ruins. In early 1860, Santana sought protectorate status from Spain, which annexed the nation in 1861. The renewed presence of the former colonial masters led many Dominicans to resent Santana. Within a year the Restoration War broke out. This European intervention in the Dominican Republic came at a time when the United States was in no position to enforce the Monroe Doctrine.[19]

United States influence in the Dominican Republic was nothing new to the Dominican people, nor was African American expatriation to the island. Black colonists had fled the United States in the antebellum period and populated the Bay of Samaná, which Grant coveted for its strategic location. In 1825, the "colony's founders resolved to escape the American racial caste system" by settling in then-Haitian territory. By the time of Grant's attempted annexation, the hundreds of colonists living there "embraced annexation because they believed that the U. S. government would extend its reconstructed institutions southward, [incorporating] Dominicans as equal citizens in the American nation." Grant's professions of equality and freedom across the Caribbean resonated more strongly with the African American colony in Samaná than it did with the rest of the Dominicans.[20] Several Republicans who opposed Dominican annexation also opposed Grant's efforts at Reconstruction, doing so through the lens of race. They cast the annexation project in the same light as attempts to move African Americans into the American political sphere. Led by Carl Schurz, they argued that African American freedom alone had been the goal of the Civil War, not equality. Schurz saw the advancement of African American rights as tied to governmental corruption. He and other "Liberal Republicans" questioned why the US should grant citizenship to Dominicans when former slaves were not up to the task in the American South. To Liberal Republicans, Reconstruction would end once the Southern states had all returned to the Union. There was no need to add additional uneducated, un-republican people into the citizenry when the Southern states were struggling to incorporate freedmen into the body politic.[21]

Grant dissented from such thinking. He believed that African Americans were indeed up to the task of citizenship and, to prove it, he needed to annex the Dominican Republic. Fish's prejudice toward the Dominicans was most certainly a significant reason for his antipathy toward annexation. Grant relied on Fish's counsel regarding matters of the State Department, and the cabinet agreed that there was not enough time for the Congress to take up the matter.[22] William T. Sherman, acting secretary of war, doubted that Caribbean nations, and by extension the people there, were ready to join the Union. "Sherman doubts the influence of the climate on free institutions," Fish wrote in his diary, "thinks our acquisitions of Texas, New Mexico and of the greater part of California have been a source of weakness and are a burden."[23] In the immediate aftermath of the Civil War, Sherman stated that the social order should revert to what it had been prior to the conflict. He did not believe in citizenship rights for freedmen, arguing that they only deserved the right not to be mistreated because of their color. Sherman articulated what many Republicans believed to be the main goal of Reconstruction: securing the South's return to the Union and a return to the status quo minus the stain of slavery. Grant's desire to bring in an additional 100,000 or more Black citizens went too far. Fish expressed a similar opinion regarding the annexation of Cuba. Speaking to German minister Baron Gerolt, Fish noted that annexing Cuba to the United States was not in the nation's best interest. "We derived forty millions [sic] a year of custom duties from Cuba, which would be lost by its annexation," Fish recorded in his diary, "[B]eside the necessity of expenditures . . . the character of the population was not homogenous with ours." The Cubans, and by extension the Dominicans, were not capable of assimilating into republican institutions because of their race and culture. The overwhelming majority was Catholic, many were Spanish or African, and some had indigenous heritage. These traits were anathema to many Americans who saw the Dominicans as not only racially, but religiously and culturally different. The Dominicans themselves historically looked down upon Black Haitians, displaying a form of Dominican nationalism that saw Black Dominicans and Haitians as less than those Dominicans of Spanish (or white) heritage. Even protestant Black American emigrants in Samana felt the ire of "Spanish Dominicans," who went so far as to limit Haitian and Black American immigration as part of an effort to "whiten" the racial makeup of the nation. To many Americans, then, the creolization of the Dominicans made them incapable of introduction into the body politic, no matter how civilized they appeared to be or how hard the ruling nationalist party tried to present Dominicans as Spanish and not Black.[24]

While Grant was preoccupied with the issue of Dominican annexation, Secretary of State Hamilton Fish was busy handling the leftover wartime disputes between the United States and Great Britain. The quarrel over the man-of-war *Alabama* derived from the fact that in 1862 a British firm had built the rebel ship in Liverpool, England, and sold it surreptitiously to the Confederate government. The British origins of the *Alabama* led American politicians to charge the British with violating US neutrality during the Civil War. American merchants and businessmen who had lost millions of dollars during the war to the actions of Confederate cruisers filed claims against the government to recoup these losses. At the same time, disagreements with Great Britain encompassed more than just the cost of Civil War maritime losses. The naturalization of British citizens in the United States, notably Irish Fenians, and fishing rights in Nova Scotia and the Great Lakes, also agitated Anglo-American relations. Efforts toward a settlement of the grievances between the United States and Great Britain began immediately after the Civil War. President Abraham Lincoln's secretary of state, William H. Seward, actively sought redress from the British for injuries to the United States. Seward also had grander motives behind his tough stand toward the British. He wanted to annex Canada to the United States and eliminate British influence throughout North America. In 1868, President Johnson's appointment of Reverdy Johnson, a Maryland senator, as minister to Great Britain led to the negotiation of a treaty that the US Senate failed to ratify, thus prolonging the diplomatic conflict between the two nations.[25]

A possible conflict with Great Britain drove Grant's desire to establish an American foothold in the Caribbean. If American diplomats could not settle the disagreements between the two nations, Grant surmised, then the US needed a base of operations for a possible war. His predecessor's choice as negotiator, Reverdy Johnson's, main task was the settlement of the *Alabama* claims, which he sought through negotiations with the British foreign secretary, the Earl of Clarendon, George Villiers. The resulting treaty, known as the Johnson-Clarendon Convention, contained several provisions that angered political leaders in both nations. The United States found the lack of an apology by the British for their interference in the Civil War unforgivable. Conceding that they had violated their own Neutrality Proclamation was equally as galling for the British. In the early months of 1869, Secretary Seward presented to the US Senate a significantly flawed treaty.[26] Reaction to the treaty in the United States was swift. The Senate overwhelmingly rejected the treaty 54 to 1, to widespread public approval. Soon after, in April 1869, Charles Sumner gave a lengthy speech charging the British with aiding the Confederacy and the cause of slavery through their economic and diplomatic support of the South. The cost for their treachery, Sumner surmised, was around $400 million in direct and indirect claims. These indirect claims became the most contentious point in the ongoing *Alabama* negotiations and Fish would eventually seek to adjudicate them in an international court.[27]

Grant inherited several other foreign policy issues that had perplexed the previous administration, particularly with Spain. Both Great Britain and Spain represented a challenge to his eventual quest for US supremacy in the Western Hemisphere. Moreover, Great Britain and Spain represented European colonialism, challenging Grant's design for hemispheric republicanism under the aegis of the United States. Grant's foreign policy envisioned displacing European monarchy and imperialism in the Americas with US-led republicanism and abolishing Spanish slavery in favor of multiracial citizenship and free labor. No territory in the Western Hemisphere offered a better staging ground for Grant's policy than did Cuba. Yet, Grant and Fish resisted Republican Party calls to support revolutionary independence efforts there. Their hesitancy derived from concerns about how United States intervention might affect other high-level negotiations with Great Britain over the *Alabama* claims. Against significant pressure from within the cabinet and from within the Congress to support Cuba, Fish convinced Grant that providing support for the Cuban rebellion would significantly undermine the United States' argument against Great Britain in the *Alabama* claims. As such, the United States officially remained neutral in the Cuban rebellion, though the plight of numerous American citizens who traveled to Cuba to support the rebels often forced the administration to intervene. Eventually, Spanish authorities captured and executed American and British insurgents on board the ship the *Virginius,* threatening Grant's policy of nonintervention in Cuba, and an enraged American public demanded action against Spain and continued to assist the Cuban insurgents.

One of the principal bones of contention between the United States and European states concerned the rights of naturalized citizens. The enormous influx of immigrants into the United States in the previous two decades had raised questions about the rights of naturalized citizens when they travelled and worked abroad. Both Cuban and Irish immigrants brought the lessons of the Civil War with them as they returned home. These immigrants shared a belief in individual liberty and self-government with natural-born Americans and they sought to transport these beliefs to the people of their former home. Because of such activities many of these naturalized Americans were arrested in their home countries, forcing Irish and Cuban Americans to look to the American government for assistance. Early on, disputes over the rights of naturalized citizens arrested in other nations caused headaches for the Grant administration. Spanish authorities arrested Cuban rebels who often claimed American citizenship and thus the protection of their adopted nation. The convoluted nature of the naturalization process did not help matters. While the courts in state governments issued official naturalization certificates to some citizens, many others had no papers to prove their citizenship. As such, when arrested in foreign countries naturalized citizens often sought refuge in the offices of the American Legation, and the charge of proving their citizenship often fell to the clerks in these offices. These clerks, then, sought advice from Fish's State Department.[28]

The development of Grant's immigration policy occurred while the Grant administration was simultaneously pursuing the annexation of the Dominican Republic and the fallout of the Cuban insurrection. Grant and Fish worked to keep the United States out of the Cuban conflict while offering to arbitrate the dispute between the Cuban rebels and Spain. In the process the administration pressed for the abolition of slavery and the establishment of self-government in Cuba. Political upheaval in Spain complicated matters, as did the clamor of American citizens who lobbied for the recognition of Cuban belligerency and a more active American role to secure Cuban freedom. Thus, the Grant administration, with its call to abolish slavery in Cuba, maintained military readiness in the Caribbean while promoting peace and republican institutions across the Western Hemisphere. Military readiness was an important factor in the proposed annexation of the Dominican Republic, as the United States looked for a safe coaling station and territory in the region. While Grant and Fish privately pursued the arbitration of the Cuban insurrection, their minister to Spain, Daniel Sickles, broached acquiring Cuba with the Spanish. Purchasing Cuba while annexing the Dominican Republic would have led the administration down an expansionist path not seen since the imperial pursuits of the Mexican-American War. Since Grant knew that he had the necessary constitutional authority to handle all diplomatic negotiations, he acted in accordance with his desire to eliminate European influence in the Caribbean and eradicate slavery.[29]

The enslaved population in Cuba grew from approximately 40,000 enslaved Africans in the 1770s peaking to nearly 440,000 enslaved by the 1840s. Cuba, then, was home to one of the largest populations of enslaved persons following emancipation in the United States. Slavery in Cuba accounted for over three-quarters of the laborers on the island, yet by 1860, with the abolition of the African slave trade, slavery began to decline. This decline in conjunction with the tenuous political situation in Spain led to a growing discontent among Spanish planters, Cuban laborers, and the enslaved that resulted in armed conflict. From the 1840s to the 1860s, Spain itself underwent complex political and religious changes. Wracked by civil wars and military coups, the country began to weaken in Europe, leaving their colonies in the Caribbean vulnerable. The Revolution of 1868, which deposed Spain's Queen Isabella II and installed military leader General Juan Prim as prime minister, further weakened Spain's control over Cuba, allowing discontent among the Cuban planters, laborers, and enslaved to boil over against the Spanish. This conflict would engulf the United States in a decade-long diplomatic crisis.[30] The perpetuation of slavery in Cuba was contingent on support from the metropole in Madrid, where Spain profited from the "peculiar institution's" productivity and the massive amount of wealth produced in both Cuba and Puerto Rico. As Grant recognized, the United States sustained this slavery indirectly through the importation of sugar and coffee from both island nations. Grant believed that a US presence in the Dominican Republic would choke slavery in Cuba and Puerto Rico because the American investment of capital would cut into the profitability of both colonies. However, he and Fish were unwilling to wait for slavery to die a gradual death. The Cuban insurrection provided an opportunity for Grant to pursue the end of slavery in the Caribbean immediately, which he saw as the next step toward the emancipation of the entire Western Hemisphere.[31]

The viability of any new Cuban republic was important to Grant's and Fish's decision-making on the granting of belligerent rights. Fish doubted the Cubans' ability to maintain a functional government, noting, "the Cubans are inefficient, & have done little for themselves."[32] Fish questioned whether the Cuban insurgents maintained control over certain provinces on the island, and whether they could sustain themselves as a republic. To Fish, the Cuban rebels would only succeed if they held significant ports, portions of land, seats of government, or seat an elected body.[33] Many American political leaders and newspaper editors argued that it was a moral imperative for the United States to intercede on behalf of the Cuban rebels. In March 1869, Senator John Sherman of Ohio, brother of Grant's comrade General William T. Sherman, introduced a joint resolution "authorizing the recognition of the independence of Cuba."[34] Cuban exiles and Republican politicians adopted resolutions at a large meeting in Steinway Hall in New York City later that month, expressing their support. Charles A. Dana, Grant's friend and editor of *The Sun,* read the resolutions to the gathering crowd, to loud applause. The group resolved, "the present struggle of the Cubans for independence and self-government, belongs in the same category as the Americans in 1776." They affirmed their support for the struggle against Spain and urged the United States government to recognize the Cubans as belligerents. Notably, "in proclaiming the abolition of slavery, the patriots of Cuba have given conclusive evidence that they share the most substantial ideas of modern democracy." The group included noted abolitionist Henry Ward Beecher, who argued that Cuba "ought to be free because her people desire it. Every people have the inherent right to self-government."[35] Such vocal support from Republican political leaders influenced Grant's consideration of Cuban belligerency, yet he struggled over the decision, holding numerous conversations with his cabinet, and asking Fish to write memoranda for both eventualities. He now faced an early test of will between his desire to see a republican Caribbean free of European influence and Fish's advocacy of a more prudent diplomatic course to deal with multiple difficulties with several European nations simultaneously. Ultimately, Grant decided not to support the Cuban insurgents, largely because of the ongoing controversy with Britain over the *Alabama* claims and the position the administration took on the question of belligerent rights during the American Civil War. His decision angered many Republicans who saw his later support for annexing the Dominican Republic as a quixotic adventure that turned his administration away from the fight for liberty in Cuba.[36]

The Cuban rebels enjoyed overwhelming support from many American political leaders and Cuban expatriates. But the ongoing *Alabama* negotiations forced the president and his secretary of state to confront Cuban supporters early on. In July 1869, Grant issued an executive order proclaiming the United States neutrality in the Cuban insurrection. This order authorized the arrest and prosecution of any American citizen and the utilization of the United States Navy for "the purpose of preventing the carrying on of any such expedition or enterprise from the territories or jurisdiction of the United States against the territories or dominions of Spain with whom the United States are at peace." Within two weeks of issuing the proclamation, District Attorney Edwards Pierrepont informed Fish that he had arrested over one hundred-sixty people in New York for aiding the Cuban rebels. Grant spent his first term avoiding entanglement in the Cuban insurrection. He and Fish understood the best method to avoid the armed conflict would be to offer mediation to restore peace. In late July 1869, Fish instructed Sickles in Madrid that he should offer "the good offices of the United States" to negotiate an armistice. Fish sought an immediate cessation of hostilities because American citizens in Cuba were caught in the crossfire or were even participating in the rebellion. "Spanish authorities in Cuba are impotent," Fish wrote to Sickles, "for protection of the lives of our citizens. Cuba and Porto Rico [sic] should not be connected in the submission or negotiation." Fish's anti-expansion beliefs may offer an explanation as to why he did not want Puerto Rico involved in Cuban negotiations, as the secretary of state was opposed to any conversations that included the US intervening in yet another Caribbean territory. Spanish Prime Minister Juan Prim followed up with an offer to sell both Cuba and Puerto Rico to the United States. Sickles, who was not authorized to purchase the two island territories, suggested a sum of $125 million. Prim noted that "Spain might arrange preliminaries with the United States and concede autonomy of Cuba and Porto Rico [sic] for satisfactory equivalent as soon as hostilities ceased," Sickles informed Fish. Fish was uninterested in purchasing the two colonies, but Grant gave the matter some thought before declining. The Spanish agreed to accept the "good offices" of the United States but only under a set of conditions that Grant and Fish were unwilling to concede. The Spanish wanted the insurgents to lay down their arms and accept a plebiscite for independence. Although Fish believed the Cubans were willing to agree to a cease-fire, he did not believe that a free and fair vote for independence would be possible. While the Spanish agreed to accept American arbitration, they were also sending 20,000 additional troops to Cuba to subdue the rebellion. Grant was displeased with this action, arguing that, while he was prepared to issue a neutrality proclamation regarding the insurrection, the actions of the

Spanish violated fundamental republican rights. "I am not clearly satisfied that we would not be justified in intimating to Spain that we look with some alarm upon her position to send 20,000 more troops to Cuba," he wrote to Fish, "to put down as Americans believe the right of self-government on this Continent." Grant then drafted a neutrality proclamation that threatened to prosecute Americans for any involvement in the Cuban insurrection and recognized the insurgents as belligerents, but he delayed issuing it because Fish argued that recognizing Cuban belligerency would undermine the administration's legal position in the *Alabama* claims.[37]

Grant intended his neutrality proclamation to counter the rising support for the Cuban rebels among the American public, especially Cuban-Americans. Many of these citizens were actively collecting weapons and materials to send to the Cubans, and hundreds were willing to enlist as rebel soldiers. The Cuban Junta, an organization of exiled Cubans, lobbied American financial and political leaders to back the rebellion. Even Grant's trusted friend, Secretary of War John Rawlins, expressed pro-Cuban views. He saw the Cuban Junta as freedom fighters who deserved recognition by the United States. His friendship with the president potentially gave him more influence on the matter than Fish and he temporarily swayed Grant toward recognition. However, Rawlins's declining health enabled Fish the chance to unite the rest of the cabinet against recognition. Instead of a neutrality proclamation, Grant extended an offer to mediate between the parties, subject to an armistice and a Spanish promise to emancipate remaining enslaved persons. Rawlins died less than a week after Grant's proposal and Fish and the rest of the cabinet backed a policy of non-recognition, mediation, and emancipation. Nevertheless, the Cuban Junta continued to push American public opinion in favor of Cuban recognition.[38]

Within a week of Grant's mediation offer, Junta leaders lobbied the State Department. Junta president José Morales Lemus called upon the assistant secretary of state, J. C. B. Davis, to ascertain the American position toward Cuba. Davis explained that the Spanish had "declared that an armistice was impossible—but that if the insurgents would lay down their arms, Spain would simultaneously grant a full amnesty." Lemus balked, stating, "We cannot trust the Spaniards. We will not lay down our arms." Lemus argued that the rebels had made several gains in Cuba and the Spanish were afraid of losing more territory. The rebels would only accept the American terms, he argued, noting that they were planning a great uprising in Havana as well as in the western agricultural region of Cuba. "To all this I said nothing," Davis wrote to Fish, "viewing the communication as an attempt to hasten the proclamation of belligerency which now seems inevitable." Davis's belief in the inevitability of recognition reflected an article of faith among many Americans that the United States would support the plight of freedom seeking peoples throughout the Western Hemisphere. The Cuban Junta's popularity was emblematic of this view and even privately Grant considered the rebels as worthy of recognition. However, Fish convinced the president to change his mind. The crux of Fish's argument drew upon the ongoing negotiations between the United States and Great Britain over the *Alabama* claims and the American positions on the questions of neutrality and belligerency.[39]

Hundreds of Cuban Americans sought aid and protection through the American legation in Havana and the State Department in Washington. Many of the claims emanated from Cuban Americans who were living under Spanish passports and working Spanish government jobs. These expatriates left Cuba for the United States, often prior to the American Civil War, where they obtained American citizenship. They then returned to Cuba and claimed Spanish citizenship, accepting jobs with the Spanish government as clerks, jobs unavailable to them as naturalized American citizens. When arrested, they claimed American citizenship and thus the protection of the United States against Spanish authority. Such cases vexed American consuls in Cuba. The State Department explained to its consuls in a dispatch: "Naturalized and native-born citizens are entitled to the same protections from the government when in a foreign country . . . and both in such case are ordinarily subject to the laws of such country and are bound to observe such laws to the same extent to which its own citizens or subjects are bound." If those American citizens decided to live abroad, they were subject to that nation's laws just like other citizens of that land. However, the dispatch also noted that any naturalized citizen who returned to their native country for the purposes of securing employment available only to citizens of that nation would negate the United States' obligation to intervene on his behalf, should the need arise. Therefore, Fish's State Department was under no obligation to protect those Cuban Americans who had violated the laws of both the United States and Cuba. Secretary Fish understood and convinced President Grant that supporting the republican movement of the Junta, either by recognizing their plight or providing material support, would undermine the important *Alabama* claims, which remained unsettled.[40]

The twin subjects of the annexation of the Dominican Republic and the recognition of Cuban belligerency dominated the early discussions in the first nine months of Grant's cabinet. The desire to support those fighting for or seeking American republicanism was important to Grant, but political and diplomatic challenges on other fronts necessitated a measured response. The Grant administration spent the first year of its term examining the situation in the Caribbean, and how it could best support liberal democracy there. It did so while balancing the necessities of relations with Great Britain and Spain. At the same time, public concern for the expansion of republicanism in the Hemisphere complicated matters. As 1869 ended, the administration began formal negotiations with not only the Spanish and the Dominicans, but officials also looked to settle the multiple concerns the United States had with Great Britain.

Chapter 2

CHALLENGES TO ANNEXATION

Grant was pleased with the information he received from Babcock following his first visit to the Dominican Republic. Babcock provided a report on the economic, political, racial, and republican makeup of the nation, as well as a selection of agricultural goods available there. He also provided the president with a memorandum of understanding signed by both Babcock and Dominican President Buenaventura Baez that dictated terms for annexation. Grant informed Fish that annexation was now a part of his foreign policy, and that the two nations needed to agree to a treaty. Grant and Fish worried about foreign control of the national debt of the Dominicans. He therefore decided to enter treaty negotiations without advising Congress, particularly the Chair of the Senate Foreign Relations Committee, Charles Sumner. Fish argued that Babcock was not authorized to negotiate nor sign a treaty of annexation, but Grant insisted that Babcock return to the island nation to initiate negotiations. The relationships Babcock made were crucial, Grant believed, to making the treaty negotiations a smooth process. As such, Fish chose a new consul for the Dominican Republic, Matthew Perry, as the existing consul, Somers Smith, had fallen out of favor not only with the Dominicans but with Babcock as well. Babcock, then, was sent back to the Dominican Republic to negotiate the treaty while Perry was authorized to sign it. As a sign of good faith, Grant ordered the secretary of navy to station an American man-of-war in Caribbean waters to protect the Dominican government from rebel forces led by José María Cabral. On his return trip to the Dominican Republic in the autumn of 1869, Babcock, his translator General Delos B. Sackett, and company took their quarters aboard the steamship *Albany,* making daily excursions ashore to meet with President Buenaventura Baez and Secretary of State Don Manuel Gautier. After some time, the two groups agreed to draft two distinct treaties. The first was a treaty of annexation to admit the Dominican Republic to the Union as a territory, with the United States providing $1.5 million toward the liquidation of the Dominican debt. The second was a treaty providing for the leasing of Samaná Bay for 99 years for $2 million if the Senate did not ratify the first treaty. Babcock then presented President Baez with $100,000 in cash and $50,000 worth of guns and ammunition.[1]

The translation of the treaties became a sticking point as the Dominicans insisted on changing the language in several articles. Babcock maintained that the American version be written in "plain English" so it would be easier for Gautier to translate into Spanish. The revisions continued for what Babcock referred to as a long "tedious day." After a short pleasure trip around the coast, accompanied by Baez and several Dominican dignitaries, Joseph Fabens reported to Babcock that the Dominican Senate had not voted to approve the treaty. At issue was Gautier's desire to add an article obligating the United States to pay off the Dominican national debt. Babcock protested that the Dominicans could not add additional articles and that the time for Dominican ratification of the treaty was soon approaching. Over the next few days, the Dominican Senate continued to delay, causing Babcock to become concerned that Gautier and President Baez were misleading him. In one instance, American businessman and translator William Cazneau even suggested creating a "secret treaty" to fool the Dominican Senate into voting for annexation. Babcock, Sackett, and Perry immediately balked at the suggestion, with Sackett stating: "anything that we got up would have to be on the square and aboveboard." On November 29, Babcock and Sackett called on President Baez to set a date for signing the annexation treaty. In Spanish, Baez explained to Sackett the reason for the delay in passing the treaty: Baez desired to confer upon Babcock a tract of land in Samaná, as a gesture of goodwill for his work on securing the treaty. There was no delay in the Senate save for a debate over how to lavish a gift on Babcock. When Sackett translated Baez's wishes to Babcock, the young officer was taken aback. He implored the president to understand that such a gift would violate American law and would certainly ruin any chance of the treaty's passage in the United States Senate. Babcock recalled, "I told him . . . that as a citizen of the United States I should like to go into business with him but could not accept a gift now." Baez relented and agreed to sign the treaties that afternoon. After securing Baez's signature, Babcock arranged for the transfer of the money and munitions to the Dominican authorities and the raising of the American flag at Samaná Bay. Satisfied with his work, Babcock returned to the United States in December and presented the treaties to President Grant who then called a cabinet meeting to discuss them.[2]

Grant's annexation proposal received a lukewarm reception in the cabinet and Fish did not think it would garner enough Senate votes for ratification. As such, Grant had to draft a series of talking points that would help him sell the treaty, not only to his cabinet, but also to the Senate and the American public. Grant asked that the cabinet members keep the annexation treaty secret until after the New Year; however, they were free to discuss the treaty for Samaná Bay. Grant then composed a memorandum that encompassed his thoughts on annexation, Reconstruction, and national security entitled "Reasons why San Domingo should be annexed to the United States." The memorandum covered a variety of topics, including the economy of the Dominican Republic, the political conventions there, and the island's strategic location. However, the memorandum brought together many of the foreign and domestic issues that weighed on the Grant Administration at the end of 1869. Grant noted how the Dominican Republic was the answer to the *Alabama* claims, the Cuban rebellion, and the violence in the Reconstruction South.

The President spent the latter days of December balancing the responsibilities of his family with those of his position. Grant had just nominated the former secretary of war, Edwin Stanton, to the United States Supreme Court on the same day that Orville Babcock returned from the Dominican Republic. Four days later, on Christmas Eve, Stanton died of a heart attack. Grant spent time that day writing checks to several charities, writing messages of condolence to the Stanton family, and jotting down his thoughts on the Dominican Republic question. The next few days saw the president and First Lady Julia Grant hosting well-wishers at the Executive Mansion and enjoying the unseasonably mild weather. Amidst the sorrow of the loss of a comrade, and the joy of the holiday season, nearly ten months after his inauguration, Grant drafted a memorandum that would come to define his administration's Caribbean policy. With edits and suggestions from Fish, Grant outlined not only his foreign policy objectives for the United States but also his intent to extend his domestic policy of Reconstruction throughout the Western Hemisphere. This memo amounted to a reiteration of Grant's position on republican values. Grant hoped to promote freedom throughout the Caribbean by eradicating slavery, supporting free trade, and expanding American economic and political systems. Doing so, Grant posited, was in keeping with the United States' oft-repeated adherence to the Monroe Doctrine. What Grant was proposing, however, was something quite different.[3]

The Grant Doctrine envisioned an American sphere of influence in the Western Hemisphere that erased the economic and cultural influences of Europe, by which Grant meant the continuation of slavery in Cuba, Puerto Rico, and Brazil. Grant's Doctrine argued for an expansion of American economic and cultural influence to open the countries of the Caribbean, Central, and South America to American trade and investment, but also to the republican ideals of freedom, free labor, and liberal democracy. To Grant, the annexation of the Dominican Republic by the United States would be an extension of the promise of the Civil War and the civil rights gains of Reconstruction. Grant's political strategy involved the extension of political and civil rights to former slaves and all African Americans in the United States. Through his proposed annexation of the Dominican Republic, Grant sought to extend these same rights to people of the Caribbean. Annexation meant the exchange of people and cultures along with American ideology. Grant sought to reshape the Dominican Republic into a liberal democracy that could achieve equal participation in the American political and economic system. Citizenship and voting rights were two pillars of Grant's Reconstruction policy at home that were crucial to the traditional Republican Party ideology of free labor and free men. By annexing the Dominican Republic and offering citizenship and equality to the Dominicans, Grant attempted to create a sphere of influence in the Caribbean that would, by its mere presence and successes, force neighboring slave-holding nations to abolish the Old-World practice and adopt American republican ideals and culture. Grant believed that the United States would throw off European influences in the Western Hemisphere by finally acting upon the liberal ideology of the nation's founders, the acceptance of men, both Black and white, as equal under the law.[4]

Grant's Reconstruction policy offered a chance to stabilize the United States both domestically and internationally in the aftermath of the American Civil War, by strengthening the nation's position in the Western Hemisphere. For many Republicans, Reconstruction offered the Republican Party a chance to restore the nation back to what it had been prior to the war, without the sin of slavery. African American rights were part of this strengthened Union, yet most Republicans envisioned that the nation after Reconstruction would remain fundamentally—a white man's republic. Grant's Reconstruction policy, though, envisioned something quite different. He sought a strengthened Union including new citizens, non-whites, and immigrants, and he saw the United States' ever-increasing sphere of influence in the Western Hemisphere expanding even further afield.[5]

Grant's ideas and ideology were more than just a corollary to the Monroe Doctrine. They were a new method of thinking about the United States' place in the world and the revolutionary nature of American ideals following the American Civil War. Global analyses of the Civil War argue that the United States was but one battleground in an international revolution of ideas. Following the defeat of the Confederacy and the establishment of the Thirteenth and Fourteenth Amendments to the Constitution, and Grant's push for the ratification of the Fifteenth Amendment, the United States was finally able to complete "the greatest civil change . . . since the nation came into life." Republican government, Grant wrote in a proclamation after the ratification of the Fifteenth Amendment, "must depend measurably upon the intelligence, patriotism and industry of these people [African Americans]." For Grant, annexing the Dominican Republic offered an initial step in healing the wounds of the Civil War and the first attempt to fulfill the true promise of the American Constitution. Citizenship and free labor finally provided African Americans the means to enjoy the republican experiment. According to Grant, offering similar blessings of liberty to the Dominican people would directly influence the surrounding nations to adopt American-style economic and political systems. Chief among these, he believed, would be the idea that nations still practicing slavery would succumb to the logic that slavery was no longer a profitable economic system, nor morally just, in a region defined by liberty and freedom. Annexation, he argued, would be another major step toward finally making a free and republican Western Hemisphere.[6]

Much like the Monroe Doctrine, the Grant Doctrine was high-minded in concept yet unsuccessful in immediate application. Not only was the primary pillar of the doctrine unattainable because annexation never stood a chance of passing the Senate, but political and diplomatic necessity forced Grant and Fish to appease European powers rather than support republican movements in the Americas. The Grant Doctrine distilled the president's ideas of republicanism and the promise of Reconstruction into an international setting, yet Grant was unable to implement his core idea of ending slavery, despite numerous attempts, forcing him and Fish to straddle the line between ideology and practical diplomacy. They chose political expediency over support for republican movements because they understood that meant the difference between war and peace with Great Britain and Spain. Although Grant toyed with the idea of supporting the insurrection in Cuba against Spain and the Irish Fenian revolt against British Canada, Fish persuaded the president that doing so would undermine significant negotiations with the British and the Spanish over perceived wrongs committed against the United States during the Civil War. Fish balanced his president's hopes for a Western Hemisphere free of both European influence and the sin of slavery with a practical need to negotiate with the British and the Spanish to prevent war with one or both nations. The Grant Doctrine, then, amounted to more than just a rationale for why the United States should add the Dominican Republic as a territory, and it was more than just an addendum to the Monroe Doctrine. For the first time in the history of the United States, a president embraced an ideology of expansion to bring freedom, equality, and the possibility of American citizenship to all inhabitants of the hemisphere, and to scuttle the influence of Europe that, according to the president, undermined republican institutions and sustained the institution of slavery economically.[7]

Grant began his memo by commenting on the agricultural and economic benefits of acquiring Caribbean territory. Hamilton Fish (or, rather his clerk) added clarifications and a few changes that he hoped would strengthen the argument in the document. "It is an island of unequaled fertility," Grant wrote, "It contains an area (that part of it known as the republic of San Domingo) of 20.000 square miles, or 12,800.000 acres." The size of the land and its fertility were important to Grant. He wrote that one half of the land "is now covered with the most valuable timbers known to commerce; at an elevation above the diseases incident to a tropical climate, and is capable of producing, when cleared of the native forest, 1500 lbs. of coffee pr. acre." The fertile soil would help the United States to produce tropical crops that could not be cultivated as successfully on the North American continent. Grant noted that "the valleys and low lands are of great productiveness, the sugar cane requiring re-setting only once in twenty years, and producing, [to the acre] with much less labor, nearly double [that] of the best sugar lands of [Louisiana]." Here Grant first discussed the notion of labor. The production of sugar cane had long been the purview of the slave-holding class. Grant believed that United States citizens would flock to the Dominican Republic to work as free laborers to grow a variety of crops previously monopolized by the Slave Power interests. "Tobacco, tropical fruits, dyes, and all the imports of the equatorial region, can be produced on these lands," Grant wrote,

"San Domingo is the gate to the Caribean [sic] Sea, and in the line of transit to the Isthmus of Darien, destined at no distant day to be the line of transit of half the commerce of the world."

Grant's experience crossing the Isthmus of Panama (Darien) as a young officer strengthened his belief that a functioning canal and transport system was needed in Central America. His journey across the Isthmus saw the death of over one hundred members of his party, with Grant nursing the sick and dying the entire time. A working canal system would have allowed for constant movement through the isthmus, saving lives and improving economic growth and military readiness. To Grant, the economic benefits of annexing the Dominican Republic grew beyond the merely agricultural: its location in the Caribbean meant that it would soon be in the middle of a growing global transit of goods across the isthmus. The construction of a Central American canal was a matter of when, not if, and the Dominican Republic would therefore sit astride the world's shipping lane. Remembering his fateful trip across Panama in 1852, President Grant commissioned several engineering and naval surveys of Central America looking for an alternative to crossing in Panama. Grant settled on Nicaragua as a better alternative because it was closer to the United States, among several reasons. Therefore, an American presence in such a vital economic hub was important to Grant's plans for the commercial growth of the United States and the growth of the Caribbean. Labor and trade were key to stabilizing the Reconstruction economy and, therefore, the Union, and the annexation of the Dominican Republic would provide that stabilizing force the Union so needed.[8]

Beyond the island's agricultural and trade potential, Grant considered the introduction of the Dominican people into the American cultural and political sphere. Grant noted that the population of the Dominican Republic was "sparse," yet the people were "in entire sympathy with our institutions, anxious to join their fortunes to ours." Like the freedmen of the American South, the Dominicans were "industrious, if made to feel that the products of their industry is to be protected; & tollrent [sic] as to the religious, or political views of their neighbors." Grant was overestimating the religious tolerance of not only the Dominicans, whom we have seen were often intolerant of Protestant Black Americans in Samaná Bay, but also the tolerance of the American people. While thousands of Catholic immigrants had moved to the United States from Europe and Cuba in the years prior to and during the American Civil War, that did not mean that Americans were tolerant of

Catholicism. The Know-Nothing party of the 1850s based its xenophobic beliefs not only on anti-immigrant policies but also its anti-Catholic attitudes. Grant, a Methodist, showed himself intolerant of Catholicism on several occasions. However he did not hold to the belief that Protestantism was a precursor to republicanism. Grant believed that their understanding of the concept of free labor for free men would enable the Dominicans to assimilate into the American system easily. "Caste has no foothold in San Domingo," he argued. "It is capable of supporting the entire colored population of the United States, should it choose to emigrate."

As evidenced by Babcock's diaries, Grant's description of the Dominicans as being "in entire sympathy with our institutions" was not entirely accurate. Babcock points to division or, at the very least, indifference to annexation and American intervention in the Dominican Republic and Babcock's own intolerance toward the superstitious practices of the Catholic Dominicans. There was a vocal majority in the Dominican government who were for annexation, an indifferent populace in the hinterlands, and a rebellion underway, which sought to use the prospect of foreign annexation to oust President Baez. As such, any statement by Grant or the Dominicans representatives that the nation supported annexation was inaccurate. American opponents of annexation knew that the Dominicans were not in agreement and exploited that disagreement to undermine Grant's annexation scheme.[9]

At this point in the memorandum, Grant began to detail how the annexation of the Dominican Republic fit into his overall goals for Reconstruction. African Americans, he believed, would be more inclined to seek their fortunes in a place like the Dominican Republic than remain in the states where they had been held in bondage for so long. "The present difficulty in bringing all parts of the United States to a happy unity and love of country grows out of the prejudice of color," Grant wrote, "the prejudice is a senseless one, but it exists. The colored man cannot be spared until his place is supplied, but with a refuge like San Domingo his worth here would soon be discovered, and he would soon receive such recognition as to induce him to stay: or if Providence designated that the two races should not live to-gether [sic] he would find a home in the Antillas [sic]." Grant was not blind to the idea that racial prejudice was a real and present fact for African Americans. Grant's hope for Reconstruction was that this racial prejudice would subside once whites allowed Black people to earn an honest wage for their labors and to invest in themselves and in their country. Grant figured that offering a refuge in the Dominican Republic for African Americans, away from the racial prejudice of whites, would allow them to enjoy the blessings of liberty, the full force of the American economy, and unobstructed participation in American political life.

Yet Grant also noted that the dream of domestic interracial harmony might just as easily remain unattainable. In that case, Grant thought that many African Americans in the South would welcome the chance to leave discrimination behind and settle in the Dominican Republic. In this regard Grant was correct, as several thousand African Americans, in the late 1870s and 1880s, left the South for the West, particularly Kansas and Missouri. Not long after the turn of the century millions more African Americans collectively migrated from the South to the industrial North of Chicago, Detroit, Cleveland, and many other cities during the Great Migration. Grant had foreseen an inevitable migration from the South to states with better economic opportunities. These African Americans hoped to migrate from the South to leave the racist former enslavers and their families behind. While Grant should have been focusing his efforts on making white Southerners accept their fellow Black countrymen as equals, he chose, however, to focus on acquiring a territory he believed would be more hospitable to African Americans seeking to leave the South. Rather than a new version of the American Colonization Society, which sought to send free Blacks to Africa to establish their own nation of Liberia, Grant's annexation attempt would create a unique Black-majority state within the United States where Dominicans and African Americans would control their economic and political life while obtaining equal representation in the federal system, thus obtaining the goal of reunification while also maintaining stability.[10]

Grant connected this plan for Reconstruction with his foreign policy. He understood that an American foothold in the Caribbean would place the United States into direct competition with European powers for control of the Western Hemisphere. "A glance at the map will show that England has now a cordon of islands extending from southern Florida to the East of the Island of Cuba," Grant wrote, "with Jamaca, [sic] and Grand Cayman south of that island, and a foothold upon the mainland in Central America, thus commanding [on both sides of Cuba] the entrance to the Gulf of Mexico . . . a gulf which borders upon so large a part of the territory of the United States." Annexation, then, was important to ensure an American economic, political, and military presence in the region. American merchant ships and men-of war were necessary to combat European economic dominance in the Caribbean. At the close of the Civil War, the United States Navy had consisted of nearly 700 ships, many of which were blockading vessels unfit for warfare; however, the government began scrapping the fleet soon after the war's end, reducing the number to a mere three dozen. Grant understood that a blue water fleet in the Caribbean was necessary in the event of a war with a European power such as Great Britain, which had a fleet of hundreds of ships.[11] Great Britain, he argued, also "has a succession of islands runing [sic] from the East of St. Thomas to South America, with another foothold upon the main land, British Guiana, thus nearly surrounding the Cariben [sic] Sea." Grant wrote his memorandum amidst serious diplomatic tensions with Great Britain, as the Senate had overwhelmingly defeated the Johnson-Clarendon convention, an attempt to settle outstanding disputes between the two nations arising from the Civil War. Soon after, Massachusetts Senator Charles Sumner delivered a scathing speech that claimed that the British owed the United States hundreds of millions of dollars for damages incurred by British-built ships utilized by the Confederate Navy. Grant considered all this when he wrote that: "The coasting trade of the United States, between the Atlantic seaboard and all ports West, and South west of the Cape of Florida, has now to pass through foreign waters. In case of war between England and the United States, New York and New Orleans would be as much severed as would be New York and Calais, France."[12]

Grant did not mention Great Britain by accident. If the United States did not negotiate a successful treaty with Britain over the *Alabama* claims, several newspapers argued, war was a possibility. British newspaper reports on the negotiations show a frustration with the United States at its unwillingness to put the matter of the *Alabama* claims to rest. In response to Senator Sumner's blistering speech calling on the British to pay for costs incurred due to the *Alabama,* the *Birmingham Daily Post* remarked: "[Sumner] likes to have it upon a truly American scale; big enough to overlap the 'universal earth,' and yet leave something to spare." British reporters contended that American politicians had thrown away a chance at peace between the two nations. The *Gloucester Journal* claimed that "quiet people, on both sides of the Atlantic, who deprecate war and rumours of war, are beginning to tremble for the peace of England and America." Sumner's speech, the *Gloucester* wrote, "roused the worst feelings of the American people," leading to the potential for "a great deal of bluster." The failure of the Johnson-Clarendon talks led the writers to lament that they were "no less surprised than annoyed" by the American decision to reject the treaty. Other newspapers commented on the massive amount of money Sumner believed the British owed the United States. The *Grantham Journal* questioned Sumner's request stating that he had passed "the narrow boundary line between the sublime and the ridiculous."

British newspaper editors worried that the negative atmosphere created by the rejection of the treaty and Sumner's speech would "check emigration from this country, which is acting so beneficially on the interests of the working classes." Rather than moving to the United States, the newspaper advised British workingmen that moving to Canada was a better choice due to the political climate. Other British newspapers welcomed the failure of the Johnson-Clarendon treaty, noting that the treaty represented a failure of a reckless British government. The *Manchester Courier* stated that its editors were "happily rid of an undertaking into which it would have been wise never to have entered." The rejection of the treaty allowed the British to reject any notion of a breach in neutrality during the war. "We should have spared ourselves some humiliation," they wrote, "and the Americans some additional irritation if we had acted on this principle throughout." The journal did worry though, that the British had provoked the United States. "We shall be greatly to blame if we do not see in it a warning that we have incurred, though by no fault of our own, the anger of a very powerful people, which has only now found out that in military and naval eminence it can rival the greatest of European powers." The *Courier*'s acknowledgement of American military power shows that the fear of an armed confrontation between the two nations was very real to the British. United States imports and exports were vulnerable in case of war with Britain. Grant argued that an American presence in the Dominican Republic would mitigate these worries. A post–Civil War United States, then, was one that was strong and able to withstand an international threat, and annexing the Dominican Republic made this possible.[13]

The United States imported significant tropical goods from the Caribbean, but their means of production and quantity worried Grant. In his memorandum, he addressed how the United States might affect the future development of agricultural production in the region, particularly regarding enslaved labor. "Our imports of tropical products, and products of slave labor," Grant wrote, "exceed our exports to the countries producing them more than the balance of trade against the United States." Tropical products, then, made up a significant portion of American imports. Yet the fact that enslaved labor produced these products made their importation unpalatable. "San Domingo can produce the sugar, coffee, tobacco, chocolate and tropical fruits for a population of 50.000.000 of people," Grant argued, "Coffee and sugar there can be produced, with free labor, at but little more cost pr. lb than wheat is now produced in our great North West." Free labor in the Dominican Republic would improve the productivity of its export crops and drive down prices. "With the acquisition of San Domingo," Grant wrote, "the two great necessities in every family, sugar and Coffee, would be cheapened by near one half." Staple goods produced by free labor would benefit the American people and undermine slave-based agriculture in Cuba, and the best way to do that was through the acquisition of the Dominican Republic. One of Reconstruction's goals, one historian notes, was to "end slavery and give that freedom more than a nominal meaning." Supporting a slave economy in the Caribbean undermined that goal.[14]

Beyond the economic and military benefits of the annexation of the island nation, Grant argued that acquisition was the moral duty of the United States as the leading power in the Western Hemisphere. "San Domingo is weak and must go some where for protection," Grant argued. "Is the United States willing that she should go elsewhere than to herself? Such a confession would be to abandon our oft repeated 'Monroe doctrine.'" Grant's memorandum represented a significant departure from the Monroe Doctrine, however, in that he envisioned a hemisphere free of slave labor inspired by the example of the United States. Whereas the Monroe Doctrine had sought to protect American interests in the early nineteenth century from those of the European powers, the institution of slavery had still been intertwined with those American interests. With the dissolution of the Slave Power, Grant's doctrine sought to protect American interests while eradicating the institution of slavery for good in the Western world. "San Domingo in the hands of the United States would make slave labor unprofitable," Grant argued, "and would soon extinguish that hated system of enforced labor." The importation of goods from the American tropics meant "the United States is the largest supporter of that institution. More than 70 pr ct. of the exports of Cuba, and a large percentage of the exports of Brazil, are to the United States." In fact, by 1860, Brazil provided over 90 percent of the coffee imported into the United States. Annexation of the Dominican Republic would allow the United States to be free of the economic and moral burden of being attached to slave powers in the Caribbean. "Upon every pound we receive from them an export duty is charged to support slavery and Monarchy. A prohibitory duty, almost, is placed upon what we have to sell. Get

San Domingo," Grant argued, "and this will all be changed." It was Grant's contention that an American economic, military, and political presence in the region would force the slave holding countries to abandon the practice and adopt the American system of free labor, liberty, and open markets.[15]

Grant concluded: "San Domingo from its exposeure [sic] to the trade winds, and its elevation is, in large part, free from the diseases of the tropics." Grant noted that "It is nearer New York City, and all the North Atlantic Sea ports, than any American Sea port in the Gulf of Mexico." He reiterated the need for American commerce to have a presence in the region, stating, "It can be reached without passing through the waters of a foreign country. In case of a Maritime War it would give us a foothold in the West Indies [sic] of inestimable value." Grant likened annexation to the grand ideas behind continental territorial expansion when he wrote, "Its acquisition is carrying out Manifest destiny. It is a step towards claring [sic] . . . all European flags from this Continent. Can any one favor rejecting so valuable a gift who voted $7.200.000 for the icebergs of Alasca [sic]?" Territorial expansion provided stability to the Union through land and economic development, all for the benefit of the republic. As he sought to garner support for annexation among congressional leaders, Grant repeated the logic and arguments set out in his memorandum. In effect, Grant's memorandum defined the essence of his administration's foreign and domestic policy. As Grant attempted to sway Congress, the memorandum provided the source for arguments that both Grant and Secretary of State Hamilton Fish would espouse to the American people.[16]

Early in January 1870 President Grant left the White House and ventured across Lafayette Square to the home of Senator Charles Sumner, chair of the powerful Senate Foreign Relations Committee. Grant arrived unannounced, where he found the Massachusetts senator dining with friends, including two newspaper reporters. Sumner invited the president into his home, whereupon Grant proceeded to share with him his desire to annex the Dominican Republic as a territory to the United States. While no transcript of the meeting exists, it is likely that Grant mentioned the benefits of annexation as he saw them for African Americans, Sumner having been the champion of abolitionism in the US Senate. Grant left Sumner's home under the impression that he had acquired his support. However, Sumner later argued that he had not endorsed the treaty of annexation, merely that he had agreed to consider it. From then on, a feud developed between Grant and Sumner that would grow to jeopardize many of Grant's foreign policy initiatives and his management of the Republican Party and its Reconstruction agenda.[17] Over the next few months Sumner and the Grant administration fought over not only the annexation proposal but also the leadership of the American Legation in London. Sumner and Grant maintained two different worldviews and viewed the direction of the Republican party differently. Whereas Sumner saw the Republicans in Congress as the leaders of the party and its agenda, Grant saw himself, as president, as the head of the party and the one who dictated the Republican agenda. As such, Grant and his allies mustered support in Congress for a vote on annexation and the president took the unusual step of lobbying members of Congress for their vote. Grant's May 1870 message to the Senate focused on annexation, reiterating his argument that the United States should be a beacon for liberty in the Western Hemisphere. In this message, Grant explained that he felt "an unusual anxiety for the ratification of this treaty because I believe it will redound greatly to the glory of the two countries interested, to civilization, and to the extirpation of the institution of slavery." Grant invoked the United States' tradition of hemispheric supremacy when he argued that no territory in the hemisphere would be subject to the transfer from one European power to another. Historians have often pointed to this message as Grant's corollary to the Monroe Doctrine, emphasizing his assertion of the no-transfer principle. More important, however, was Grant's call for the United States to divest itself of all imports from slave holding nations and, more radically, for the eradication of slavery throughout the hemisphere.[18]

Grant sought to forestall hardline conservative anti-expansionists—those who sought to limit American acquisition of foreign soil—including his own secretary of state, by acknowledging that the idea of annexing the Dominican Republic was the brainchild of the Dominican leaders themselves. "The government of St. Doming [sic] has voluntarily sought this alliance," Grant wrote. "It is a weak power, numbering probably less than 120.000 souls, possessing one of the richest territories under the Sun, capable of supporting a population of 10.000.000 of people in luxury." Grant again brought up the specter of European influence in the region by claiming that he had "information, which I believe reliable that a first class European power stands ready now to offer $2.000.000 for the possession of Samana Bay." Here Grant was referring to rumors in the diplomatic corps that either Great Britain or Germany was interested in acquiring Samaná Bay. In that case, Grant argued, what good was the Monroe Doctrine? "If refused by us what grace can we say to any foreign power who may come in for the prize we refuse, 'hands off'? The people of St. Domingo," he claimed "are not capable of maintaining themselves in their present condition and must look for outside support. [They] yearns [sic] for the protection of our free institutions and laws, our progress and civilization. Let us give them." Unlike other imperial expansion attempts by the United States either before or after, annexation of the Dominican Republic would mean the overseas expansion of the rights and privileges of the US Constitution as well as the cultural and economic benefits of American influence to non-whites in the territory. Grant and the Dominican leaders both envisioned a path to statehood, but Grant understood that would be a difficult sell to both his cabinet and the Senate. Secretary Fish informed the president that many members of the Senate were unwilling to support a path to statehood as they did not want to acquire new territories and many did not want more non-white citizens, but he offered the idea of establishing a protectorate as an olive-branch to hesitant legislators. Grant therefore offered the Senate another option by stating "if in good time providence should make it clear that a Confederation of all the Islands of the Caribian [sic] Sea, and Gulf of Mexico, under a protectorate or other supervision of the Unites States should be desirable, there will be nothing in this treaty to prevent such an arrangement." If not statehood, then, at least the United States would provide protection for those who asked. "Shall we refuse them?" he asked rhetorically.[19]

In his message to the Senate, Grant sought to convince Senators of the strategic value of an American presence in the Caribbean. "The acquisition of St. Doming is desirable because of its geographical position," he argued. "It commands the entrance to the Caribian [sic] sea and [the] Isthmus transit of Commerce. It possesses the richest soil, best and most capacious harbors, most salubrious climate and the greatest abundance of products of the forrest [sic], mine and soil, of any of the West India islands." Grant continued to argue that this Caribbean acquisition would lead to the growth of the American economy. "Its [sic] possession by us would build up a coastwise Commerce of immense magnitude in a few years, which will go far towards restoring to us our lost Merchant Marine. It will give to us those articles which we consume so largely and do not produce, thus equalizing our exports with our . . . imports." Grant hoped that the members of the Senate saw the enhanced standing in the world and the stability that annexing the Dominican Republic would provide. Producing goods with free labor and expanding the American economy, then, enhanced the goals of his Administration to eliminate the post–Civil War debt.[20] The "lost Merchant Marine" was a clear statement to the Senate that he understood the importance of the *Alabama* claims and the disagreements that had led to difficulties in the diplomatic relations with Great Britain. "In case of foreign war," Grant argued, the Dominican Republic "will give us a command of all the islands refered [sic] to," instead of leaving them to a future enemy of the United States. The Dominican Republic then would mitigate the problem of foreign control of vital waters in a time of war. "Now our coast trade between the States bordering on the Atlantic and those bordering on the Gulf of Mexico, is cut in two by the Bahamas and Cuba," Grant told the Senate, "Twice we must, as it were, pass through foreign countries to get, by sea, from Georgia to the West Coast of Florida." War with Britain was a possibility on the minds of both the British and the American publics and the ever-present rebellion in Cuba continued to engulf American citizens. Grant used these to justify the annexation of the Dominican Republic as an important contingency measure for the security of the United States.[21]

Beyond added security in time of war, Grant reiterated that the acquisition of the Dominican Republic would become a beacon for freedom in the Caribbean. "St. Domingo, with a stable government," Grant envisioned, "under which her immense resources can be developed will give remunerative wages to tens of thousands of laborers not now upon the island." Rather than drawing labor from the American South, as he argued in his memorandum, however, he curiously suggested to the Senate that "the labor will come in canoes, and in every conceivable way from [and] take advantage of every available means of transportation to abandon the adjacent islands both for and seek the advantages [and] blessings of freedom, and its sequence; each inhabitant receiving the reward of his own labor." Grant argued that an American presence in the Dominican Republic would lead to mass immigration to the island, either from free laborers on neighboring islands and Haiti, or from the enslaved self-emancipating. "Porto Rico [sic] and Cuba will have to abolish slavery as a measure of self preservation [sic]; to retain their laborers," he told the Senate.[22]

As an outpost of freedom in the Caribbean, the Dominican Republic offered the United States a way to promote economic recovery from the Civil War. Not only would the Dominican Republic produce materials for the American market, but it could also provide a new outlet for the consumption of American goods. "St. Domingo will become a large consumer of the products of Northern farms and Manufactures [sic]," Grant argued, "The cheap rate at which her citizens can be furnished with food, tools and machinery, will make it necessary that the other islands . . . should have the same advantages (in order) to compete in the production of Sugar, Coffee, tobacco, tropical fruits etc. (This will open) to us a still wider market for our products." Once the Dominican Republic integrated into the American economy, then, the neighboring island nations would ultimately follow suit.[23]

Producing American goods and shipping them to the Caribbean opened new markets, and the production of these goods by an American territory within the United States would add to the nation's treasury. "The production of our own supply of these articles will cut off more than One Hundred Millions of our (annual) imports[,] besides largely increasing our exports" Grant explained to the Senate. "With such a picture it is easy to see how our large debt abroad is ultimately to be extinguished." This debt had reached over $2 billion in 1869, with over half of the debt in foreign loans. Again, Grant tied the annexation of the Dominican Republic to the regeneration of the domestic economy and to extinguishing foreign interests in the United States. "With a balance of trade against us (including interest on bonds held by foreigners, and money spent by our citizens traveling in foreign lands) is greater than (equal to) the entire yield of the precious metals in this country," he wrote, "it is not so easy to see how this result is to be (otherwise) accomplished." The Civil War left the United States dependent on foreign loans, and during the period of Reconstruction the Grant administration attempted to transition the federal Treasury away from government held foreign loans. At the same time, the Republican governments of the Southern states sought foreign investment to stimulate their local economies. Therefore, the investment of foreign capital hindered political and diplomatic discussions of the annexation of the Dominican Republic. Grant understood that foreign loans also burdened the Dominican economy, and that the repayment or cancellation of these loans was important to securing Senate support for annexation. Economic stability was a key component of the administration's Reconstruction policy and the ability of the Southern states to reenter the Union and to strengthen the republic. Grant hoped that acquiring the Dominican Republic would alleviate the economic burden of the national debt.[24]

Grant's reluctance to procure foreign loans was an extension of his fidelity to the Monroe Doctrine. "The acquisition of St. Doming is an adherence to the 'Monroe Doctrine,'" he wrote, "it is a measure of national protection: it is assuming (asserting) our just claim to a controlling influence over the great

Commercial traffic soon to flow from West to East by way of the Isthmus of Darien." In advocating for annexation, Grant argued that an American presence in the Dominican Republic would "build up our Merchant Marine; it is to build up (furnish) new markets for the products of our farms, shops and maunfacturies [sic]; it is to make slavery insupportable in Cuba and Porto Rico, at once, and ultimately so in Brazil; it is to settle the unhappy condition of Cuba, and end an exterminating conflict." Annexation, then, would "provide honest means of paying our honest debts, without a long period of privation and want (without overtaxing the people)." Grant ended his message by stating that annexation would "provide our citizens with [the] necessaries of every day [sic] life at cheaper rates than ever before; and it is in fine a rapid stride towards that greatness which the intelligence, industry and enterprise of the Citizens of the United States entitle this country to assume among nations."[25]

Grant's message to the Senate in May 1870, combined with his memorandum from earlier in the same year, therefore amounted to a new doctrine. Grant revolutionized the application of the ideas of the Monroe Doctrine in the new world that the Civil War created. The Grant Doctrine was both an outgrowth of the Monroe Doctrine and something distinct. Prior to the Civil War, enforcing the Monroe Doctrine meant doing so to aid a slaveholding American society. President James K. Polk had invoked the Monroe Doctrine when he justified the Mexican American War and the United States' demands for Mexican territory in the 1840s, which Grant experienced as a young officer. Not only was expansion into the southwest during the antebellum period responsible for the coming conflict of the 1860s, but it was also rooted in the expansion of American power to the West coast as well as the replication of slave society in new territories. The intent of the Monroe Doctrine was to strengthen republican governments in Latin America, but the republican government of the United States in the 1820s and 1840s sustained the system of slavery. The Monroe Doctrine, then, was a tool with which the United States hoped to push out European influence in the hemisphere to grow its slave-based economy. The Grant Doctrine sought to expand liberty throughout the hemisphere, championing free republican societies over the institution of slavery. As a tool of Reconstruction, expanding the blessings of liberty and freedom were central to Grant's philosophy of American hegemony in the hemisphere.[26] As a Doctrine, Grant's ideas were offered up as an honest articulation of American republican ideology and economic freedom. His doctrine represented a realignment of purpose for the United States following its Civil War, a purpose that Grant understood was the price to be paid for the bloody conflict. National reunification required national stability, and Grant saw the Grant Doctrine and expansion into the Caribbean as that stabilizing force. Grant hoped to advance American ideals of freedom, free labor, and citizenship throughout the hemisphere. He would do so by exporting an ideology which sought, through economic and social change, to bring about an end to slavery in Cuba and Puerto Rico, and as a result, an end to European influence. Grant desired to see the republican experiment replicated throughout the Caribbean and Central and South America, and he understood that the process could begin on a small scale with the acquisition of the Dominican Republic.

From the moment of his visit to Charles Sumner on Lafayette Square, Grant would encounter one roadblock after another to his hopes for Dominican annexation. Due to political infighting within his own party, and personal animosity between Sumner and the President, Grant was unable to convince enough senators to support his plan even though he was willing to limit his vision by embracing Secretary Fish's suggestion to jettison annexation in favor of a United States protectorate in the Caribbean. Grant's desire to bring the Dominican Republic into the Union as a territory with a path to statehood similarly attracted little attention from the American public. Members of the press traded volleys over the annexation scheme with pro-administration editors lauding the possibilities of annexation while others condemned the process as corrupt. Republican leaders in Congress were focusing their attentions on strengthening the republic and building up the national economy, rather than focusing on equal rights and expansion. Grant proved unable to convince Congress and the American public that acquiring the Dominican Republic would enhance the nation's economic and social well-being. Rather, Americans seemed to be more interested in westward expansion, economic development, or the increasing agitation over the Cuban rebellion against Spain, in which they urged Grant to intercede on behalf of the Cubans.[27]

A main sticking point to implementing Grant's doctrine of extending freedom and republican ideology throughout the Western Hemisphere was the litany of diplomatic disagreements that he had inherited with Great Britain. These disagreements were rooted in both conflicts over boundary lines and fishing rights in Canada and in the claims lodged by northern merchant ship owners against the Civil War exploits of British-built Confederate raiders, namely the *Alabama, Florida, Georgia,* and *Shenandoah* (referred to collectively as the "*Alabama* claims"). Many Republicans, particularly Charles Sumner, wanted Britain to cede Canada to the United States in lieu of payment for the *Alabama* Claims. Grant and Fish both believed that American annexation of Canada was inevitable, but until that day, the two nations would have to settle their differences diplomatically and annexation efforts were pointed south.[28] The Canadians had petitioned the British government in 1866 for independence and the establishment of a confederation. The cancellation of American and Canadian trade reciprocity in 1866 by the United States, the continual problem of Irish-Fenian raids and riots originating in the United States, the 1867 American annexation of Alaska from Russia, and the clash of American and Canadian fishermen in both the Great Lakes and northern Atlantic compounded American–Canadian–British animosity, as did the unresolved *Alabama* claims. Grant sought peaceful negotiations with the British, and therefore ordered US marshals to arrest all Fenians invading Canada and he thwarted the attempts of American politicians who wanted to hasten the acquisition of Canada, regardless of whether the Canadians wanted to join the United States. Grant prioritized settling the numerous outstanding financial and political claims with Britain and instructed Fish to negotiate an advantageous settlement. However, if these arguments were not settled, having an American presence in the Dominican Republic made a potential conflict with Britain an easier prospect.[29]

Grant compromised on his vision for a free and democratic Western Hemisphere, in part, because of the pragmatism of his secretary of state and his own belief in the ultimate inevitability of Canadian annexation. Fish and Grant understood that the difficulties between the United States and Great Britain represented the most urgent diplomatic challenge facing the administration. While Grant spent the better part of 1870 focusing his attentions on the Dominican Republic treaty, Fish remained in constant communication with the British minister to the United States, Sir Edward Thornton. Most of their conversations centered either on the Cuban insurrection or on the rights of Canadian fishermen and traders, but Fish continued to press the president on when he could begin negotiating the settlement of the *Alabama* claims. Grant preferred to settle all the difficulties between Britain and the United States in a single treaty, but in December 1870 he relented and authorized formal negotiations with the British. Canadian annexation was no longer an objective of those talks because numerous correspondents and acquaintances had convinced Grant and Fish that the Canadians would choose to join the United States of their own free will sooner rather than later.[30]

A further test of the Grant Doctrine was the ongoing Ten Years' War between Spain and the independence movement in Cuba. Many Cuban farmers and abolitionists sought to overthrow Spanish control of the island and embrace republicanism. The Ten Years' War was a perfect opportunity for Grant to test the viability of his doctrine, as many Americans were supportive of Cuban independence and emancipation there. However, Grant, and more specifically Fish, decided against support and recognition of the Cuban belligerency. Although Grant initially wanted to intercede on behalf of the Cuban rebels, Fish understood that recognition of Cuban belligerency would undercut the American legal argument against the British over the *Alabama* claims, which was based on the position that the British had illegally intervened in a domestic conflict. The British would view American recognition and support of the Cuban rebels as interference in a similar civil conflict between Spain and its subjects. Therefore, Fish convinced Grant, it was better to act as an honest broker to resolve the differences between the Spanish and the Cubans. Such an approach would allow the United States to maintain its stance against the British while, at the same time, advancing Grant's goal of a free and independent Cuba. Grant and Fish therefore tried to forestall armed conflict with Spain while the Cuban rebellion raged even as Americans inspired by abolitionism argued that the United States should intercede on behalf of the rebels and the enslaved there.[31]

As had been the case in the American Civil War, the Atlantic Ocean did not separate the United States and its Reconstruction travails from larger international forces. While diplomatic intrigues were happening in the Western Hemisphere, revolutionary change erupted across the European continent. European states were realigning and the long conflict between France and the German states culminated in the Franco-Prussian War. In fact, the turmoil and upheaval throughout Europe directly affected American foreign and domestic policy. During the Franco-Prussian War, shipments of American-made weapons to Europe tested the Grant administration's policy of avoiding involvement in foreign conflicts and buoyed charges of corruption. The administration had to answer for how American rifles fell into the hands of French soldiers. American citizens, some of German and French birth, traveled across the Atlantic to participate in or observe the conflict, including several American elites who found themselves trapped in Paris and Berlin in the early part of the 1870s. The development of the Paris Commune in the spring of 1871 exacerbated former Confederate fears of African American leadership in the South and northern industrialists' fears of rising organized labor as Northern Republicans, newspaper editors, and Northern laborers employed the rhetoric of the Commune as a fear tactic against African American laborers throughout the United States. Black workers "relied on government jobs handed out by politicians who relied on their support," Southern whites claimed, reifying the specter of the Paris Commune as socialist madness in Europe. As a revolutionary movement, the short-lived Paris Commune might have won support from Grant, who professed liberty and equality. Yet the Commune struck many Americans as a crude and violent rebellion and not a true republican movement. Grant instead supported the French Republic, and the Paris Commune became an American bogeyman, a metaphor for socialism and government gone awry.[32]

The decision not to assist revolutionary moments abroad, which Grant held was an important tenet of American republicanism, was underscored by the violent reaction to Grant's Reconstruction idealism in the American South. African Americans secured the rights of citizens through the Reconstruction amendments but whites in the South were unwilling to recognize these rights. Much as Grant had predicted in his memorandum, white Southerners exhibited their animosity against African Americans through violence and intimidation. Grant's doctrine of freedom, equality, and citizenship for all people in the Western Hemisphere proved to be unobtainable in his own country when Americans chose racism and reconciliation over republican principles. Despite the presence of federal troops, Grant could not stem the tide of violence and tumult in the South, and Secretary Fish was unwilling to support forcible attempts to create a society based on freedom and equality. As Grant and Fish were struggling with their foreign policy, they were also attempting one of the greatest social changes in the nation's young history. Grant's exhortations on the idealism of the republican experiment and the notion of African American participation in American democratic processes were undercut by the unwillingness of many Republicans to support the rights of African Americans and the indifference of white Americans who were weary of political violence in the name of social change. Reunion was the goal for most white Americans, not equal rights, and once the reentry of the Southern states had restored the Union, many whites were ready to move on. Grant's Doctrine, then, was untenable from the start, as he and many white Americans were unwilling and unable to support freedom and democracy at home just as they were unable to support those rights for non-white people abroad.[33]

Chapter 3

ANNEXATION'S FAILURE

On May 31, 1870, Secretary of State Fish attended a cabinet meeting carrying a proposed message on US foreign policy in the Western Hemisphere. Fish's message discussed neutrality in the Cuban rebellion, "American policy respecting the West Indies," and the topic of annexing the Dominican Republic. Attorney General Hoar and Secretary of the Navy Robeson thought such a message should be sent to Congress right away, while Secretary of the Treasury Boutwell worried that the message "may be regarded as discourteous to the Senate." Other cabinet members either remained silent or doubted the necessity of such a message. President Grant, however, let Fish know that he "approves every word in it." Yet, there was one passage that vexed Grant, a short paragraph "speaking of John Quincy Adams in terms of warm eulogy." Grant hated the Adams family, writing to friend Adam Badeau, "The Adams' do not possess one noble trait of character that I have heard of from old John Adams down to the last of all of them, [Henry Adams]." Fish agreed to edit the message and submit it to the president later. Grant then expressed his desire to issue a proclamation against the Irish Fenians and other immigrants engaged in violations of US neutrality. Grant railed against the "proceedings [such] as those of the 'Irish Republic' the 'organization of a government within the U. S.' the 'holding of a Congress' and the 'assumption of the power to raise armies and fit out expeditions.'" Fish recorded Grant's diatribe in his diary later that day, noting that the president directed his ire at "this thing of being a Citizen of the U. S. for the purpose of voting, and being protected by this [Government] and then claiming to be Citizens of another [Government] must be stopped." Fish agreed to consult with the Attorney General and to help prepare a proclamation that clarified the rules of citizenship for immigrants. Leaving the meeting, Fish must have assumed that he and the president were on the same page regarding the foreign policy objectives of the nation.[1]

Later that month, Fish prepared a message to Congress in which he laid out the administration's policy on neutrality in Cuba. President Grant, then, drafted an accompanying statement condemning Spanish policies there, referring to "the cruelties practiced in Cuba," which he intended to add to Fish's message and send to Congress. Grant wanted to attach the memorandum to Fish's report to Congress to show his administration's objections to Spain's actions toward the United States and her citizens. Hoar and Robeson concurred with Grant, but Fish balked, arguing that his message offered a better approach to Congress. "I contend that my draft presents a just & impartial summary of the case," Fish wrote in his diary, "[it] condemns each party—that by adding what the [President] has written, its [sic] logical effect will be destroyed." Fish counselled that Grant's grievances against Spain were more akin to a declaration of war. He argued that the president's claims were inaccurate and that to include them in an official message would lead the nation down a dangerous path. Fish eventually succeeded in convincing Grant to soften the wording. The president confirmed his mistake weeks later when Grant pulled Fish aside and remarked: "[Y]ou led me against my judgment at the time, you almost forced me, in the matter of signing the late Cuban message, and I now see how right it was, and I desire most sincerely to thank you. The measure was right & the whole country acquiesces in it."[2]

Grant's harsh language toward Spain seemed out of step with his foreign policy which—while acknowledging that a war with Spain was possible, if not inevitable—sought to embrace republican ideas in the Western Hemisphere peacefully. "Let Us Have Peace" was Grant's campaign slogan, and the president's policy, both domestically and internationally, had been for the United States to maintain a peaceful coexistence in the world. However, war hawk cabinet members such as Robeson and Hoar pushed the president toward intervention in Cuba. The statement Grant submitted to Fish was a move away from Grant's policy in that it sought to rush into military intervention against Spain without regard to the diplomatic or political needs of the Cubans or the American people. Fish's final version of the president's message softened Grant's ire toward Spain, bringing his message back to a singular statement of neutrality while managing still to argue that Spain was guilty of abuses against American citizens. Grant's first term was only a year old, and Fish was working hard to keep the United States at peace. War hawks and the Cuban Junta had convinced many in the American public that intervention in Cuba was a just cause. Grant himself believed as much, but he was wary lest embroilment in Cuba frustrate Dominican annexation.

Intervening into the Cuban rebellion while simultaneously negotiating a treaty of annexation might destabilize the Caribbean even further. Fish, then, led Grant down a pragmatic path, where the United States would remain neutral in the Cuban rebellion, thus keeping the nation out of war and keeping Grant from undermining the United States' position against Great Britain in the *Alabama* claims. Grant surmised that by remaining neutral in the Cuban rebellion, the mere presence of the United States in the Dominican Republic would strangle Spanish control over the enslaved, and Cuba would fall to his domino theory of liberty.

Grant and Fish's neutrality message arrived in Congress just as the House was set to vote on a resolution to recognize the belligerency of the Cuban rebels. Some members of Grant's cabinet urged Fish to send Grant's more bellicose message to sway the vote in favor of recognition. Fish, however, did not believe recognizing the Cuban rebels was in the best interest of US foreign policy. Fish's softer message received a mixed reaction from legislators. While some members of Congress cheered Grant's decision to condemn the "failure of Spain to protect American citizens, or to give them time to prove their innocence of complicity in conspiracy against Spanish authority," others balked at his lack of support for the Cuban Junta and the rebellion. For Fish, the message had the desired effect, as the House Republicans voted against recognition of Cuban belligerency. It was the first time in the fifteen months of the Grant presidency that Fish believed the administration and the Republican Party had coalesced around his foreign policy. Following a cabinet meeting, Fish and other members congratulated one another on the defeat of the belligerency resolution. "All concur in the opinion that the movement was wise and beneficial in its results," Fish wrote in his diary, "that it has served to concentrate and consolidate the party, and to exhibit a policy, and the capacity of rallying the party." Fish conceded that the Republican Party had long been at odds without a single issue to coalesce around, "the presentation of some issue on which they should be required as party men, to say 'yea' or 'nay' distinctly upon some issue presented by the Administration." Fish knew Grant was hesitant to support his secretary's course of action with Cuba, yet Grant trusted him, and they "consolidated the party." Fish understood that the administration was setting a precedent of foreign policy that was more important than "a momentary excitement of popular sympathy." From this point forward the Grant administration would speak with one voice on foreign policy, even if the Republican Party was not always in agreement.[3]

With the issue of the annexation of the Dominican Republic in the hands of the Senate in the summer of 1870, Fish had time to tackle the complicated subject of immigration. While the Congress was debating the recognition of the Cuban rebels, a Naturalization Act was working its way through the congressional process. Initially submitted by New York Republicans Noah Davis (in the House) and Roscoe Conkling (in the Senate), the Naturalization Act proposed that the federal government establish a centralized authority for the purpose of streamlining the naturalization process. Prior to 1870, any foreign-national could apply for naturalization in any state or local court—with the influx of hundreds of thousands of new immigrants to the United States during and after the Civil War, naturalization had become a tool for election fraud. Noted political scientist Francis Lieber wrote to Grant in 1868 that "If you are elected President we here will do our utmost to make Congress pass a statute giving back the power of naturalization to the U. States Courts, or U.S. Commissioners, as it was originally, and we hope we shall not have a veto on such a bill. The present unlawful naturalization is *gigantic*."[4] In New York, the Tammany Hall political machine used the disorganized nature of the naturalization process to its advantage, naturalizing thousands of immigrants just in time for the 1868 election. As a result, New York Democrats won local elections thanks to thousands of citizens naturalized just a few days before. In response, Davis and Conkling wanted to create legal guidelines for local and state courts to prevent any local magistrate from bestowing citizenship on any immigrant without time constraints. The immigrant community did not respond favorably to the legislation.[5]

Some immigrant groups and members of Congress fought the passing of a new naturalization law on several grounds. They argued that the proposed law violated the spirit of the Expatriation Act. The Expatriation Act of 1868 declared the right of expatriation "a natural and inherent right of all people," and that all naturalized citizens of the United States were entitled to the same protections as native-born citizens. Placing undue burdens on immigrants, centralizing the process of naturalization, and extending the time it took to receive naturalized status deprived immigrants of rights to move freely about the nation and throughout the world. The proposal galvanized immigrant support in the Democratic Party and added to the split in the Republican party with Liberal Republican Carl Schurz using the legislation to gin up the support of German immigrants in the mid-West. The legislation looked like Know-Nothingism to many European immigrants who worried that a new xenophobia was overtaking the Republican party. At the same time, immigrants, whites, and many Black Americans objected to the inclusion of Chinese immigrants in the naturalization process. While the legislation was intended merely to streamline the process of naturalization for white immigrants, Charles Sumner offered an amendment that would remove race as a defining factor for citizenship. The prospect of thousands of Chinese immigrants becoming American citizens frightened politicians and laborers in the West and South, who saw Chinese immigrants as a cheap source of labor who were uncivilized and unworthy of citizenship and who, more importantly to many, would undercut existing laborers.[6]

While many African Americans decried the loss of wages to Chinese immigrants, Black leaders such as Frederick Douglass saw immigration to the United States as a proving ground for Reconstruction and citizenship. When Charles Sumner advocated the end of the coolie trade and full citizenship for Chinese immigrants, Douglass informed him of his robust support for such measures. "Upon the Chinese question I rejoice to see you in the right place, far in the advance and the country as usual behind you," Douglass wrote to Sumner. "A bitter contest, I fear, is before us on this question. Prejudice, pride of race, narrow views of political economy, are on one, humanity, civilization and sound policy are on the other." Their support for Chinese citizenship went further than Grant, who only sought to end the coolie system which was "marked by all the horrible and infernal characteristics of the slave trade," but he did not support citizenship rights for Chinese immigrants.[7] Douglass's *New National Era* supported Chinese immigrants as fellow victims of Democrats who claimed that Chinese laborers stole jobs from whites. "They profess to fear the competition of cheap labor and at the same time advocate free-trade," Douglass and his editors wrote, "[w]hich would bring not only the labor of the Chinamen but the labor of all the paupers of Europe in competition with American labor." The newspaper argued that the Republican party would ensure equal rights for all laborers, regardless of race or origin, noting that the party that ended slavery was best suited to protect the rights of Black and Chinese labor. Four months later, though, several members of the Republican Party would vote down Sumner's amendment to remove race from the naturalization process. Douglass also chastised business owners who forced all laborers to work for wages so low that Chinese immigrants could replace them, as happened in Massachusetts when a shoemakers' union went on strike. Yet as Chinese laborers were immigrating to the South, African Americans were moving increasingly to the West. Many Black Southerners, who grew weary of constant violence from former Confederates, believed that they would find better opportunities and labor conditions in the Western territories. Black Americans joined whites as they settled former Native American land, spurred on by federal spending, private investments in railroads, and Black activists leading the charge to move West. Laborers in the West, regardless of race, feared a sudden influx of Chinese laborers who might drive down compensation. Many Black Americans attempted to differentiate themselves from Chinese immigrants and Native Americans by pointing to their own Christianity as an example of their embrace of modernity and civilization. Chinese immigrants were labeled "heathens" and Native Americans "barbarians," and both were "alien of our customs" and incapable of being American citizens. Black Americans embraced these stereotypes against the Chinese and Native Americans to position themselves as politically superior and economically competitive.[8]

The naturalization of citizens complicated United States relations with Cuba, as Cuban-American citizens claimed the Spanish government was violating their rights as Americans. The State Department handled hundreds of claims from Cuba that both clarified and muddled the situation there. At the same time, Irish Fenian nationalists imprisoned by the British were also claiming American citizenship. Both Grant and Fish considered these claims to be potential roadblocks to settling the *Alabama* claims as well as other potential diplomatic issues. In August 1870, Grant wrote to Fish that he was considering issuing pardons for Irish Fenians imprisoned for their raids into Canada. Fish urged caution and asked the President to hold off on issuing the pardons, writing, "political prisoners are the worst kind of birds to keep caged . . . I would however suggest whether it may not be well to postpone the action . . . the pardon will produce some irritation among the Canadians, who may in their excitement annoy some of our fisherman." Fish suggested postponing until after the fishing season, since the complicated fishery situation was one of the main sticking points between the United States, Great Britain, and Canada that he hoped to negotiate into the *Alabama* claims discussion. Grant then postponed the pardons until October, choosing, however, to issue a proclamation of neutrality that would admonish not only the Fenians, but also the Cuban Junta, and for good measure the German Americans who felt the need to get involved in the Franco-Prussian War. Fish recalled the cabinet meeting in his diary, noting that he "Submitted the draft of a proclamation of warning against violation of international duties." He clarified further that the proclamation was against those who "by such means as the assumed Governmental organizations which claim to exercise Legislative Military Powers within the US (for example the Fenian Congress & the Cuban Junta)." The proclamation was "to be issued simultaneously with the granting of the Pardons (which the President has decided to issue to the Fenians convicted in connection with the late raid upon Canada)." Grant issued the neutrality proclamation the same day as the pardons so there could be no denying its meaning toward the Fenians and the Cubans: American citizens, natural-born or naturalized, were not to involve themselves in the military expeditions of other nations.[9]

Many Black leaders in the United States disagreed with Grant when it came to the Cuban insurrection and support for emancipation there. Black writers challenged the president's stance on the Cuban rebels, claiming that the mission of the Junta and the Republican party were inseparable. "There is no halting an idea at a national boundary," P. B. S. Pinchback's *Semi-Weekly Louisianian* opined in August 1871. "From being the gloomy bulwark of slavery and the accursed African slave-trader, we have become by the silent force of our example the pioneers of freedom and emancipators of nations." Such a statement echoed the Grant Doctrine as Pinchback, and other African Americans, proclaimed that it was now the duty of the United States to support the emancipation of enslaved persons in the Western Hemisphere and to support those seeking liberty and freedom. Although Grant and many of his cabinet members agreed with these sentiments, the significance of the *Alabama* claims took precedence over Reconstruction's aims. Though many Republicans sympathized with the plight of enslaved persons in Cuba, many white members of the Party split over whether to intervene in the rebellion. Conservative Republicans decried expansionism and worried that intervention was the first step to annexing Cuba and introducing the island's inhabitants into the body politic of the United States.

The emancipation of the Cuban enslaved, not the acquisition of Cuba, was a central tenet of the Republican Party's ideology, and African American leaders believed that the president should take a proactive stance toward recognizing Cuban belligerency and intervening in the insurrection on behalf of the rebels. When Grant chose political expediency in the *Alabama* claims over intervention in Cuba, he alienated African American leaders whose sympathies lay with the enslaved in Cuba. Chief among Grant's critics on the subject of Cuba was the abolitionist and African American preacher, Henry Highland Garnet. Speaking to the Cuban Anti-Slavery Committee meeting at the Cooper Institute in New York, Garnet harkened back to the same imagery that abolitionists had used in the antebellum period of the bloody and violent slave South. "Slavery shall be blotted out from every island in the Western Sea," Garnet declared in a manner akin to the Grant Doctrine, "as it has been banished from the Western continent. The shores of our continent shall not be washed by the waves made bloody by Cuban slavery." Garnet told the assembled Cuban expatriates and supporters that he was sorry that the federal government prohibited him from sending material support but that the Cuban people, particularly the Cuban enslaved, had the moral support of the African American people and former abolitionists in the United States. He and the Cuban Anti-Slavery Committee voiced their displeasure when President Grant announced he would not recognize the Cuban rebels.[10]

In contrast, Frederick Douglass, who like Henry Highland Garnet, P. B. S. Pinchback, and many other African American leaders hoped that the United States would help emancipate the enslaved persons in Cuba and Puerto Rico, was less critical of Grant. As both an African American and a Republican, he hoped that Grant would champion pro-Cuban views. When Grant decided not to recognize Cuban belligerency, Douglass admitted his confusion and disappointment in the president's stance. In a letter to African American inventor Samuel Raymond Scottron, Douglass proclaimed that he fully supported Cuban freedom, but trusted that Grant knew what he was doing. "The first gleam of the sword of freedom and independence in Cuba secured my sympathy with the revolutionary cause, and it did seem to me that our government ought to have made haste to accord the insurgents belligerent rights," Douglass wrote. "Why it did not is still a mystery to me. Nothing but my high confidence in its wisdom, knowledge and good intention has restrained me from joining in reproaches." Douglass told Scottron that he supported Grant, arguing "I have deemed our government, with all the facts of the situation before it, a safer guide than my own feelings. I have assumed that President Grant and his cabinet were better judges than myself of the international duties of the Republic though I think with my limited knowledge that a great opportunity has been lost." Douglass believed that an anti-slavery feeling was growing in Spain and that emancipation was inevitable in Cuba and he favored any course that led to the eventual end of slavery in Cuba and in Puerto Rico. Douglass understood that Grant and Fish were juggling several diplomatic issues and that Cuba was a single spoke in the wheel of foreign policy. Douglass's acknowledgment that the Cuban decision might be part of a wider foreign policy process shows an adept understanding of the international complexities facing the Grant administration.

In late 1870, the Dominican Republic annexation and the *Alabama* claims required most of Fish's attention and the secretary was happy to, temporarily, have the Cuba question off the docket.[11]

The Senate received the Dominican Republic annexation treaty in early January 1870 and it became an immediate sensation in Congress and in the press. Little did Grant know that it was dead on arrival in the Senate. Issues of racism among the Republican Party, charges of corruption against the Grant administration, personal animosity between the president and Senator Sumner, and institutional jealousies between the foreign policy wings of the executive and legislative branches all lead to the downfall of the treaty. Grant's primary mistake was his failure to include the powerful chair of the Senate Foreign Relations Committee, Massachusetts senator, Charles Sumner, in the early treaty deliberations. Fearing that a loan between the Dominican Republic and a London banking house could derail the annexation attempt, Grant and Fish had decided to maintain secrecy not only of Orville E. Babcock's mission but also of the entire annexation plan. With the Hartmont Loan, as it was known, set to expire on New Year's Eve 1869, Grant did not allow anyone outside of the cabinet to view the treaty until after the New Year. The early January 1870 meeting at Sumner's home was the beginning of a long, drawn-out feud between Sumner and Grant that revolved around the Dominican Republic, Anglo-American relations, and the fates of junior officers and diplomats who swore allegiance to either man. Eventually, due to this feud, Sumner lost his committee chairmanship.[12]

    Contemporaries believed that the animosity between Sumner and Grant was due to a cultural clash between the Harvard educated Senator and the hardscrabble former soldier, a judgment in which most modern historians concur. Sumner decried such a charge claiming that his "early life" had nothing to do with his dislike of Grant, nor was his early life as grand as the public assumed it was. Fish argued, though, that the genesis of Sumner's hostility to the treaty was his belief that the Senate Committee on Foreign Relations should be the source of United States foreign policymaking. He believed that Sumner was angry at the way the administration had negotiated the treaty, specifically through Orville E. Babcock. "The Senate has been for two or three years accustomed to originate measures and to resist what the Executive originated," Fish noted. "The habit of criticism, if not of opposition became somewhat fixed, and on the ascension of a friend to the Executive Chair, the habit could not entirely and at once subside—it is difficult to voluntarily relinquish power." Sumner had battled the Johnson administration over the direction of foreign policy, yet Grant was a Republican, and thus, nominally a friend. Rather than attacking the president outright, Sumner originally took aim at Babcock as the object of his ire, noting that the young officer had exceeded his authority in his mission to the Dominican Republic. Sumner charged that Babcock's September memorandum represented a treaty engineered by a military officer, not a diplomat, who styled himself as the "aide-de-camp" of the president. The senator also sensed corruption in Babcock's claim to Baez that the American president would use his influence to assure annexation's approval in Congress. Sumner, an acquaintance wrote, "became the enemy of the whole scheme [because he] did not believe that the President of the United States should be made a lobbyist to bring about annexation."[13]

Charges of corruption against political opponents was a common practice in the era. Sumner believed that Babcock was at the center of a corrupt scheme perpetrated by Joseph Fabens and his confederates in the Dominican Republic. This corruption, Sumner claimed, enveloped the President and the State Department, thus calling the entire scheme into question Sumner was able to cast a shadow over the entire annexation scheme by labeling Babcock and his colleagues in the Dominican Republic, Fabens and William Cazneau, as corrupt. Sumner used his connections with journalists in Washington (indeed Sumner was dining with journalists the night President Grant knocked on the Senator's front door to discuss annexation) to promote the idea that Babcock, Fabens, Cazneau and Dominican President Buenaventura Baez were planning an illegal scheme to bring about annexation. Babcock did not help matters by ignoring the needs of American citizen Davis Hatch, who the Baez regime had imprisoned as an enemy to its administration and an enemy to annexation. Babcock also notes in his diary that Cazneau and Fabens offered him a significant parcel of land (nearly 1,000 acres) in the Dominican Republic if annexation succeeded. This is the best direct evidence of Babcock's corruption in the annexation scheme. Babcock notes that such a parcel of land would make his fortune and provide financial stability for his family. However, the land transaction never took place and never amounted to more than just talk between the men. When called before Congress to testify about his actions in the Dominican Republic, it was the Davis Hatch case that vexed Babcock and the Grant administration more than any talk of bribes and land deals.[14]

The case of Davis Hatch also represented the biggest obstacle to annexation for the American consulate in the Dominican Republic. In the intervening time between Babcock's missions, a Dominican court found Hatch, an American citizen living in the Dominican Republic, guilty of insurrection through his support of the previous regime led by former Dominican President Jose Maria Cabral. The court sentenced Hatch to death, but Baez commuted his sentence to banishment and, as far as anyone in the State Department was concerned, the Dominicans had exiled Hatch from the country. In fact, Hatch remained in prison, eventually reaching out to the new American consul in the Dominican Republic, Raymond Perry. Hatch's continued imprisonment, he claimed, was because he opposed annexation, and Perry requested guidance from Secretary Fish on how he should assist him. Fish instructed Perry to demand that the Dominicans release Hatch immediately. However, Perry found that the Dominicans were stonewalling him in the hopes that Hatch would remain in custody until after the United States Senate approved of annexation. When Perry approached Babcock about Hatch's situation, Babcock declined to get involved. Eventually, Hatch brought a lawsuit against the United States and the Dominican Republic, which resulted in congressional hearings focusing on Babcock's conduct during the annexation process. Though most of the committee members cleared Babcock of any wrongdoing, the minority opinion (written by annexation opponent Missouri Senator Carl Schurz) leveled the charge that Babcock's relationship and correspondence with filibusterer William Cazneau was "most suspicious," and that Babcock's conduct was "so extraordinary, so unsoldierlike [sic], so utterly un-American, [and] unnatural." President Grant was so furious at these accusations of corruption that he told Ohio Governor Rutherford B. Hayes. "'I can defend myself, but he is merely a major of engineers with no opportunity to meet a Senator,'" and that he felt "'much embitterment' against Sumner and Schurz for unjust attacks on Major Babcock."[15]

Though Fish did not fully support Grant's annexation scheme, he did not share his reservations with members of the Senate. He did, however, try to convince the president that there were other ways to garner their support if he was willing to make a few changes. Notably, Fish underscored that bringing the Dominican Republic into the Union as a territory with a path to statehood would certainly sink the treaty since the issue split Republicans. One faction, including Sumner and Schurz, led the charge against annexation by utilizing racist science, arguing that the Dominicans were not up to the task of citizenship and civilization. On March 24, 1870, the *New York Herald* claimed that Sumner, in executive session, referred to the Dominicans as "a turbulent, treacherous race, indolent and not disposed to make themselves useful to their country or to the world at large." Sumner argued that due to constant fighting with Haiti they had proven that "the character of the people would render acquisition of their country undesirable." The *Herald* also reported that Sumner's speeches explicitly referenced the race of the Dominicans and that he did not hold them in as high esteem as he did Black Americans. Historian Eric T. L. Love notes that while it was possible the writers of the *Herald* were twisting Sumner's words, several Sumner biographers agreed that race played a factor in the senator's opposition to annexation. As for Schurz, he was more overt in his racist evaluation of the Dominicans. Love notes that Schurz "condemned the Dominicans as 'immoral, vicious, and lazy,' people."

With these two leading voices in the Senate adamantly against annexation, Fish looked for other ways to placate Grant's desire for a foothold in the Caribbean. Fish told Grant that any promise of statehood would undercut support for annexation in the Senate, as he had learned from numerous senators that the establishment of a Caribbean protectorate would gain support for, at least, a lease of Samaná Bay, but not outright annexation. Fish agreed with these senators that the economic influence of the United States in the Caribbean was beneficial to the economies of the United States and the island nations, but political acquisition of these territories would only hinder the development of both. To maintain national and international stability, Fish contended, a base in Samaná Bay was preferable to annexation. In his diary, Fish noted that "Senator Morril [sic] of Maine this morning urged the President should not press the treaty—says it has no 'earnest' friends in the Senate—that the weight of Argument & fact is against it." Grant flatly rejected Fish's suggestion of a protectorate, arguing "it was Schurz suggestion . . . and he [Grant] regards it as the suggestion of an opponent." Fish countered that it was his idea only, stating "I express the conviction that the Treaty will be rejected unless some of its opponents are gained over by some new feature, or principle & that this [a protectorate] had occurred to me as possibly capable of gaining some." With Grant appeased that the idea had originated with Fish, he authorized the secretary to mention it to Sumner.[16]

The constant disagreements between the administration and key Republican senators caused a strain in Fish and Sumner's personal relationship.

The two had been close friends prior to the Civil War and observers assumed that they would have a good working relationship as the heads of foreign relations in their respective branches of government. However, Sumner's hatred of Grant fractured his relationship with Fish, which played out in public on the Senate floor and in private correspondence between the men and mutual acquaintances. Sumner died in the middle of Grant's second term but not before these severe clashes with the president led to the fracturing of the Republican Party. This animosity forced Fish, long an admirer of Sumner, to admit that the Massachusetts senator had possibly lost his mind. Fish noted in his diary: "I express the opinion that Sumner is 'crazy—a monomaniac upon all matters relating to his own importance— & his relations toward the President.'" The secretary continued that Sumner, "more than once in speaking of the Presidents [sic] interviews with him last Winter at Sumner's house, about San Domingo had said that Grant was drunk." Fish concluded, "[Secretary] Boutwell, who was present at the interview says 'he was no more drunk, or excited than he was when we left him upstairs five minutes since—no more than Sumner himself.'"[17]

On March 15, 1870, Sumner's Senate Foreign Relations Committee voted against recommending ratification of the Dominican Republic annexation treaty to the full Senate. A successful treaty did not require a favorable vote from the Foreign Relations Committee; however an unfavorable vote would create roadblocks to receiving the necessary two-thirds majority of the full Senate. The senator delayed the committee vote for months, leading Grant to claim that Sumner had lied to him in their meeting at Sumner's home. As Fish recounted, Sumner accused the president of drunkenness and the vitriol between Sumner and Grant severed any relationship that Fish had with the Senator. Grant wrote to Fish warning him against sharing information with Sumner, stating "[Sumner] is an enemy of the treaty; will kill it to-morrow if he can, and only favors delay probably to better secure its defeat. I do not think it good policy to trust the enemies of a measure to manage it for, (and to speak in behalf of), its friends." This personal animus helped end Grant's chances of getting the treaty through the Senate and subsequently ended any hope of implementing the Grant Doctrine in the Caribbean. However, Grant was not yet willing to let go of the possibility of acquiring the island territory and promoting his vision of American democracy abroad. In response to the Senate Foreign Relations Committee's vote against sending the treaty to the floor, Grant went to the Capitol to lobby for a full vote on the Senate floor. Sumner balked at the idea that Grant would enter his territory and the turf war prompted the secretary of state to join the president on the Hill to temper rumors that he was against the treaty, rumors which were due to Fish himself uncharacteristically confessing to a friend his lack of support. Grant, though was successful, and the Senate brought the treaty to the floor for debate, even though Sumner's committee voted unfavorably against it in a closed session.[18]

Grant had hoped that annexation would be embraced as an outgrowth of Reconstruction, as a haven for African Americans to express their newfound freedoms. His position on the equality of the races and the advancement of civil rights for African Americans should have found allies among the Republicans in the Senate, but tying his policy to annexation was a nonstarter. Several historians have noted that Grant, though supportive of African American movement to the Dominican Republic in memos and private conversations, never broached the idea in official communications to Congress. Many of the Senate leaders had been strident abolitionists before the Civil War and Grant expected them to remain loyal party men who upheld the Republican platform of civil rights. Republicans such as Carl Schurz possessed views on race that were not as thoroughgoing as their support for abolition had made them seem. Therefore they could never be counted on to help the president implement a policy that sought to bring even more non-white voters into the American polity. Schurz believed that the Dominicans were intellectually inferior to whites and that they were unable to shoulder the burden of citizenship. He told the members of the Senate to read the history of the tropics and they would find the people there lacking. "Read that history," he argued, "read that of all other tropical countries and then show me a single instance of the successful establishment and peaceable maintenance, for a respectable period, of republican institutions, based upon popular self-government, under a tropical sun." Senator Matthew Carpenter of Wisconsin reminded Schurz "that it is only very recently that the Senator could point to a tropical negro that was not in the condition of slavery." However, Schurz countered that the island of "Santo Domingo" had been free of slavery longer than the United States, yet the people there had shown no ability to embrace republican institutions. Schurz argued that the climate was at fault, a tropical climate that destroyed Anglo-Saxon progress and made the darker skinned inhabitants "shiftless." Both Schurz and Sumner subscribed to the biological racism of the era, which held that whites could not physically function in the tropics and that the environment was too oppressive for all races, therefore the annexation of the Dominican Republic would be of benefit neither to the white citizens of the United States nor to the Dominican people. Grant was hopeful that, as the treaty made it to the Senate floor for a full vote, more Republicans believed as he did rather than subscribed to the views of Sumner and Schurz.[19]

The annexation of the Dominican Republic, by which Grant proposed to increase the non-white citizenry of the US by over one hundred thousand, and the way he had pursued annexation, ran counter to many Republicans' vision of republicanism. Republicans and Democrats alike saw corruption and scheming at work in the Dominican annexation effort. They blamed Grant for what they saw as failures in Southern legislatures in South Carolina and Mississippi, legislatures with numerous Black members, and opposed his attempted racial Reconstruction. To them the inclusion of thousands of Black and non-white citizens from the Dominican Republic would prove as disastrous as it had in the South. They reasoned, as one historian wrote, "in its own sleazy way, Santo Domingo was exotic, and exotic meant a foreignness in culture and habit that went with the climate and stood very little chance of being eradicated." With that foreignness was the assumption of graft and nefariousness as well. As one historian has written, "from very early critics knew that behind the Santo Domingo proposal schemes, seedy or shady, must lie." By negotiating the treaty without the consent of the Senate Foreign Relations Committee, Grant's administration had further expanded executive power at a time when members of his party feared an expansive presidency and the federal government in general. Republican senators, then, chose to challenge the president on annexation to check his executive overreach in the Reconstruction era.[20] Heated debates ensued in the Senate in the three months following the decision of Sumner's committee. During that time, the original deadline set in the treaty for ratification expired, but Grant directed Fish to work out an extension with the Dominicans while he continued to lobby senators to his cause. Sumner and Schurz continued their assaults against the treaty and the Dominicans as they also levied charges of corruption against Babcock. Grant fumed as the Senate Investigative Committee took the word of Raymond Perry, the American Consul, over that of the president's aide. In a letter to fellow Grant confidante, Adam Badeau, Babcock expressed his frustrations with the entire process. "We are in the midst of a terrible struggle in the Senate, Sumner, Schurz, etc. 'versus the President,'" he wrote. "[Sumner] made a most cowardly attack upon me in the Senate . . . as he is a coward, I simply intend to denounce him as a liar and coward, and let the poor sexless fool go." Since the Senate investigation of Babcock centered on his poor handling of Davis Hatch's case in the Dominican Republic, this mistake proved to be just what the anti-treaty group needed to sow doubt surrounding Babcock's involvement in the scheme.[21]

Grant hoped to export republicanism to the Caribbean while also protecting the electoral rights of African Americans across the South. The state legislatures in South Carolina and Mississippi elected Black majorities and Black men were soon thereafter sent to Congress. When Mississippi rejoined the Union in January 1870, the newspaper owned by Frederick Douglass commented on Hiram R. Revels' selection to the Senate as the first African American member of that chamber. The *New Era* extolled the revolutionary act of admitting Revels, noting, "Escorted by Senators representing the two opposite complexions of the continent, Mississippi returns to her place in the Union. She comes with a proud pre-eminence of loyalty over all Southern States. She brings [a] forty thousand majority for the Republican Party." The editors understood that the event was but one small act for Mississippi to show whites that African Americans belonged in the political sphere. "Here is a repentance that needs not to be repented of. Mississippi, more than any other State in the Union, will furnish the proof our friends I have been anxious about, that, namely, of negro capacity in statesmanship." Douglass's paper understood the fraught nature of admitting Revels into the Senate, noting that "Senator Revels and the Hon. James Lynch went down into the State with only the experience of Methodist preachers, without political training, without even an elector's knowledge. They went into a community chagrined under defeat, spiteful in feeling against the colored victims who had helped to overthrow oppression into a community destitute of capital, bristling with Ku-Klux rifles and bowie-knives, Slippery with blood from assassination." As the former Confederate states reentered the Union, Black voters reshaped the face of politics in the state legislatures, much to the chagrin of the white electorate. While this era of Reconstruction created a revolutionary political atmosphere, at the same time, Black Southerners faced an onslaught of Klan violence and oppression from former Confederates attempting to nullify African Americans' right to vote. At this same time, Grant attempted to gain support for annexation from this constituency of like-minded Republicans.[22]

Grant's presence in the capitol caused a stir among members of Congress, most notably Sumner himself, who complained bitterly to Secretary Fish about the President's violation of Senatorial conventions. During the debates over the treaty, annexation proponent and Grant ally Senator Oliver P. Morton of Indiana presented goods and materials which Babcock had brought back from the island nation, including hemp products and large blocks of salt. Curious senators proceeded to lick the salt block, causing quite a commotion when Revels joined racist Democrat Garrett Davis of Kentucky and simultaneously licked the sodium deposit.[23]

Sumner continued to aggravate the Grant administration with his hostility toward annexation. Their mutual dislike for one another led to a showdown on the Senate floor in which the old Bay Stater unleashed his greatest weapon, his oratory skills, against his president. In a series of speeches, Sumner railed against Grant and the treaty, questioned Grant's motives in annexing the Dominican Republic, charged Grant with attempting to steal the entire island, including Haiti, and mocked Grant's grammar. A month after the swearing in of Senator Revels, Sumner delivered a speech arguing that Grant was acting like a despotic monarch, "all this has been done by kingly prerogative alone, without the authority of an act of Congress." Sumner accused Grant of acts of terrorism against the sovereign people of the Dominican Republic, arguing that the president had spent little time worrying about African Americans in the Southern states, while he allowed the rise of the Ku Klux Klan, focusing instead on annexation. "I insist that the Presidential scheme, which installs the Ku-Klux on the coasts of St. Domingo," Sumner charged, "and which at the same time insults the African race in the Black Republic [Haiti], shall be represented. I speak now of that Ku-Klux of which the President is the declared head, and I speak for the African race, whom the President has trampled down." Sumner's charge was a stinging rebuke of the president's policy, and Sumner's Republican colleagues who supported Grant let the old abolitionist know he had gone too far.[24]

Sumner's speech particularly disturbed Revels, whose elevation to the chamber had only occurred the month prior. In a letter he sent to the Massachusetts Senator two days after his fiery oration, the former pastor argued that the annexation of the Dominican Republic was one of Christian magnanimity. Revels viewed "the question from a Christian standpoint, that is, whether it is not the duty of our powerful, wealthy, and Christian nation, regardless of the trouble and expense which may attend it, to extend the institutions or various means of enlightenment and intellectual, moral and religious elevation with which God has blessed us." The new senator argued that it was a moral right for the United States to extend its republican institutions "to the inhabitants of that Republic" questioning whether such a feat "cannot be done more effectively by annexation than in any other way." For Revels, the blessing of American liberty and republicanism were best exported to the Caribbean by the United States through the annexation of the Dominican Republic. Revels, expressing the ideals of the Grant Doctrine, saw the moral and social reasons for annexation along with the strategic and economic reasons and, as such, he defied his friendship with Sumner and voted for the treaty. In the end, though, the treaty failed to receive the necessary two-thirds majority, falling by a vote of 28–28.[25]

Though African Americans were willing members of the Republican Party, they were not always accepting of the party's policies or, for that matter, the policies of the party's president. Grant's plan to incorporate more peoples into the body politic, particularly Dominicans, met resistance from some white Republicans and received mixed support from Black Republicans. His diplomatic handwringing on the Cuban question angered many Black leaders who believed that the United States was morally obligated to support the cause of liberty and freedom in a slave rebellion so close to its shores. At the same time, many African American leaders lined up just as strongly against Grant's annexation scheme for the Dominican Republic. Rather than follow Grant's lead as the head of the Republican Party, several Black leaders agreed with Sumner that the annexation of the Dominican Republic would be the first step toward the eventual overthrow of the Black Republic of Haiti. Thus, Grant struggled to build a coalition of African American leaders behind his various Reconstruction policies. However, when it was time for his reelection bid in 1872, most Black voters cast their vote for Ulysses S. Grant.[26]

For all their disagreements on policy, Ulysses S. Grant and famed African American political thinker and orator Frederick Douglass knew that they could rely upon one another as staunch Republicans. The Grant Doctrine of exporting republicanism throughout the Western Hemisphere appealed to Douglass's sensibilities as both a member of the Republican Party and an African American activist who championed freedom and liberty. Douglass saw the United States as part of a global movement towards liberty and supported a new American imperialism that reflected the Grant Doctrine. Douglass eventually supported Grant's pet project of annexing the Dominican Republic. He begrudgingly accepted Grant's and Fish's decision to remain neutral in the Cuban rebellion, and he favored rapid settlement of the American West, although he later decried the exodus of thousands of Black

Southerners to Kansas. Through all these initiatives, Douglass championed the Grant administration's domestic Reconstruction plan of enforcing freedmen's civil rights across the South. As Douglass wrote to Orville E. Babcock, late in the second term, "[Grant's] name stands for national peace, Liberty prosperity and stability. He has been the shelter and savior of my people in the hour of supreme danger and naturally enough we feel great concern as to who is to come in his stead." Grant's actions had earned him political capital with African American leaders such as Douglass, who endorsed his party, backed his reelection, and even considered supporting him for a third term. Buoyed by thousands of new voters, with African Americans reporting 90 percent voter turnout in elections, Grant hoped that the Republican Party would reshape the political landscape of the South and provide a template for the incorporation of additional territories and citizens into the body politic.[27] From his position as a leader in the African American community, Douglass championed the cause of the Republican Party in the Reconstruction era. He edited a national newspaper, *The New National Era*, as a voice for Black issues in the United States. His sons, Frederick Jr. and Lewis, assisted him in publishing the newspaper, printing articles and editorials that challenged the Southern Democrats and the rise of the Ku Klux Klan, and offered support for the Republicans in the Southern states. African Americans relied on *The New National Era* as a leading voice "in the political center of Reconstruction." Thus, Douglass's steadfast support for Grant and the Republican Party against newspaper editor Horace Greely, Senator Carl Schurz, and even long-time friend Charles Sumner and the Liberal Republicans in the 1872 election, showed that he considered Grant was a better alternative than the Liberal Republicans who wanted to end federal protections in the South.[28]

The treaty's defeat did not dampen Grant's desire to acquire the island nation. Grant signed a lease with the Dominicans for the port at Samaná Bay and he continued to insist that annexation was the key to the future of race relations in the United States. To convince the Senate that he was correct, Grant asked the Congress to establish a commission of experts to travel to the Dominican Republic to report on the nation's willingness to join the United States, and to see the economic and republican possibilities of bringing the nation and its people into the Union. Congress agreed. The commissioners he proposed were Andrew White, the President of Cornell University; Samuel Gridley Howe, a reformer and advocate of the Freedmen's Bureau; Benjamin Wade, a former Ohio Senator; Allan Burton, former minister to Colombia, who was selected as commission secretary. Franz Siegel and Frederick Douglass were named assistant secretaries.[29] Meanwhile, Sumner argued against the commission, labeling it as a scheme to corrupt the republican nations of the Caribbean. In a speech which became known as Sumner's "Naboth's Vineyard" speech—as the senator likened Grant's annexation attempt to the biblical tale of King Ahab's coveting of the vineyard of the farmer Naboth—Sumner focused much of his derision on Babcock. He challenged Babcock's qualifications and argued that the young officer had been duped by supporters of the Dominican president and he also complained about Grant's decision to lobby publicly on behalf of the treaty. Sumner parsed Grant's words from his annual message, focusing on the fact that Grant referred to the "island of San Domingo," arguing that the president was thus clearly signaling his desire to annex Haiti as well! "Nine times in this message," Sumner claimed, "the President has menaced the independence of the Haytien [sic] republic." He concluded his initial remarks with: "I protest against this legislation as another stage in a drama of blood."[30]

Despite Sumner's vitriol, the commission was approved. The commissioners set sail for the Dominican Republic in January 1871 for a two-month fact-finding mission. During their investigation, the commissioners traveled throughout the Dominican Republic to ascertain the situation on the ground and to determine what form of relationship with the United States the Dominicans themselves desired. The commission concluded that the Dominicans had never truly known independence, being either under the thumb of European powers or under assault from their Haitian neighbors. The commission witnessed the Dominicans' poverty and concluded that the United States could help. As they recorded in their report: "There is but one chance for that republic ever to recover its independence — to become, after a proper period of probation, one of a union of states, the freedom and substantial independence of each being guaranteed by the strength of all." While Congress barred the commission from advocating the US annexation of the Dominican Republic, the commissioners and secretaries believed that annexation would undoubtedly benefit the Dominicans.[31]

Douglass was particularly moved by what he witnessed in the Dominican Republic. He concluded that his old friend, Sumner, was on the wrong side of the debate. Sumner, along with many Black leaders, decried that Douglass was not selected as a full member of the Commission of Inquiry, but was made Assistant Secretary. Douglass, though also disappointed, accepted the position to better inform himself on the annexation issue. Like

Grant, Douglass viewed the incorporation of the Dominican Republic into the body politic of the United States as a positive good not only for the Dominicans but also for his fellow African Americans. He agreed with Grant that the people of the Dominican Republic were offering annexation willingly and acceptance of their offer would mean the expansion of citizenship rights for non-whites and the strengthening of the Republican Party. As for his disagreement with Sumner, Douglass wrote in his 1881 memoir, "To Mr. Sumner, annexation was a measure of extinguishing a colored nation and to do so by means of selfish motives." However, to Douglass, annexation meant "the alliance of a weak and defenseless people having none of the attributes of a nation, torn by internal feuds and unable to maintain order at home or command respect abroad, to a government which could give it peace, stability and civilization, and make it helpful to both countries." Like Grant, Douglass envisioned the United States as a stabilizing and civilizing force for a nation ready to accept the ideals of liberty and the blessings of the American political system.[32]

As a member of the President's Commission of Inquiry into the purchase of Samaná Bay, Douglass's interactions with the Dominican people, who expressed the desire to become Americans, intensified his annexation convictions. This visit to the Dominican Republic opened a fissure between him and Sumner, who continued to oppose annexation and a US presence in the Dominican Republic in any guise. Through the pages of the *New National Era* and in his speeches, Douglass stumped for Grant's expansionist proposal. The newspaper warned against division and strife within the Republican Party over the Dominican Republic at a time when unity in defense of African Americans' rights and liberty was essential to keeping Democrats from power. "We shudder at the possibility, and every enlightened colored man," the newspaper opined, "must shudder at the possibility of the accession of this old party of rebellion and slavery to power." Moreover, Douglass saw annexation in the same terms as Grant, as a method for exporting the republican virtues of the United States to the Dominican people, enveloping them into the body politic of the nation as citizens, and protecting them with the Reconstruction amendments. Douglass likewise saw Dominican territory as a haven where African American citizens could escape the violence of the South and make their way as citizens of the United States. He also believed that the Dominicans needed the guiding hand of American Protestantism to lead them away from the superstitious Catholicism of the Old World.[33]

Not every member of the Republican Party agreed with racial equality as the purpose of Reconstruction, and the annexation scheme widened numerous fissures within the party. For most Republicans, the overriding goal of Reconstruction was the preservation of the Union, and the passage of the Fifteenth Amendment, strengthening the nation forever more. The Liberal Republicans pushed back against racial equality, arguing that Grant's Dominican scheme would import people "incapable of the self-discipline necessary for productive free labor and active citizenship." Liberal Republicans were more interested in a Reconstruction that produced a United States that "rekindled the sentimental nationalism of the antebellum period, with Northerners and Southerners accepting a common destiny borne of common feeling rather than coercion." Reunion was their goal, and when they achieved "a reunited nation, a free labor system, and a formal guarantee of equal treatment before the law," they considered Reconstruction complete. This contrasted with the radical Republican view, that the national government's role was to protect African American rights against white Americans' disdain for equality.[34]

Both Charles Sumner and the Liberal Republicans attempted to use Douglass's position as assistant secretary of the commission as a wedge to pull African American support away from President Grant in the upcoming 1872 election. Sumner focused upon a White House dinner for the Dominican annexation commissioners, to which Douglass was not invited. Democrats latched onto Sumner's stance echoing many of his anti-annexation speeches and, charging Grant with racism for failing to invite Douglass to the event while the white commissioners dined in the Executive Mansion. Douglass thought that the entire affair was ridiculous. "When did any Democratic President invite any Negro to dinner," Douglass asked a crowd in Maine. "That the President has no prejudice of color that debars him from recognizing all men alike I know from the fact that he extended all the courtesies to the Black Minister from Hayti [sic] that he has to white Ministers from other countries." Douglass noted that Grant did not invite the white Franz Sigel, also an assistant secretary to the commission, to the dinner and that the group had called upon the president informally and was only invited at the last minute. Douglass also pointed to the president's friendship with Native American Ely S. Parker as further proof that Grant would not shun him based on his race because Parker, "darker than I, has dined with him," and Grant assured him that he would have been invited had he been with the commissioners on that day. The supposed dinner scandal came on the heels of a very real scandal in which a ship's captain had refused to allow Douglass to dine with the white commissioners while traveling up the Potomac River. Douglass's colleagues rebuffed the captain in solidarity, yet Grant's silence on this slight to Douglass did not help matters. Sumner conflated the two events to cast aspersions on Grant, which Douglass refused to endorse. During the 1872 election campaign, Douglass's stump speeches defended Grant's record as a Republican leader and friend of African Americans.[35] Douglass, like Revels, split with his former abolitionist ally Sumner, offering his support to the president. "If Mr. Sumner after [reading the commission's findings] shall persevere in his present policy," Douglass stated, "I shall consider his opposition fractious, and regard him as the worst foe the colored race has on this continent." Sumner, though, maintained that Grant had rebuffed Douglass because he was Black and that Douglass was angry over the dinner incident and the Dominican commission. Sumner likened Grant's annexation scheme as an assault on the entire Black race, as was, he argued, the incident on the Potomac. Douglass, who had admitted to abolitionist Gerrit Smith that he was disappointed by Grant's silence on that incident, noted that "he was so used to being snubbed" that the incident was not worth holding over the president's head. Sumner, however, wrote to Smith that Douglass "*in my own house*" complained of the "President's conduct as an indignity." Smith, for his part, believed Douglass when he wrote that "the insult [to Douglass and by extension the Black race] exists but in Mr. Sumner's imagination."[36]

Fish considered the Dominican commission's report a vindication of the position he had maintained throughout the process, while Grant saw it as confirmation that his doctrine was correct. According to Fish, Grant was excited by early reports from the commission. Grant also believed that the report vindicated Babcock "against the charges & insinuations against [him]." Fish agreed that sending the report to Congress was wise, because "In the main it is right—it submits the whole question to Congress & the Peoples [*sic*]—asks no action." In the end, Congress took no action on the report, and, despite the public insistences of both Grant and Douglass, the idea of annexation faded from the minds of the public and the Senate. As the lease for Samaná Bay expired in October 1871, neither the Congress nor the cabinet was interested in pursuing the matter further. According to Fish, Grant, after having read a message from the Dominican diplomat Gautier regarding the Samaná lease, "very promptly says 'We will then drop the whole matter—and leave the whole question for Congress & the People.'" In October 1871, Fish confided to his journal, "thus, a troublesome, vexatious & unnecessary question, is, as I trust, finally got out of."[37]

Other former abolitionists and Black leaders were not as supportive of Dominican annexation as Douglass and Revels. Louisiana Governor P. B. S. Pinchback's newspaper, *The Semi-Weekly Louisianian,* argued that the scheme was splitting the party and "should never had been an administration scheme. . . . Let San Domingo stand on its own." Gerrit Smith echoed Sumner and deployed biological racism against annexation. "The tropic belongs to the sable races of men," he argued, noting that Black men were free to live among whites, but they were biologically predisposed to living in the tropics. He also charged that Grant was interested in annexing the entire island. "I say the island—for, I see that the President goes for annexing the whole of it" including Haiti. Though a supporter of the president, Smith believed Grant's arguments on behalf of the Dominican people to be disingenuous. He thought that Grant meant to enrich the nation by exploiting Dominican resources. Douglass disagreed, believing that it was possible both to enrich the United States and uplift the Dominican people by bringing them into the institutions of the American republic. Former abolitionist leader Peter H. Clark recognized the annexation scheme as central to Grant's policy agenda but hoped that the president would be willing to move on for the betterment of the Republican Party. In a speech honoring the anniversary of emancipation in the West Indies, Clark acknowledged that Grant had near complete support from African Americans because of his record as both the general who won the Civil War and as the president who championed Black rights through the Reconstruction amendments. However, Clark conceded that many Black Americans believed that Grant had deviated from his promise to "not enforce [ideas] in opposition to the will of the people" by pursuing the annexation of the Dominican Republic. By submitting the Commission of Inquiry report to Congress and leaving the matter to the chamber of the people, Clark noted, Grant had ultimately remained true to his pledge by allowing the Congress to decide rather than pushing the question further. More important to Clark, though, was the hypocrisy of the Democrats who now opposed annexation because, prior to emancipation, Southern Democrats had been strong proponents of Manifest Destiny, including annexation of the Dominican Republic, to expand the slave empire. Surely, the addition of thousands of free Black and brown men into the body politic, rather than as enslaved, was now undesirable to Southern Democrats and a factor in their opposition to Grant's plan.[38]

The demise of the Dominican treaty did not end the drama between Grant and Sumner. Sumner's decision to defy Grant and block the treaty in the Senate Foreign Relations Committee led Grant to vow vengeance against him and anyone else in the Senate who opposed annexation. According to Fish, Grant stated, "he will not consider those who oppose his policy as entitled to influence in obtaining positions under him—that he will not let those who oppose him 'name Ministers to London.'" This was a reference to Sumner, who had used his position as committee chairman to request the nomination of his friend, John L. Motley, as minister to Great Britain. Grant initially acquiesced to Sumner's request but, after their relationship soured, looked for any reason to recall Motley from his position. The position of minister to Great Britain was particularly important as the United States was amid negotiations on numerous claims and disagreements with Britain in what would eventually become the Treaty of Washington. Motley's reckless conduct as American minister to Britain obstructed early negotiations and Grant allowed his feelings toward Sumner to color his dealings with Motley. Fish recorded in his diary that Grant "intended to remove Motley, who he said represented Sumner more than he did the Administration, & spoke with much warmth of feeling, about Sumner." Fish replied that he "thought [Grant] was mistaken as to the extent of Sumner's present exercise of influence over Motley . . . [that] there had been a tendency to follow Sumner when he first went out." However, Fish believed that Motley had not done so in recent months, and he hoped "to induce the [President] to withhold action as to the removal of Motley—at least for the present."[39]

Grant worried that Sumner's power in the Senate would undermine his entire Reconstruction agenda as Sumner had previously objected to all the Reconstruction amendments, arguing that they were redundant to what the Constitution already provided to the freedmen. His rejections of the Thirteenth, Fourteenth, and Fifteenth Amendments were also political machinations since Sumner had previously entered legislation with similar language to the Fourteenth Amendment. His opposition, then, was merely so other senators and rivals in Massachusetts would not get credit for passing such an Amendment. Since Sumner likened himself, and not the president, as the captain of the ship of foreign policy, Grant could not trust the senator to support any measure that originated from the White House. Sumner's speech against the British position on the *Alabama* claims exacerbated an already fraught relationship between the two nations, and his personal animosity toward the president began to threaten his relationship with Fish. Grant remarked to the cabinet that he understood "that Sumner has said to several persons that he intends to oppose everything the Administration proposes." None of the other cabinet members could corroborate Grant's fears, though Secretary of the Treasury George S. Boutwell could only say about Sumner, "'no he did not say that, to me.'" Even so, Secretary Fish spent the first three months of 1871 intriguing to have Sumner replaced as Chairman of the Senate Foreign Relations Committee. For Fish, the troubled relationship between Sumner and Grant threatened the upcoming negotiations with the British. By March 1871, Grant believed removing Sumner from his chairmanship was essential to the passage of the administration's agenda in the Senate.[40]

Fish initially contacted Timothy Howe, chairman of the Senate Committee on Committees, to make the case that the Republican Party no longer wanted Sumner as chairman of Foreign Relations. Fish argued that Sumner was blocking important administration initiatives, purely out of spite toward Grant. Fish repeatedly noted in his diary his suspicion that Sumner was suffering from a physical and mental breakdown. "He exhibits what I believe is a very common incident to insanity," Fish wrote. Sumner had charged publicly that Grant and Babcock were threatening him with physical harm, and he used that charge to arouse sympathy from colleagues who recalled the vicious attack Sumner had suffered from South Carolina Representative Preston S. Brooks years before. Such arguments were enough for Howe, who believed that the chairman of the Foreign Relations Committee should, at a minimum, be on speaking terms with the president and the secretary of state. As such, Howe removed Sumner from his position as chair. Sumner's allies were furious and directly blamed Grant and Fish. Schurz alleged that Grant had removed Sumner solely because of his opposition to the Dominican treaty rather than because of any personal animosity on Sumner's part. Senator James Nye's argument, though, swayed the Senate, when he noted that the legislative body could not remove Grant or Fish but could remove Sumner for the betterment of American foreign relations. Sumner subsequently lost his chairmanship by a vote of 33 to 9. Grant denied any direct involvement in the event, but it was clear that Fish, on behalf of Grant, had worked to rid the administration's toughest critic of his power base. This, historian Charles W. Calhoun notes, "marked an extraordinary exercise of executive power and demonstrated the strength of Grant's influence in Congress."[41]

Sumner's ouster from the committee meant that Grant and Fish could more successfully prosecute their foreign policy, but it did not mean the annexation of the Dominican Republic. Grant continued to refer to annexation throughout his presidency, including his second inaugural address and his final message to Congress. In subsequent interviews published around the world, he discussed the lost opportunity with reporter John Russell Young during his post-presidential World Tour. Even in his final days, while working on his memoirs, Grant focused on the Dominican Republic in one of the very few references he made to his presidency and its legacy. Grant reiterated his position that he had hoped that the Dominican Republic would aid in the settlement of the question of the freedmen. "He was brought to our shores by compulsion, and he now should be considered as having as good a right to remain here as any other class of our citizens," Grant wrote. "[I]t was looking to a settlement of this question that led me to urge the annexation of Santo Domingo during the time I was President of the United States." Until the end, Grant maintained that annexing the Dominican Republic would have meant a better life for African Americans and the republic at large.[42]

Though Grant's desire to annex the Dominican Republic did not come to fruition, the attempt reaffirmed the principles of American hegemony in the Western Hemisphere as expressed in the Grant Doctrine. Grant signaled to the world his vision of a united hemisphere, free from European influence and free from the sin of slavery. His decision to send a novice diplomat, Orville Babcock, to negotiate the terms for annexation illustrated his belief in executive supremacy in matters of foreign policy while also showing his inexperience as a politician. The fact that he even bypassed his own secretary of state when presenting the treaty to Congress shows that Grant believed that the power to negotiate treaties was his alone. Babcock's missions to the Dominican Republic illuminated Grant's foreign policy objective to strengthen United States hegemony in the Western Hemisphere. It also revealed Grant's desire to export the ideals of Reconstruction beyond the borders of the American South, exerting American influence over the remaining slave-holding nations to bring about the abolition of the practice of slavery. Babcock's missions reveal Grant to be a naïve politician who failed to grasp the nuances of diplomatic protocols. Internal strife within the

Dominican Republic should have signaled to Grant that the Dominicans were undecided upon annexation. Having just defeated a rebellion in the United States, Grant should have realized that Baez's control over the Dominican Republic was tenuous at best. The annexation scheme was a venture that ultimately failed.

As for Babcock, he approached his missions as he would any orders given by General Grant during the Civil War, by obtaining the objects set forth by Grant and Fish and reporting the information accurately and quickly. Unfortunately, Cazneau, Fabens, and Baez drew Babcock easily into their machinations, tempting him with land and convincing him to withhold assistance to Davis Hatch. As such, he failed in his duty as a representative of the US government to protect the rights of American citizens in a foreign land. Ultimately, Babcock's mission was the first major foreign policy failure of the Grant administration. Even so, the proposed annexation of the Dominican Republic struck a new note for the United States' ambitions in the Western Hemisphere, one that presidents William McKinley and Theodore Roosevelt carried forward in the late nineteenth and early twentieth centuries, albeit without the idea that the people of the Caribbean were equal to Americans. In the meantime, however, Grant, Fish, and the State Department would turn their attention to the more pressing matter of the *Alabama* claims and relations between the United States and Great Britain, and to the rising violence in the American West. The administration would use the opportunity to yet again flex control over foreign and domestic relations, wresting the power from not only Congress, but also from its own diplomats. Fish and his colleagues in the State Department came to an agreement with the British to settle all disputes in what was known as the Treaty of Washington. The *Alabama* claims went to an international arbitration in Geneva, Switzerland, resulting in a $15.5 million award for the United States. All other claims were settled either by commission or arbitration in the subsequent decade.

Reminiscing in the years after the Grant administration, African American Congressman John R. Lynch of Mississippi argued that Senator Sumner's opposition to the annexation of the Dominican Republic had been justified because his political authority reached beyond the borders of Massachusetts. Lynch likened Sumner's humiliating loss of his chairmanship of the Senate Committee on Foreign Relations to a misstep in Congressional history. "[Sumner] knew and appreciated the fact that when he spoke and voted as a senator," Lynch wrote, "he did so, not merely as a senator from the state of Massachusetts, but as a senator of the United States. He belonged to no one state, but to the [nation]." Lynch's lauding of Sumner exemplified the dilemma that many Black leaders confronted in the Dominican scheme: forcing them to choose between President Grant and his Reconstruction policy and Senator Sumner, long known as a champion of African Americans' rights. Both Grant and Douglass believed the annexation of the Dominican Republic was an important step in exporting the civilizing force of republicanism. The freedom and equality that came with republicanism and the prosperity and progress that came with civilization were the foundation of Grant's plan to export the ideals of Reconstruction to the Caribbean. While the Grant Doctrine sought to bring liberal democracy to the Caribbean, Grant was also focusing on "civilizing" the American West. As more white and Black settlers crossed the Mississippi River into Western territories, clashes with Native Americans increased. As such, Grant spent the first few years of his presidency balancing not only the Grant Doctrine in the Caribbean and the *Alabama* claims, but also a significant shift in relations with the "uncivilized" Native Americans.[43]

Part II

RECONSTRUCTION IN THE AMERICAN WEST

Chapter 4

RECONSTRUCTING THE "UNCIVILIZED"

Grant's first inaugural address offered his ideas about who should be included in the republican experiment. For the first time in a presidential inauguration, the plight of Native Americans was featured, including outlining a path to citizenship for them. "The proper treatment of the original occupants of the land, the Indian, is one deserving of careful study," the new president told the crowd, "I will favor any course towards them which tends to their civilization, Christianization and ultimate citizenship." Grant's short statement encapsulated his republican ideology: a faith that men who, once made civilized and faithful Christians, were welcome into the body politic of the United States. While Grant painted with a broad brush, by 1869 many Native Americans were already Christians. Christian missions in the West, however, had mostly failed to "Christianize" the indigenous people there. In fact, several indigenous nations had moved to reservations, embraced western education, transitioned to an agricultural economy, and developed political structures that were similar in practice to those in the American states. The "Five Civilized Tribes" of the Cherokee, Creek, Choctaw, Chickasaw, and Seminole nations represented the type of industrious and educated Native American that Grant hoped would become American citizens. His statement in his inaugural address prefigured the themes of the Grant Doctrine. Grant saw the Reconstruction era as a time when people long left out of the republican experiment could finally enjoy the blessings of liberty. So Grant envisioned a policy in the West that sought to incorporate Native Americans into the body politic while helping them along on, as he saw it the pathway to civilization. Native Americans, with their concept of communal ownership of land, could not be republican citizens until they embraced homesteading and property ownership. The pathway to citizenship, through civilization, then, went through the route of land ownership. This would become Grant's Peace Policy. Grant's desire to provide a path to citizenship for Native Americans, though, aroused support from reformers.

The *National Republican* quoted a missionary from Indiana who stated, "at last the race [Native Americans] has found a President who understands them, for, said he, 'I have long thought the Indian was a man.'"[1]

For Grant and the Republican Party, the American West represented a new frontier for exporting Reconstruction across the continent, but his administration faced significant challenges. American business, technology, and labor was moving West, and Grant understood that Native American culture stood in the way of this progress. The growing railroad expansion in the West led white settlers and gold hunters to consistently encroach on Native American land. The federal response was to either force Native Americans onto new, less desirable land, or to send in the army, ostensibly, to keep the peace. Most often, however, the military took the side of white invaders of native land rather than enforcing the terms of sovereign treaties. Though many indigenous people were pushed aside onto reservations, the Peace Policy sought to incorporate them into the body politic once they embraced the civilizing forces of republicanism and Christianity. Native Americans who exhibited the traits of free labor, through farming or business, and who embraced Christianity were welcome members of the body politic.[2]

Grant's Peace Policy represented a series of reforms of the ways the federal government interacted with Native Americans, particularly those in the West. The Peace Policy began with the basics of "civilization, Christianization, and citizenship" as the central tenets of the administration's policies. However, there were several stops along the pathway to citizenship. The administration sought the following reforms to United States-Indian relations: the movement of Native Americans to reservations where they could cultivate their own plot of land, Seneca leader Ely S. Parker's appointment as Commissioner of the Bureau of Indian Affairs (BIA), the transfer of the BIA from the Department of the Interior to the War Department, the creation of a Board of Indian Commissioners by the House of Representatives to audit BIA funds, and the increase of appropriations for educational, agricultural, and religious needs of Native Americans on their pathway to Christianity. Enacting these reforms, Grant believed, would lead to the assimilation of Native Americans into American culture, Western civilization, and the body politic of the United States.

Of all the reforms in the Peace Policy, the most controversial was the request to transfer the BIA to the War Department. Grant and Parker both believed that the transfer to the War Department would allow the US Army to maintain peaceful relations with Native Americans. They envisioned a similar use of federal troops in the West like those troops in the South, stationed to protect the rights and lives of African Americans there. The BIA was dominated by agents who received their positions through political patronage. As such, fraud and graft permeated throughout the Indian agencies, to the detriment of Native Americans the United States was bound by treaty to protect. The paradoxical nature of the War Department protecting Native Americans was not lost on Parker when the army was so often responsible for massacres and killings of Indians. However, Parker saw two distinctions that made him believe the War Department was better suited to protect the rights of Indians in the West. First, the killings of indigenous people at the hands of American soldiers were, he argued, the result of incompetent soldiers and officers, and not indicative of the entire army. Second, Parker understood that the Civil War had forced the War Department to become administratively competent, capable of supplying millions of people spread across thousands of square miles. With such a bureaucracy already in place and working for African Americans in the South, supplying the food and material needs of Indians on reservations in the West would not be a problem.

Access to food and goods, access to education and land, and military security, would allow Native Americans, Grant and Parker believed, to assimilate into the American cultural and political system A military presence in the West that embodied his Peace Policy, would strengthen the Union, and by increasing the roll of citizenship there by including Native Americans as members of the body politic (and members of the Republican Party), Grant believed he was creating a stronger United States, one that could withstand the economic and political upheaval of the Reconstruction-era. Nevertheless, Grant still held to nineteenth-century racist concepts of Western civilization that dismissed Native American culture as something that could never be considered civilized. Once Native Americans accepted republican norms, by abandoning their culture, Grant believed that they would be worthy of being counted as equal citizens of the republic. Grant, however, was painting Native American interest in his Indian policy with a broad brush. While some indigenous people accepted his path to citizenship, most were uninterested in the plan, nor did they care about his desire to strengthen the Union by adding them as citizens.[3]

Grant's idea of a pathway to citizenship for Native Americans aligned with his larger vision for the United States during the Reconstruction era.

He believed that the Civil War had fundamentally changed the United States into a nation that was finally living up to the ideals of its founders. African Americans now enjoyed freedom and citizenship, and Grant hoped to export these tenets of republicanism to the Caribbean through the Grant Doctrine. This Doctrine spurred Grant's attempt to annex the Dominican Republic to the United States as a territory with a path to statehood, guaranteeing citizenship rights for the Dominicans and offering the island as a haven for African Americans fleeing the onslaught of racist whites in the former Confederacy. Grant's Peace Policy would mirror this approach. Much like his Dominican scheme, Grant relied on the assistance of a former military aide, this time to implement his plan to civilize Native Americans with a view to organizing the Indian Territory in Oklahoma with a path to statehood. The Peace Policy envisioned that Native Americans would organize the Indian Territory on a path to statehood and Native Americans, as full citizens, would enter the Union as equals.

Grant's ideas about Native American citizenship reflected his belief in the tenets of republicanism that rewarded hard work with political participation. Grant drew from his personal experience with his military aide, Ely S. Parker, a Seneca leader and Union staff officer who had been present at Appomattox. Grant thought that Parker epitomized the civilized Native American; he was an educated man, an engineer by trade, and a veteran of the Civil War who embraced the cultural and political norms of the west. As such, Grant named Parker his Commissioner of the Bureau of Indian Affairs (BIA), the highest position for any non-white man in the entire administration.[4] Under Parker's leadership, Grant envisioned an American West composed of distinct Native American territories, populated by American Indians who embraced Western civilization, modern agricultural methods, Christian religious beliefs, and, most importantly, a republican form of government. Grant hoped that the United States Congress would accept these Indian territories just as he envisioned that they would accept the Dominican Republic, as a territory with a path toward statehood. Native American leaders would populate the governments of these territories and exercise the rights of United States citizenship enshrined in the Fourteenth and Fifteenth Amendments. For Grant, the key to Native American participation lay in their willingness to embrace the trappings of civilization and the authority of the federal government. By accepting the Peace Policy, Native Americans were as welcome into the body politic as any other citizen of the United States and then free to move anywhere in the country.

Conversely, the failure to incorporate themselves into the fabric of American society, Grant surmised, meant leaving natives vulnerable to the onslaught of approaching American businesses, railroads, and settlers moving further west. These entities would then encroach upon their land and Native Americans would have no recourse or support from the federal government. The United States military was unwilling to honor its treaties with Native Americans in the face of such settler colonialism. This inevitably led to violence and the death of Native Americans.

One problem with Grant's civilizing path for Native Americans was that the United States Constitution did not require "civilization" as a precursor to citizenship. The Fourteenth Amendment required only birth or naturalization for citizenship. Other than the reference to Native Americans not taxed (that is, not counted for purposes of Congressional representation unless they had paid taxes), there was nothing else in the amendment that specifically disqualified Native Americans for citizenship. Yet Grant placed the requirement of civilization on Native Americans as a precursor to citizenship. Grant's ideas of civilization, however, were ambiguous and open to interpretation by both whites and Native Americans. For many white Republicans, no amount of assimilation would suffice to consider Native Americans equal to whites as citizens. For many Native Americans, the ambiguity of Grant's call for civilization offered possibilities for them to convince whites that they had assimilated into white society, accepted republican norms, and willingly participated in the body politic, but all the while maintaining their distinct culture.

Parker attempted to use this ambiguity to his advantage to develop an Indian policy that incorporated Native American culture and political structures into republican forms of government that would meet with Grant's approval.[5] Parker had first met Grant in Galena, Illinois before the outbreak of the American Civil War, where the Treasury Department had sent Parker to build a customs office. His work as an intermediary for the Seneca kept him traveling back and forth between Galena and Washington where he worked to prevent whites from settling on Seneca land. This included convincing the federal government to purchase land once taken from the Seneca and then deeding it back to the tribe. His work on behalf of his people impressed many of the leaders of the Treasury Department who described him as a gentleman and a testament to his race. Thus, when Parker joined Grant's military staff in 1863, whites accepted him in both the army and the federal government as an example of a "civilized Indian." Parker, though, had learned to navigate his dual worlds and, as Commissioner of Indian Affairs in the Grant administration, he hoped to impart the lessons he learned to Native Americans in the West so they might participate in the American republican experiment.[6]

Grant anticipated that his political opponents would have questions about the constitutionality of Parker's selection as Commissioner of Indian Affairs. As a Native American, Parker did not have full citizenship rights until the ratification of the Fourteenth Amendment. Although he had voted in municipal and some statewide elections in New York, he was not a citizen of the United States. Nevertheless, he had served in numerous positions in the federal government prior to the Civil War and been an officer under Grant. The Grant administration seized on the transformative nature of the Reconstruction era laws to overcome a major hurdle in the question of Parker's eligibility as a citizen. With Grant's election in 1868, the previous commissioner, Nathaniel Taylor, offered his resignation in early March 1869, and Republican Senator John M. Thayer of Nebraska wrote to Grant two days after the inauguration to nominate Parker for the post. "I desire not to be officious, but I will take the liberty of recommending the appointment of Gen. Parker, of your late Staff, to be commissioner of Indian affairs," he wrote. "I can think of no one whose appointment to that position would give greater satisfaction to the country. What appointment so appropriate? Who could exercise so favorable an influence upon the Indians?" Thayer articulated what Grant was thinking as well: that Parker was in the best position to represent the interests of both American Indians and the Grant administration, and to facilitate the path to civilization and citizenship for Native Americans. However, Secretary of the Interior Jacob Cox was unsure if an indigenous person could serve in such a high-level administration position, so he asked for an opinion from Attorney General Ebenezer R. Hoar. Hoar wrote to Cox that "on the facts presented, I do not perceive that he is disqualified from holding such office under the Constitution and laws of the United States." According to the attorney general, Parker qualified as a citizen under the Fourteenth Amendment which stated that representatives to Congress were apportioned by the whole number of persons in the state "excluding Indians not taxed." As Parker had been a taxpayer in the state of New York, Cox argued, he qualified as a citizen and was eligible for any post in the federal government. Based upon this legal opinion, Cox recommended to the president that the nomination of Parker take effect immediately.[7]

This constitutional inquiry into Parker's eligibility was an important episode in the early days of the Grant administration. Republicans redefined the Constitution's racial boundaries through the Reconstruction amendments, securing African American freedom, citizenship, and voting rights. Grant hoped to expand these same rights to other races as well. By examining whether the Constitution expressly prohibited allowing Native Americans, or any other non-whites for that matter, from serving in high-level positions, the Grant administration created a precedent that gave heft to Grant's ideas. It showed that Grant was willing to support and appoint people of color to positions within his administration. Parker was one of several unprecedented appointments by Grant. He also assigned a Jewish superintendent to a Bureau of Indian Affairs district office, Dr. Herman Bendell, and he appointed an African American educator as minister to Haiti, Professor Ebenezer Don Carlos Bassett. While such appointments immediately broke new ground, his policies toward Native Americans evolved more gradually.[8]

Initially, Grant continued his predecessors' policy, recommending the removal of Native Americans to designated reservation territories. Where he differed was in how he intended to run these reservations. Rather than the political appointees who had managed the BIA in previous administrations, Grant intended the military to oversee the reservations, thus removing political appointees from the administrative process. Parker wanted Native Americans to exercise decision-making on the reservations, consigning whites to the local peripheries. Grant acquiesced to Parker's policy because it fit more closely with his views of self-determination and a republicanism that allowed civilized men to control their own economic and political lives. Much as African American men were asserting political responsibility in the American South, Grant accepted that Native Americans should make their own political decisions in the Indian Territory—to a point. Grant believed that Native Americans needed the guiding hand of the federal government to help them along the path to civilization, but Parker convinced him that they would find their way "to assimilate into the expanding United States at their own pace." In this way, Grant's plan for Native Americans paralleled his plan for the Dominicans.[9] An important aspect to Grant's Native American policy was the military administration of Indian reservations. Much like Congress had used the army in former Confederate states to implement Reconstruction, Grant believed that it was also best suited to protect the interests of Native Americans against the encroachments of white settlers. Grant understood that the Civil War had fundamentally transformed the United States into a more centralized nation. When Congress passed the Thirteenth Amendment, abolishing slavery, it became "the first amendment in the history of the American Constitution that increased, rather than limited, the power of the national government." The Fourteenth Amendment further augmented this power by expanding the number of citizens, thereby increasing representation in Congress. Grant believed that a military presence in the South made up of mostly African American garrison troops could contain the inevitable violent outbreaks that would occur in the South. He hoped that the presence of the military in the West would likewise mitigate violence perpetrated by white settlers against Native Americans. By controlling the violence, Grant intended to buy time to allow the federal government's Reconstruction policies to take hold and for economic and political change to stymie racial violence in both the South and the West.[10]

As commander of the entire United States Army following the Civil War, Grant had recommended transferring the Office of Indian Affairs from the Department of the Interior to the War Department. For Grant, the only way to ensure that Native Americans could become civilized republican citizens was by protecting their autonomy in Indian Territory with the army. Grant believed that "if Indians acted badly, it was because they were treated badly." He thought that Native Americans would be more apt to accept Western civilization if they were treated with kindness. The Indian agents and traders with whom they routinely dealt had cheated them, and white settlers had stolen their land. With good reason, Native Americans had responded to settler colonialism with animosity and violence toward the white encroachers. Grant and Parker both believed that if the army assumed the functions previously performed by the Indian agents, it could keep the peace more effectively. Grant sided with the 1868 report of an Indian Peace Commission (which was heavily influenced by Parker) which investigated the violence perpetrated against Native Americans in the West. The Commission found that the blame for violent outbreaks was "squarely at the feet of the Americans [whites], not the Indians." The commissioners questioned whether the white interlopers were acting civilized. "If the lands of the white man are taken, civilization justifies him in resisting the invader. Civilization does more than this: it brands him as a coward and a slave if he submits to the wrong." Yet, the commissioners wrote, these same civilized men were not honoring their treaties with the supposedly "savage" Indians. "If the savage resists [invaders of their land], civilization, with the ten commandments

[sic] in one hand and the word in the other, demand his immediate extermination." The commissioners recognized this hypocrisy and believed reform was in the best interest of peace with Native Americans, though they worried that transferring the Bureau of Indian Affairs to the War Department would only incite war. Grant took many of the commission's recommendations to heart.[11]

The president's plans suffered a blow, however, when Congress blocked Grant's proposal to transfer control of Indian Affairs from the Department of the Interior to the War Department. Congress sought greater oversight of Indian affairs, thereby undercutting a fundamental component of Grant's Peace Policy. This further escalated tensions between the army and the Interior Department, which had been neglectful in providing reservations with needed supplies, had contributed to Native American attacks on white settlers, and had forced the army into action. Military leaders such as Phillip Sheridan and William T. Sherman worked well with Commissioner Parker but often clashed with the Indian agents who played on white settlers' fears of a large standing army in their territory. These agents claimed that they were working to civilize the Native Americans while the army was only there to pacify them, leaving them to their savage state. Sheridan and Sherman viewed Native Americans as a nuisance that should be eradicated from the continent, yet they still worked to implement Grant's Peace Policy. Grant, however, continued to believe that the army was the best civilizing agent because it would create the peaceful environment in which Native Americans could be secure and embrace republican ideals and it had a centralized bureaucracy capable of supplying Native Americans with the goods they needed to survive.[12]

Throughout Grant's presidency, Native American delegations visited the White House to make representations on behalf of their people as leaders of sovereign nations. Grant, however, saw them not as foreign representatives but as Americans whom he hoped would become citizens. As wards of the nation Native Americans were considered Americans but they had no constitutional rights. They could not vote, they could not serve on juries, they had no freedom of movement around the nation, and they had few legal rights in the judicial system. As shown in his dealings with Congress over the annexation of the Dominican Republic, Grant believed it was his prerogative as president to negotiate treaties with foreign entities, but Native American peoples were a different matter. He was seeking to replace the customary bonds of allegiance and leadership within Indian nations and replace them with individual citizenship rights and allegiance to the Constitution and laws of the United States.

In late January 1870, Grant welcomed a delegation of chiefs from the Cherokee and Creek nations to the White House, who spoke warmly of their relationship with the president. "Mr. President," a representative offered, "we call here to-day to offer our fealty to you as our recognized guardian and ward, and to pray to you, Sir, to continue as our good friend and father." The chiefs used submissive language to flatter Grant and show that they accepted his civilizing policies. Grant turned the language back upon the chiefs to show that he viewed them as his equals as Americans. "You are welcome," he replied, "and in reference to continuing your 'good father,' as you say, I must answer that I have long thought that the two nations which you represent, and all those civilized nations in the Indian country, should be their own wards and good fathers." Grant continued, "I am of the opinion that they should become citizens, and be entitled to all the rights of citizens, -cease to be nations and become States." Grant saw the path forward for the Cherokee and the Creek the same as he saw as the path for the Dominicans: an organized territory of non-white citizens, accepted into the United States with the civilizing force of republicanism, which would lead these territories to inevitable statehood. With statehood would come participation in the body politic through representation in Congress, municipal and statewide elections, taxation, and military service. Late in Grant's first term, Congress passed a rider to an appropriations bill that effectively ended Native American sovereignty. This rider stated that "hereafter no Indian nation or tribe within the territory of the United States shall be acknowledged or recognized as an independent nation, tribe, or power with whom the United States may contract by treaty." This did not negate existing treaties, but the administration could not negotiate new treaties in the future. The government treated Native Americans as wards, people who were no longer members of sovereign tribes but rather were stuck in a limbo between sovereign and citizen.[13]

Significantly, Grant and Parker saw the civilizing force of the federal government in different ways. While Grant desired that Native Americans accept Western civilization and turn from their cultural heritage, Parker wanted Native Americans to hold on to their traditional structures of power and culture. As a young man, Parker had studied English and other subjects in white schools while also learning the cultural ways of his people, such as archery, fishing, canoeing, as well as learning the stories and legends of great

Tonawanda warriors of the past. As a translator for his people, Parker straddled the line between the white and Native American worlds. He was soon meeting with presidents of the United States and other political dignitaries in New York and Washington to secure his people's lands in the face of white settlers. As such, he believed in protecting native culture while also assimilating into the white "civilized world." Prior to the Civil War, while working as a federal bureaucrat, Parker had designed a system of tribal governments, modeled after republican forms of government, which reclassified traditional tribal ranks of chiefs and warriors into a municipal administration made up of justices of the peace, clerks, and treasurers. Parker encouraged tribes to establish this structure of governance to ensure control over their own political development. White control would mean a total loss of their culture and traditions. Following the war, Parker hoped to implement a similar political structure under the Grant administration, with the president's blessing. Parker's concept evolved into Grant's plan for an Indian territory that would enter the Union as a state with a citizenry made up entirely of Native Americans. Native Americans organized such an enclave in 1871 in the Oklahoma area known as Okmulgee.[14]

On January 30, 1871, Grant prepared a message to Congress relating to the Council of tribes held at Okmulgee. The tribes had adopted "a declaration of rights, and a constitution for their Government." This constitution represented the first step along the path that Grant had laid out for them, and he presented it to Congress as a positive step toward their inevitable citizenship. "It [would seem] highly desirable that the civilized indians [sic] of the country should be encouraged in establishing for themselves forms of territorial government," Grant informed the Congress, "compatible with the Constitution of the United States, and with the previous custom towards other communities laying outside of State limits." This was an important point for Grant. The Native Americans at Okmulgee were taking the proper steps that any territory should take toward applying for statehood, the same steps that other territories in the West were taking, the same steps just denied to the Dominican Republic. Grant believed that the Okmulgee territory was not ready for statehood, and the Native American tribes there had a long way to go before they could qualify for statehood. But he believed that the Congress should accept the proposal for Native American sovereignty over their own legislative affairs. This would allow them to establish a territory with republican institutions that would lead them to become better citizens. The territory was in its infancy and was just beginning to establish institutions of governance, but Grant agreed with Parker and his new secretary of the interior, Columbus Delano, a former Ohio Congressman (who would resign amid scandal in 1875), that Native Americans should hold the local positions of power. "I do not believe that it would not be advisable to receive the new territory with the constitution precisely as it is now framed," he advised, "So long as a territorial form of government is preserved Congress should hold the power of approving or disapproving of all legislative action of the territory." By this, Grant meant that Congress should have the power to approve the text of the constitution of this Native American territory. Grant advised, though, that it was within his power to appoint the officials in the territory and, undoubtedly taking Parker's advice, informed Congress that "It might be well to limit the appointment of all territorial officials, appointed by the Executive, to native citizens of the territory. If any exception is to be made to this rule I would recommend that it should be limited to the Judiciary." Like the Dominican Republic, Grant envisioned a racially distinct state, managed, and populated by Native Americans that would enable them to participate in the body politic insulated from the animosity of white settlers. "It is confidently hoped that the policy now being pursued towards the indian [sic] will fit him for self government," Grant concluded, "and make him desire to settle among people of his own race where he can enjoy the full privileges of Civil, and enlightened government."[15]

Grant saw the constitutional meeting at Okmulgee as a positive step toward the inevitable inclusion of a Native American state into the Union. Expanding the Union would strengthen the republic's economy and increase the rolls of the Republican Party. Parker saw the Okmulgee constitution as "a chance for [Native Americans] to block any future attempt 'of having territorial government forced upon them.'" However, Grant suggested just such a plan of enforcing congressional control over the territory, albeit while allowing Native American officials to remain in place. Grant's vision, though, was what one historian called "a paternalistic action that effectively killed the constitution itself." Indeed, by March 1871, Samuel Checote, Chief of the Creek Nation, had written to Grant to protest the congressional interference in the Indian territorial government. Checote expressed the hope that "our constitution . . . may remain unchanged—and that the Teritorial [sic] forms of Government may be of our own creation—and not one created by parties who are entirely unacquainted with our manners, Customs—or wants." The Creek chief expressed the worry of many nations in the Indian Territories that the federal government would force them to abandon their entire culture and customs, something Parker was unwilling to concede but which Grant accepted as a precondition for assimilation into the body politic. Grant believed that the Native Americans assembled at Okmulgee were well on their way toward the path to citizenship; their declaration of rights and constitution demonstrated their understanding of republican political ideology. Like the Dominicans, they needed the guiding hand of the United States government to lead them to the inevitable finish line of statehood. Parker lobbied the secretary of the interior for individual allotments of land for the Native Americans in Indian Territory as he understood that Grant saw private land ownership as one of the first steps toward citizenship and republicanism.[16]

In late February 1871, Nag-ga-rash, chief of the Iowa tribes, and thirty-six other chiefs, petitioned Grant, Parker, and Secretary Delano to authorize a reservation for their tribes. They asked for a farm "to each of our young men and young women" and they "also request[ed] that a manual labor boarding School may be established for the education of our children." Such a request was just what Grant and Parker were looking for as further proof that their policy of transforming Native Americans into republican citizens was working. Later, the same chiefs claimed "that we are adopting the habits and Customs of Civilized life. That we are opening Farms, building Dwelling houses, raising Cattle, using Agricultural implements, and educating our children in school houses." All they asked in return was for the proceeds from the sale of their ancestral lands in Iowa, now that they had relocated to Nebraska and Kansas. The Iowa tribes had done everything that Grant had asked of them in his inaugural address. They had embraced the ways of Western civilization, accepted his Indian reservation policy, and educated their children in the republican tradition. Now what they sought was direct access to the funds raised from the sale of their ancestral lands, which the Interior Department had deposited in a trust fund. The Iowa tribes never received these funds because Interior departmental leadership subscribed to the racial stereotype that indigenous people could not be trusted with money.[17]

As commissioner of Indian affairs, Parker endured similar assaults on his character due to the racist views of his detractors and, although he enjoyed the full support of President Grant, he grew weary of the position. Early in his presidency, Grant appointed nine men to the Congressional Board of Indian Commissioners (BIC), a body designed by Congress to provide oversight of the Grant administration's control over Indian policy. William

Welsh, a well-known leader of the Episcopal church in Philadelphia, and no friend of Ely S. Parker, ostensibly led the BIC. The BIC had the authority to "inspect the records of the Indian Office and to obtain full information as to the conduct of all parts of the affairs thereof." Welsh initially took this charge as his personal mission to root out perceived corruption in the Indian Office, corruption that he believed was firmly due to Parker. However, he soon believed that the commission was too weak to challenge Parker's alleged corruption. Welsh resigned from the commission, charging Parker with fraud in his resignation letter. Welsh believed that the BIC, as an arm of Congress, should be responsible for disbursing all funds for Indian Affairs and not the BIA. Grant and the secretary of the interior disagreed, seeing the disbursement of funds as under the purview of the administration.[18]

Even though he had resigned from the commission, Welsh continued his attacks on Parker by lobbying friends in Congress to investigate the commissioner of Indian affairs. Welsh used Parker's absence from the office while he attended the Okmulgee convention as an opportunity to levy charges against him and the Office of Indian Affairs (OIA). Utilizing the House Committee on Appropriations, Welsh introduced his "claims to have discovered irregularities in [the OIA's] management, especially in the matter of purchasing goods." Welsh had previously reported to Secretary Delano and President Grant that Parker was guilty at the very least of sloppy accounting, if not outright fraud, in the contracting and sale of nearly a million dollars of goods and livestock in Texas and Missouri. Welsh charged that Parker had failed to notify the BIC of these purchases and requested a congressional inquiry into him and his office. He also charged Parker with falsifying documents, accepting bribes, and purchasing materials in the open market rather than through the competitive bid system. The real crime, though, was not asking the approval of Welsh and the BIC for the sale. Parker told Delano that Welsh was seeking to replace him to secure "religious management of Indian affairs."[19]

Once Grant lost the chance to have Indian affairs under the management of the army, he agreed to allow religious groups into the management of Indian agencies to supplant political patronage. This became the final pillar of the Peace Policy, religious management of Indian Affairs, particularly the Christianization and civilization of Native Americans. Parker worried that as the Grant administration's Peace Policy incorporated more religious groups into the jurisdictions as Indian agents that Native Americans would lose their sense of culture and that the OIA would lose control of its resources to outside influences. He did not understand why Welsh, who was no longer a member of the BIC, had so much influence. "I also think it proper to remark, that during the past and preceding year," Parker wrote to Delano, "the communications from Mr. Welsh, relative to Indian affairs, have not always been couched in those terms which might be expected from one not authorized to dictate or control." Though Welsh had no authority, Parker wrote, "but as there was a probability that his motive was a desire to promote the welfare of the Indians, his wishes have, as far as the same were practicable and not incompatible with existing laws, been complied with." In other words, Parker had tried his best to work with Welsh, even though he was under no obligation by law to do so, because he thought it was the best thing to do for the sake of the Native American people whose welfare were Parker's responsibility. Welsh, however, had constantly undermined Parker's position without possessing any real authority.[2]

The House Committee on Appropriations took up the matter of Parker's alleged fraud in January 1871. The committee gave Welsh, though not a member of Congress or a member of the BIC, prosecutorial privileges, and a surprising amount of influence over the testimony. Though the investigation was Welsh's brainchild, Congressman Aaron A. Sargent (R-CA), who chaired the investigation alongside Willian Lawrence (R-OH) and James Beck (D-KY), orchestrated the hearing to lend credibility to Welsh's charges by allowing Welsh to submit a list of witnesses and to sit with the committee to cross-examine them. The committee accorded Parker his own attorney to cross-examine witnesses on his behalf, so Parker selected former Union General Norton Chipman, the famed prosecutor of the commander of the Confederate Andersonville prison.

Welsh began the hearing accusing Parker of orchestrating a vast conspiracy of fraudulent practices from small time graft to bribery. He accused Parker of purchasing goods outside of the bids system and without congressional appropriations, and of paying too much for beef and purchasing inferior goods, doing all without consulting the BIC. Chipman, on the other hand, pointed to testimony indicating that Parker was unaware of any such illegalities and questioned whether such practices had even taken place. Eventually the committee compelled Parker to testify, and Welsh spent hours meticulously going over each transaction hoping to force the commissioner into an admission of guilt. Chipman similarly detailed each transaction to allow Parker to explain his actions and describe his consultations with the BIC. Welsh's trump card involved a purchase of beef sent to Native

Americans on the Missouri River by a subcontractor, James Bosler. This contract, signed on June 15, 1870, represented, according to Welsh, Parker's most egregious act of defiance against the BIC. Bosler explained that Parker had acquired such a large quantity of meat from him on short notice because of an emergency on the Missouri River. Bosler claimed that he had charged higher rates than usual to make up for the increased manpower costs and to cover any damages he might incur. Significantly, Chipman's cross-examination of Bosler revealed that Welsh had coached him in his testimony and that he had already identified Parker as his target in the investigation before the committee had even met.[21]

According to Bosler, Welsh admitted that his motivation to bring charges against Parker was to force him out of the department because he was racially unfit for the job. Welsh told Bosler that Parker "was the representative of a race only one generation from barbarism, and he did not think that he should be expected to be able to withstand the inducements of parties who were his superiors in matters of business." Parker was barely civilized and was thus more susceptible to bribery or to manipulation and therefore was not worthy of his position. Welsh also told Bosler that he had resigned from the commission over a disagreement about the "receiving and inspecting" of goods and that "if the balance of the commissioners had followed his example [and resigned], they would have had General Parker out of office at that time; that the matter would have ended there." Welsh attributed Grant's loyalty to Parker to his "goodness of heart" and he pressed Bosler as to whether he had seen Parker drunk. Welsh again demeaned Parker's abilities as a civilized man, arguing that he "did not have the moral courage to withstand temptation" as he was being "feasted and wined" in New York by special interests. Bosler claimed that Welsh told him, "That he had gone to Secretary Cox and told him the condition of affairs, and the manner in which they were treating Parker, and asked Secretary Cox if he thought he (Cox) could withstand inducements of that kind [being feasted and wined] and that Secretary Cox said he did not believe he could." Bosler's testimony revealed Welsh had always sought to remove Parker from office because he believed that any Native American was morally incapable of conducting the business of the Office of Indian Affairs. Welsh thought that only white, Christian men could conduct such work. Curiously when given a chance to cross examine Bosler, neither Congressman Sargent nor Welsh asked a single question about this testimony of his recollection of conversations with Welsh.[22]

Throughout the investigation of Parker and the BIA, Grant remained silent, never offering any words of support or encouragement for his commissioner of Indian affairs. However, many interpreted Grant's message to Congress recommending the Okmulgee constitution, two weeks after the conclusion of the investigation, as a gesture of support for the commissioner. By supporting the Okmulgee constitution Grant was, in fact, supporting Parker. However, this stood in marked contrast to his openly vocal support of Orville E. Babcock throughout the Dominican Republic investigation, but this probably had more to do with their respective positions within the administration. While Babcock was Grant's private secretary and closest confidante, he was still technically a major in the Army Corps of Engineers. Grant therefore viewed the investigation into Babcock as a congressional overreach and unduly deploying the weight of an entire branch of government against one low-level officer. "He [Grant] said he felt 'much embittered' against [Charles] Sumner for unjust attacks on Major Babcock," future President Rutherford B. Hayes recorded in his diary. Parker, on the other hand, was a member of the Department of the Interior, a cabinet officer and commissioner who had the support of the executive branch at his disposal. To Grant, Parker was using the proper channels to answer the charges, he was providing the House Appropriations Committee with the information it requested, and he and the secretary of the interior provided a defense of the actions of the department. Thus, his personal intervention was unnecessary.[23]

In late February 1871 the House Committee on Appropriations rendered its verdict on both the department and Parker. "To the mind of the committee," members wrote "the testimony shows irregularities, neglect, and incompetency, and, in some instances, a departure from the express provisions of law for the regulation of Indian expenditures, and in the management of affairs in the Indian Department." Even so, the committee noted, they did not find "evidence of fraud or corruption on the part of the Indian Commissioner." The committee placed some of the blame for the mistakes and incompetency on the "vicious system inherited from the past," the corrupt system of Indian agents which Grant and Parker were trying to reform. However, the committee also ascribed some of the blame to "errors of judgment in the construction of statutes passed to insure economy and faithfulness in administration." Here, the committee referenced Parker's decision not to consult the BIC on the Bosler purchase. The committee found that

Parker had acted in error, but this did not constitute fraud. The report therefore exonerated Parker, but it also showed the tension between the BIA and the BIC and the need for continued reforms in the administration of Indian affairs.[24]

After over a year of harassment from the BIC, Parker angrily resigned on June 29, 1871, citing the constant harangues from William Welsh and the hamstringing effect of congressional legislation and ongoing investigations of the BIA. While the investigative committee found Parker not guilty of fraud, and to have acted within his rights as the commissioner of the BIA, the political fallout proved too much for Parker to bear. Parker, though, had added to the agitation between the BIA and the BIC by continuing to act without their approval. After the investigation concluded, Parker failed to notify the BIC of several purchases made on behalf of the BIA, even though the investigative committee had noted that such a failure was an "error in judgment." Members of the BIC were furious with Parker, and they vowed to have him removed. When Secretary of the Interior Delano demanded Parker send all vouchers and sales to the BIC for approval, Parker resigned. "The effect of Congressional legislation," he wrote, "has been to almost wholly divest the Indian Bureau of all its original importance, duties and proper responsibilities." Parker complained that the BIC had weakened his position to the point that he was working more for Congress than for the Department of the Interior. "Under present arrangements the Commissioner of Indian Affairs is nearly a supernumerary officer of the government," he argued, "his principle [sic] duties being simply that of a clerk to a Board of Indian Commissioners, operating wholly outside of and almost independently of the Indian Bureau." Parker told Grant that it was his sincerest desire to "aid in forwarding and promoting to a successful issue, the Presidents [sic] wise and benificent [sic] Indian policy, but I cannot in justice to myself longer continue to hold the ambiguous position I now occupy." The president accepted Parker's resignation, taking the opportunity to reflect on their friendship and careers together. "Accepting it severs official relations which have existed between us for eight consecutive years," Grant wrote to Parker, "without cause of complaint as to your entire fitness for either of the important places which you have had during that time. Your management of the Indian Bureau has been in entire harmony with my policy, which I hope will tend to the civilization of the Indian race. It has also been able and discreet."[25] With Parker's departure from the Bureau of Indian Affairs, Grant lost a strong ally in his efforts to advance Native Americans along the path toward citizenship. More importantly, Parker had been a guiding force in Grant's policy for Native American autonomy. Parker had convinced Grant that Native Americans should hold leadership positions in their territories and that while the army and the federal government could implement laws and supply Native Americans with the goods and materials they needed to establish farms and schools, the Native Americans themselves should be the ones to institute the changes on their reservations. With Parker gone, Grant lost an important voice on behalf of Native American rights and culture, and Welsh and his allies were able to transform Grant's Indian policy into an effort led wholly by religious groups focusing solely on the Christianization of Native Americans rather than their path toward citizenship.[26]

In the years after his resignation, Parker continued to support the Indian policy of the Grant administration, but that support would not last. Parker moved to New York where he took a position as a clerk for the Board of Commissioners of the New York City police department and made a home for himself and his wife. He mostly stayed out of national affairs, save for continuing to represent the interests of the Seneca in land deals. However, he began to sour on the religious interests of the BIC and the methods by which the board attempted to "Christianize" and "civilize" the indigenous in the West. In an undated letter to poet Harriet Maxwell Converse, Parker laid out his problems with the Peace Policy noting that he had "little or no faith" in the Christianization methods toward Native Americans. "It has not been honest, pure or sincere," he wrote, noting that "Black deception, damnable frauds and persistent oppression has been its characteristics." The policy of the United States, he noted, was that the "only good Indian is a dead one" and he believed the government was ready to prove that policy. He compared the plight of Native Americans to that of African Americans arguing that whites in the United States would not respect the rights of either minority group. White religious leaders argued that the only hope for Native Americans was their "absorption ... into the great body politic," a view with which Parker continued to disagree. "The only salvations for the Indians, and the only solution for the Indian problem" he wrote, "is to give them secular and industrial schools in abundance.... The Indian wishes to be let alone in his wigwam. His good life is bound up and interwoven with his land, his women and his children." The BIC, the Indian Aid Association, and the Indian Rights Association all were leading the extermination of Native American culture in the guise of citizenship and civilization, Parker averred, and he believed that any claims of progress by these groups were false. Native Americans resisted the Peace Policy, he argued, noting that "it is very evident to my mind that all schemes to apparently serve the Indians are only plausible pleas put out to hoodwink the civilized world that everything possible has been done to save the race from total annihilation, and to wipe out the stain on the American name for its treatment of the aboriginal population." Education, Parker concluded, was the first goal, "above all. Other good things will follow." Thus even Parker, one of the principle authors of the Peace Policy, deemed it a failure.[27]

Grant's Peace Policy in the West sought to define who could and could not be a citizen of the United States and what was required of a civilized citizen. For Grant, the best way to establish his Indian Peace Policy was to place a civilized Native American man in charge of the Bureau of Indian Affairs. Grant and Ely S. Parker sought a pathway toward citizenship for Native Americans in various Indian territories once they were "civilized." For Grant, civilization meant assimilating into Western social, cultural, and political norms, particularly republican norms. For Parker, this meant assimilating existing indigenous political structures into republican political structures. Both, though, envisioned a United States where Native Americans were equal to all Americans, where they practiced the tenet of republicanism of free labor, and where Indian territories entered the Union as a Native run state. While many Native Americans agreed to this Peace Policy, most did not. The policy was not helped by the fact that Parker and the Bureau of Indian Affairs were both under siege from Congress and special interest groups hell bent on Christianizing Native Americans, but not treating them equally. Though the loss of Parker meant Grant's policy suffered, he and his administration continued to seek out ways to bring Native Americans into the American body politic. As Grant moved into his second term, implementing his civilizing path to citizenship in the West remained one of his top domestic priorities.

Chapter 5

NATIVE AMERICANS, CHINESE IMMIGRANTS, AND CIVILIZATION

As it entered its second term in 1872–1873, the Grant Administration continued to grapple with the question of citizenship as redefined by the Fourteenth Amendment. While the State Department managed the question internationally, focusing on the citizenship qualifications and rights of immigrants, the Department of the Interior sought to do the same for Native Americans. The Constitution did not clarify immigrant and Native American citizenship status, thus creating a murky situation for the administration. Beyond the inclusion of these "new" citizens, the administration also grappled with the protection of the citizenship and electoral rights of African Americans in the South. For Grant, republican citizens possessed the traits of Western civilization—hardworking, land-owning Christians who put their faith in the Constitution above their culture and religion. Expansion in the American West provided a laboratory for the question of equal citizenship for the civilized. President Grant's Peace Policy of the inclusion of Native Americans into the body politic failed in the West due to a variety of reasons. The ambivalence of Native Americans to becoming citizens of the United States, the federal government's violation of treaties with Native American nations, and white settlers' violent clashes with Native Americans on their own land meant the end of the Peace Policy and the devolution of the West into all-out war. The racism of his fellow Republicans and Democrats toward Chinese laborers led to the establishment of the first of the Chinese exclusion acts, as well. These cases in the West showed the Administration's desire to codify citizenship rights for the civilized, as well as demonstrating Grant's naiveté that a color-blind citizenry was possible. Finally, thousands of African Americans, tired of the constant outbreaks of violence in the South, sought their fortunes in the West, where land was in abundance and where they could farm beyond the reach of their former enslavers. The Grant Doctrine, which sought the annexation of the Dominican Republic for this exact purpose, would ultimately fail in the laboratory of the West.

In late October 1874, Secretary of the Interior Columbus Delano submitted a report to President Grant that addressed the complexities of Native American citizenship. Delano was a strong supporter of Grant's Peace Policy, and he worried that conflict in the West, particularly in the Black Hills region of the Dakotas, would lead to a protracted war. In his report, he looked at the historical treatment of Native Americans and the variety of ways citizenship would change their experience in the United States. Primarily, Delano hoped that the United States Congress would implement a change in status for Native Americans and make them citizens rather than wards. One of his central arguments was that Native Americans needed to participate in homesteading to become citizens. "To aid in prosecuting the work of Indian civilization, I recommend the extension of the homestead-laws to Indians, with certain modifications," he wrote. "These laws at present apply to citizens of the United States only, and their provisions cannot be enjoyed except by that small portion of the Indian race who are legally entitled to the privileges of citizenship," such as Ely S. Parker. Delano noted that the Department of the Interior was charged with examining the rights of Native Americans as citizens and their rights under the homestead laws. According to an 1855 treaty, the Ottawa and Chippewa tribes were dissolved, under the condition that they were compensated for this dissolution. "This payment having been made," Delano noted, "the question was submitted for decision whether these Indians then became citizens of the United States and entitled to make homestead-entries. This question involved a consideration of the civil status of Indians after the dissolution of their tribal relations had been accomplished with the consent of the Government." To find the answer to this central question, Delano looked to the Reconstruction amendments, particularly the Fourteenth Amendment. In his report to Grant, Delano noted the following sections of the amendment germane to the question of Indian citizenship: "All persons born and naturalized in the United States, and subject to the jurisdiction thereof, are citizens of the United States and of the States wherein they reside," and "Representatives shall be apportioned among the several States according to their respective numbers, counting the whole number of persons in each State, excluding Indians not taxed." As such, Delano concluded that, "These Indians were born in the United States, and, therefore, expressly included in the provisions above quoted, provided they were '*subject to the jurisdiction thereof.*'" Federal law, prior to Reconstruction, did not reach the various tribes, meaning that members of the tribe were self-policing. "They were, however, in some sense subjects of the United States," Delano wrote, "but not citizens in mere right of home birth."[1]

With the passage of the Fourteenth Amendment Native Americans became citizens by birth. Delano surmised that, while prior to Reconstruction members of Indian tribes were "domestic subjects" they were not the "sovereign constituent ingredients of the Government." Delano noted that the dissolution of tribes, which he saw as a positive good rather than the cultural destruction that it was, meant that individual Native Americans were no longer part of a communal group, but rather were individual members of the United States population and, thus, had "become subject to the jurisdiction of the United States. They are then liable to taxation and are to be counted in the enumeration for representation." Delano was making a legal argument that used the monumental changes of Reconstruction to reconsider Native American membership in the body politic. For Delano, it was as simple as being a member of the American public, one naturally born in the territories of the United States, to be included as a citizen. The key to conveying citizenship on Native Americans, Delano argued, was through taxation. "By the fourteenth amendment, Indians not taxed are excluded from the basis of representation. This embraces simply such Indians as are not liable to taxation." The Supreme Court, he wrote, ruled that the government could not tax Native Americans while the tribal relation continued. "Thus the Department arrived at the conclusion, that when an Indian tribe is dissolved and its tribal relations ended, with the consent of the United States, either by treaty or legislative enactment, the member of such tribe become *ipso facto* citizen, of the United States, and entitled to all the privileges and immunities belonging to other citizens."[2]

Delano sought to answer another question posed to his Department from the Administration—whether legislation was required to make Native Americans citizens. "In the absence of congressional legislation," Delano quoted from the administration's questionnaire, "can an Indian, by mere act of voluntarily abandoning his tribal relations and ceasing to claim or exercise any of the special privileges, immunities, or exemptions incident to such a political condition, and by adopting the habits and customs of civilized life, become without further action on his part, a citizen of the United States?" This question was at the heart of the Grant Peace Policy. Delano's answer was "that an Indian cannot, voluntarily dissolve his relations with his tribe, and thereby become a citizen of the United States." Before an Indian became a citizen a complex dissolution process had to be followed that included the dissolving of the tribe as an official tribal unit and that tribal dissolution can only be done so through Congressional legislation. "Reviewing these opinions," Delano argued, "I feel assured of their correctness. It was, in my judgment, inconsistent with sound law, as well as with public policy, to permit an individual Indian, by voluntarily withdrawing from his tribe, to become a citizen without some act of the Government recognizing his citizenship." While Delano agreed with the assessment that individual Native Americans could not become citizens without the dissolution of their tribe and without Congressional legislation, he did support a change to this policy. "Under these circumstances, and in view of the importance of this subject," he wrote, "I deem it proper to invite the attention of Congress to the recommendation of the Commissioner of the General Land-Office in favor of legislation in behalf of Indians who desire to withdraw from their former associations, become citizens of the United States, and avail themselves of the benefit of the homestead-laws."[3]

Homesteading was an important feature of citizenship to both Delano and Grant. The Republican Party's ideology revolved around the concept of free soil and free labor. Free republican citizens were hard-working property owners. The Homestead Act, passed in 1862, allowed individual white homesteaders up to 160 acres of farmable land. In 1866, the Southern Homestead Act granted land to African Americans who had been cultivating said land for five years or more. Delano and the Grant administration wanted to expand these provisions to Native Americans to make them good republican landowners and citizens. Doing so led them to civilization and the destruction of their cultural norms that were antithetical to republican citizenship. "A common ownership of property is the normal condition of the Indian race," Delano claimed, "and with it are found nomadic habits totally inconsistent with the idea of permanent habitations, individual ownership, and domestic industry. The work of civilization can never be completed until these habits are abandoned." "Every proper inducement, therefore, ought to be offered the Indian," Delano argued, "which will prompt him to individual ownership of property, and such habits of industry and economy as are incident to our civilization."

The homestead laws of the United States, though, were complex and required significant buy-in from Native Americans willing to take such a pathway to citizenship. The homestead laws required people to live on and work on the land for at least five years before they were allowed to apply for ownership. "These five years afford considerable guarantee that no one will apply to make homestead-entries unless he possesses the qualities essential to citizenship," the secretary argued. The complex and time-consuming nature of American homestead laws, then, precluded those who were uninterested or unable to become fully formed citizens. Delano also worried that white settlers would swindle Native Americans out of their land. "Should it be suggested that the extension of this privilege to Indians would furnish inducements to speculators to use them in acquiring titles to our public lands," Delano asked, "I would reply that this danger can be prevented by providing that the patent to be issued shall contain a clause rendering the title inalienable except by consent of the President. This would insure ample security against the abuse of this privilege, as well as necessary protection against improvident sales without adequate consideration." Delano argued that President Grant, and future presidents, had the right to decide if Native American land claims were legitimate or if they were part of illegal land speculation schemes. "An extension to the Indians of the benefits of the homestead-laws, under the safeguards mentioned, and such others as the wisdom of Congress may suggest, will greatly facilitate the work of their civilization," he wrote. "It will rapidly break up tribal organizations and Indian communities; it will bring Indians into subjection to our laws, civil and criminal; it will induce them to abandon roving habits; and teach them the benefit of industry and individual ownership, and thus prove highly advantageous in promoting their prosperity."[4]

Homesteading was not unheard of in Indian Territory. In the years prior to the Civil War, whites forced Choctaw, Cherokee, Chickasaw, and other Native American nations in the South to leave their ancestral homes and to settle in Indian Territory in present-day Oklahoma. Many of these Native Americans brought enslaved persons of African descent with them to this new territory. These nations aligned themselves with the Confederacy in the hopes of perpetuating the system of slavery. With the war's end came emancipation and the enslaved Black people in Indian Territory were given their freedom. Historian Alaina E. Roberts notes that these formerly enslaved people represented a unique case in the history of Reconstruction as the federal government offered them land (forty acres each) as reparations for their enslavement. The tribes did not offer citizenship to these freed people within the tribal nations where they lived and, in order to receive a homestead, they had to move to land outside of the tribal territory. This land allotment,

Roberts notes, was "a clear violation of Indigenous sovereignty," but doing so provided freed people with the opportunity to own their own land and to become citizens of the United States. With homesteading underway in Indian Territory, Delano's call for Indian homesteading as part of the pathway to citizenship did not come from nowhere.[5]

In June of 1834, the US Congress passed the modified Indian Intercourse Act, which delineated between the territories of the United States and "the frontier," or Indian country. According to Delano, this act of Congress was "the only general law under which Indian affairs have been conducted." The act established a territorial boundary along the Mississippi River, save for Louisiana and Arkansas, that required Native Americans to live in the frontier lands of the West, with support and protection from the US Army. Of course, whites quickly began settling in this "frontier" and the army acted as antagonist to Native Americans rather than protectors. Forty years later, Delano argued, "the provisions of this act are entirely inadequate to meet the present requirements of the service, and the experience of the past has shown that they are not sufficient for the protection of the Indian." Moreover, Delano worried that the existing laws hamstrung the government from prosecuting both Indian and white criminals who committed crimes against Native Americans. "It has been held, for example, by a territorial judge that he has no power, for want of jurisdiction, to try and punish an Indian who murdered one of his race," Delano recounted, "although the crime was committed in his own district and outside of an Indian reservation." Federal officials, he noted, had no "authority to punish Indians for crimes committed on an Indian reservation. There is no law enforcing obedience to the injunctions or compliance with the requirements of an agent, and hence he is to a great extent powerless unless aided by military authority." Beyond Native American crimes, "depredations are daily committed by white men upon Indians on their reservations, and the only punishment that can be inflicted is expulsion from the Indian country." White settlers were more often committing violence on Native lands without fear of repercussions. Delano argued that Americans were just as likely to be the victim of a crime in New York City as among Indian tribes. However, in New York, prosecutors would more likely arrest the criminal for said crime.[6]

Delano believed that the government should treat Native Americans fairly, especially through the enforcement of existing treaties. However, Delano also viewed Native Americans paternalistically, seeing them as not only uncivilized but also possessing an almost childlike ignorance of Western economic and political norms. He and Grant supported the slaughter of bison in the West as a means of forcing Native Americans into the more civilizing practice of farming. Delano also exploited Native Americans and the Bureau of Indian Affairs, resigning from his position as secretary of the interior amid scandal, accused of embezzling BIA funds to enrich himself and his son. His tenure as secretary of the interior was marked, then, with hypocrisy.

Delano's bigoted viewpoint is evident in his report to Grant when he discussed the payment of cash to Native Americans. "In many instances we have treaty stipulations requiring annuities of cash and property to be paid to Indians per capita," he wrote. "In some cases the only evidence of such payments consists of receipts given by the chiefs of the tribes." These receipts, though, did not show any ability by Native Americans to understand the importance of these cash payments, Delano argued. "The improvidence and want of intelligence which characterize most Indians entitled to such annuities, render the [repayments] not merely useless, but absolutely unprofitable; nay, even demoralizing." Native Americans, he claimed, were not intelligent enough to appreciate how to handle such payments. "On receipt of the money or goods, the uncivilized Indian hastens to dispose his portion for a toy, a trifle, or, what may be worse, spirituous liquors, which render him troublesome and dangerous." Delano relayed the ubiquitous stereotype that Native Americans were more interested in procuring alcohol with their payments, which he deemed destructive to their civilization. If Congress passed legislation enabling the Grant administration to not only manage the daily affairs of Native Americans on reservations but also to allow Native Americans the civilizing effects of land ownership, then the work of the Department of the Interior would be eased. "The work of civilization will be greatly accelerated by enactments which shall define as far as possible the relations between this race and the Government," Delano wrote, "which shall furnish authority for enforcing the orders and requisitions of agents, which shall be sufficient to punish Indians for crimes against each other and against white people *wherever* committed, and which shall also inflict adequate punishment upon white people who trespass upon territory belonging to Indians or commit crimes against them."[7]

Delano's emphasis on white predation and Native Americans is important to understand both his and Grant's views of civilization. While both sought to "civilize" Native Americans into Western cultural norms, Grant did not see whites who committed crimes against Native Americans as civilized. An examination of Grant's rhetoric shows that he often reserved the use of pejorative terms usually reserved for Native Americans, such as "savage," for white Southerners committing violence against African Americans or Mormons who practiced polygamy. He occasionally referred to the "savage tribes" who continued to roam the West in search of hunting grounds, and, on his post-presidency World Tour, referred to the "savage natives" of foreign lands. Often, though, he used such rhetoric for white violence committed against minority groups. In his report to the Senate on the so-called "Colfax massacre," he wrote that "a butchery of citizens was committed at Colfax, which in blood thirstiness and barbarity is hardly surpassed by any acts of savage warfare." He referred to the "late barbarous massacre of innocent men at the town of Hamburg—South Carolina." The massacre "at Hamburg, as cruel, bloodthirsty, wanton, unprovoked, and as uncalled for as it was," Grant wrote, "is only a repitition [sic] of the course that has been pursued in other Southern States within the last few years—notably in Mississippi and Louisiana." Mississippi, he noted, was "governed to day [sic] by officials chosen through fraud and violence, such as would scarcely be accredited to savages, much less to a civilized and christian [sic] people." Again, Grant here notes that white Southerners committing violence against African Americans were acting less than civilized, noting that they were worse than the so-called "savages" of the West. Such white men violated the norms of Western civilization, acting like uncivilized Native Americans. They upended republican society by undermining the body politic through violence towards African American voters or by seizing land that belonged to Native Americans. For the United States and Reconstruction to succeed, all peoples had to buy into the republican agreement of free labor, free men, and free elections. White settlers and Southern whites who committed violence should know better since they were theoretically civilized. In contrast, Native Americans, once civilized, would be able to prove themselves by living and acting as republican citizens.[8]

Delano's report continued to call for Native American citizenship in the United States. "The time has arrived when some general law regulating Indian citizenship is, in my judgment, indispensable," Delano wrote. "Occasionally, treaty-stipulations with Indian tribes are expiring, among whom is found a greater or less degree of civilization. This compels the Department to determine the status of such Indians in regard to citizenship. There are also many who desire to separate from their tribes, adopt the habits and customs of civilized life, and become citizens." Delano and Grant both believed that there were individual Native Americans who were sufficiently civilized and able to become citizens of the United States, such as Ely S. Parker. Grant and Delano wanted to see legislation that would allow Native Americans more generally to enter the body politic as citizens, and, ostensibly, as members of the Republican Party. Delano looked to the Mexican American War to show that thousands of Native Americans had already proven themselves as civilized citizens. "It must also be borne in mind that by our treaties with Mexico we acquired, with the territory then obtained, a large number of Indians. These are, for the most part, Pueblo or Mission Indians, and in either case is to some extent civilized." After the Mexican American War many Native Americans, who were previously citizens of Mexico, were living on lands ceded to the United States. The United States treated these Native Americans as wards of the country. "They are peaceable, inoffensive, and industrious," Delano argued, "before being attached to the United States, many of them were under the care and instruction of Roman Catholic priests. It is claimed that our treaties with Mexico guaranteed these Indians citizenship, because, as is asserted, they were citizens of Mexico previous to the treaty attaching them to this government." The Treaty of Guadalupe Hidalgo (1848) gave all citizens in the former Mexican lands the right to either move into Mexican territory, thus keeping their Mexican citizenship, or to stay on their land and become citizens of the United States. Any citizens, regardless of race, who stayed in the ceded territory "after the expiration of that year, without having declared their intention to retain the character of Mexicans, shall be considered to have elected to become citizens of the United States." The United States government did not, however, honor these treaties with Mexico. They have, Delano wrote, "never been recognized as citizens by the department, but have been treated like other Indian tribes. They have accepted assistance, received agents, and come under the general system of management applied to other Indians of the United States." In the past, the Department of the Interior experienced problems declaring these Native Americans citizens entitled to homestead land in the Southwest. Delano, though, was of the opinion "that a large number of these Pueblo and Mission Indians are sufficiently intelligent, well-disposed, and industrious to be allowed at once to become citizens, under such conditions and restrictions as Congress may deem it wise to impose." Congress just needed to act.[9]

Grant received Delano's report on October 31, 1874, and he soon thereafter added reference to it in his annual message to Congress. "The attention of Congress is invited to the report of the Secretary of the Interior and to the legislation asked for by him. The policy adopted for the management of Indian Affairs, known as the peace policy, had been adhered to with most beneficial results," Grant informed Congress. "It is confidently hoped that a few years more will relieve our frontiers from danger and Indian depredations. I commend the recommendation of the Secretary for the extension of the Homestead laws to the Indians; and for some sort of territorial government for the Indian Territory." For Grant, civilization continued to trump citizenship and he argued to the Congress that "a great majority of the Indians occupying the territory are believed yet to be incapable of maintaining their rights against the more civilized and enlightened white man." Native Americans were not civilized enough to withstand the incursion of white settlers yet, ironically, "civilized and enlightened" white men were the obstacle to Native American civilization. As such, Grant argued that "any territorial form of Govt [sic] given them therefore should protect them then in their homes and property for a period of at least twenty years, and before its final adoption should be ratified by a majority of those effected." Native American land ownership was the key to civilization and, subsequently, the legal rights of citizenship. With citizenship came the organization of a territorial government that was required to protect its Native American citizens from the depredations of settler colonialism. Grant did not see the paradox of his statement.[10]

The next day, Congressman Isaac Parker, a Republican from Missouri, introduced legislation that answered Grant's call. Parker introduced H. R. 3864, "to enable Indians in certain cases to enter public lands of the United States under the homestead law, and for other purposes." The House referred the bill to the Committee on Indian Affairs, of which Parker was a member. Parker, who Grant later appointed to the new US District Court for the Western District of Arkansas, where he earned the nickname "the hanging judge," introduced several pieces of legislation that sought to provide Native Americans with the opportunity to own land and to organize territorial governments. None of his Native American bills, including H. R. 3864, became law.[11]

In his 1875 Annual Message, Grant took the opportunity to call upon Congress to outlaw the practice of polygamy. "In nearly every annual message that I have had the honor of transmitting to Congress," Grant wrote, "I have called attention to the anomalous, not to say scandalous, condition of affairs existing in the Territory of Utah, and have asked for legislation to correct it." Grant was incredulous: "[T]hat polygamy should exist in a free, enlightened, and Christian country, without power to punish so flagrant a crime against decency and morality, seems preposterous." Though Grant considered it an immoral practice, he also looked to republican institutions to end polygamy in the United States. "True, there is no law to sustain this unnatural vice," he argued, "but what is needed is a law to punish it as a crime, and at the same time to fix the status of the innocent children, the off-spring of this system, and of the possibly innocent plural wives." While Grant held sympathy for the innocent, he insisted that polygamy "should be banished from the land." Mormonism, in his views, was an uncivilized and unrepublican religion that put the desires of their prophet Brigham Young above the Constitution. Mormons' unwillingness to abandon the practice of polygamy meant turmoil in the Utah territory and its quest for statehood. It would take until the Supreme Court ruled anti-polygamy laws constitutional in 1879, and the passing of the Edmunds-Tucker Act of 1887 which dis-incorporated the Mormon Church, for the United States to outlaw polygamy completely. These rulings, along with the Mormon Church's suspending the practice of polygamy in 1890, led to the eventual elevation of Utah to statehood in 1896.[12]

Interestingly, Grant's 1875 message also asked the Congress to consider another supposedly immoral and uncivilized act occurring in the West that violated his republican sensibilities. He invited, "the attention of Congress to another, though perhaps no less an evil, the importation of Chinese women, but few of whom are brought to our shores to pursue honorable or useful occupations." This surprising admonition against the importation of Chinese women enslaved as sex workers shows that Grant remained true to the Grant Doctrine's intent to end slavery in the Western Hemisphere, in all its forms. By linking sex slavery to polygamy, Grant showed that he viewed both immoral practices as wholly uncivilized and unrepublican. They were entirely out of step with a modern United States and unwelcome in a post–Civil War America.[13]

In an effort to normalize relations between the United States and China, the two countries had agreed to a set of policies under the terms of the 1868 Burlingame Treaty. These included reciprocal trade and immigration, but Chinese immigrants could not become naturalized citizens of the United States. This provision stood in marked contrast to the Republican Party platform embracing immigration and naturalization for European and African immigrants. The treaty did grant Chinese immigrants the right to practice their religion, study in the public schools and universities, and travel freely in the United States. Espousing a basic tenet of republicanism, the treaty made it "a penal offense for a citizen of the United States or Chinese subjects to take Chinese subjects either to the United States or to any other foreign country . . . without their free and voluntary consent respectively." This provision hit at the heart of the Chinese immigrant labor movement and Grant's republican policies toward immigration and slavery in the Western Hemisphere. Grant defined forced Chinese labor, or "coolie labor," as slavery. The Burlingame Treaty defined forced Chinese labor in the United States and elsewhere in the Western Hemisphere as an illegal act. As Grant tackled the question of Chinese immigration in the West, he did so in the belief that he was upholding the republican principle of free labor and the nation's treaty obligations toward China. The problem was that the prohibition against forced Chinese labor "would remain practically unenforced."[14]

The issue of Chinese immigration in the West reflects the complications of labor, race, and republican ideology. The California legislature designed exclusionary policies, which Grant believed to be fully in line with republican principles, to prohibit the trafficking of Chinese women for the purposes of sex slavery. Regardless of their intent, though, these policies became the foundation for later racist immigration legislation which targeted the Chinese specifically because of their race and their impact on white laborers. For Grant, however, ending this form of enslavement of Chinese women aligned squarely with the Grant Doctrine's emphasis on liberty and free labor. The Grant administration already struggled to come to grips with the meaning of naturalization for European immigrants who became American citizens. The introduction of Chinese immigrant labor in the West complicated the issue further as questions of labor and race collided in California and cut across party lines. Both Democrats and Republicans engaged in anti-Chinese rhetoric and advocated limiting the level of Chinese immigration. Grant entered the fray as he sought to restrict the flow of forced labor and Chinese sex slavery coming through American ports. His support for the Page Act of 1875, which barred Chinese women from entering the United States, signaled to Americans his support for limits on Chinese immigration, even if the legislation had little effect on the flow of immigrants from China. Grant believed that his position was consistent with his goal of eradicating slavery in the Western Hemisphere, as enshrined in his Doctrine.[15]

Grant began receiving reports of anti-Chinese fervor in the West as early as his first year in office. Nevada Governor Henry G. Blasdel drew attention to the growing ill-will toward the Chinese in the West in the hope of obtaining military protection for the immigrants. "They are peaceable, industrious and very usefull [sic] in the development of our resources," the Republican governor wrote to Grant, "they have . . . been driven from their homes . . . It has come to my knowledge that organised bodies of men are threatening to drive them from the State [California]." The governor noted that many of the local militia members were also anti-Chinese, therefore he suggested to Grant that he might require outside military assistance. The problems of Reconstruction in the West, then, mirrored the South. Like the freedmen and Native Americans, Chinese workers required a military presence to protect them from harassment driven by racial animosity. Grant addressed these developments in his first annual message in December 1869.[16] He framed the Chinese issue in terms of the larger republican commitment to free labor and anti-slavery. Grant and the Republican Party sought legislation that would specifically bar the involuntary immigration of Chinese workers and the continued enslavement of people in the Caribbean nations of Cuba and Puerto Rico. The United States could enforce penalties against those who brought Chinese laborers to the United States under false pretenses under the auspices of the Burlingame Treaty, yet the administration did not do so. A report commissioned by the Chinese government found that "eight or nine out of every ten [Chinese laborers in Cuba] have been conveyed there against their will." Grant's annual message therefore requested legislation that would "forever preclude the enslavement of their people, upon our soil . . . and also prevent American vessels from engaging in the transportation of 'Coolies' to any country tolerating the system." From the outset, the Grant administration made clear that the enslavement of peoples in any form would not be tolerated in the Western Hemisphere and that any participation in such trade violated the core republican principles of the Grant Doctrine.[17]

At the same time, Grant pledged to support the rights of Chinese immigrants who came to the United States of their own volition to labor industriously. The story of immigration to the United States is a story about labor. Anti-Chinese fervor in the West, much like anti-Irish and anti-German threats in the East, was rooted in the fragility of labor. Anti-Chinese anger was based in the racist beliefs of both white and Black Americans that

Chinese workers were barbaric, uncivilized, and unrepublican and unworthy of taking jobs for lower pay that should have gone to Americans. Such language was quite often used to describe the Irish by nativist Know-Nothings and white laborers upset by the influx of Irish immigrants in the years prior to and after the Civil War. In the Reconstruction era, Irish Americans were often discriminated against because of their cultural backgrounds, and they were denied access to good jobs and advancement. But they were not denied citizenship as were Chinese immigrants. Irish immigrants, as well as some African Americans, joined anti-Chinese groups in the West as a means of expressing their American-ness versus the otherness of the Chinese. Anti-Chinese sentiment in the West, however, threatened to undermine Grant's pledge of support for their rights, and in California, party loyalty took a backseat to anti-immigrant sentiments. Republicans and Democrats alike vowed to end Chinese immigration and won election to local, state, and Congressional offices by promising to send Chinese laborers back across the Pacific. Such rhetoric raised fears of violence and Attorney General Amos T. Akerman consulted Grant on the prudence of applying the 1870 Enforcement Act, often referred to as the anti-Ku Klux Klan Act, against the anti-Chinese agitators. While Akerman questioned the necessity and legal basis for federal intervention, he worried "where popular passions are so inflammable, it may grow to be serious. Possibly it may be well to have some of the military at hand for emergencies." Whether it was violence against African Americans in the South or against Chinese in the West, the Grant administration expected the Reconstruction-era civil rights acts to sustain order if necessary and to maintain republican norms of peaceful labor relations.[18]

One of the aspects of Chinese immigration that Grant took up as a pillar of republican virtue was the plight of Chinese women forcibly brought to the United States as sex slaves. Their condition, Grant argued, contributed "to the disgrace of the communities where settled and to the great demoralization of the youth of those localities." Prostitution and slavery, both moral failings, were unrepublican and required legislative action to protect not only Americans but Chinese women as well. However, studies show that Grant and the Republicans in California who reported this supposed immorality significantly overestimated the number of Chinese women forced into sex slavery. Grant claimed that "hardly a perceptable [sic] percentage of [Chinese women] perform any honorable labor." According to one study only half of the nearly 2,000 Chinese women in the city of San Francisco were prostitutes; the remainder were wives, daughters, mothers, and grandmothers who had arrived with their families. Thus, while the Chinese sex slave trade was problematic, and worthy of Grant and the Republican Party's attentions, the anti-Chinese rhetoric in California lumped all Chinese women together and Grant latched onto it because it fed into his republican anti-slavery agenda. Therefore, all Chinese women who immigrated to the United States found their status in jeopardy.[19]

Representative Horace F. Page (R-CA) spearheaded his party's adoption of anti-Chinese rhetoric for political purposes after witnessing California Democrats successfully employ the same tactic. Page, like Grant, had focused on the Burlingame Treaty's article that prohibited contract Chinese laborers immigrating to the United States. While Republicans viewed such laborers as no more than slaves, local California labor groups viewed them as competition and stirred up anti-immigrant sentiment in the state Democratic Party. As that party enjoyed electoral success in the California state legislature, as well in the US House and Senate, Page and fellow California Republicans jumped on the anti-Chinese bandwagon. Page introduced several anti-Chinese bills to restrict Chinese immigration. Though his bills ultimately failed in the House, Senator Charles Sumner's actions the following year presented Page with a new opportunity. Sumner proposed amending federal naturalization laws to include Chinese immigrants as candidates for citizenship, along with European immigrants, negating the prohibition in the Burlingame Treaty. Sumner argued that Chinese immigrants had just as much of a right to citizenship as any other civilized immigrant who wished to become American. This prospect enraged Californians of both parties and the senators from California voted against the measure.

Page introduced a bill in the House that would not only keep the Burlingame Treaty clause preventing Chinese naturalization but would also forbid anyone of Chinese descent from becoming a citizen. Although this bill also failed, Page began gaining traction for his anti-Chinese legislation. In 1875, he drafted a bill consistent with the Burlingame Treaty but took the first step toward barring Chinese entry into the United States by banning the immigration of Chinese women. Page based his legislation on the clause in the Burlingame Treaty that prevented forced immigration of laborers from China. He claimed that Chinese immigrant women were slaves of the Chinese underworld, unwitting pawns of a barbaric culture. Under the treaty, he argued, the United States was obligated to prevent this slave trade which violated republican morality. Like Grant, Page conflated all Chinese women with prostitutes, concluding that the United States should not allow them into the country. As the new bill comported with both the Burlingame Treaty and the Republican Party's anti-slavery principles, it successfully made it through Congress "with virtually no opposition," and President Grant signed it into law on March 3, 1875.[20]

Grant considered the Page Act's exclusion of Chinese women to be consistent with his republican ideals as it squared with his anti-slavery principles and notions of morality and civilized society. When Grant left office in 1877 for his famous three-year World Tour, his time in China only reinforced his belief that underworld gangs enslaved Chinese laborers and forced them to work abroad. Many Chinese diplomats and elites asked him about the Chinese exclusion bills making their way through Congress in 1879, but the former president, speaking only in generalities, argued that he had been out of the country too long to comment. Grant did, however, support a moratorium on Chinese immigration as a means of quelling anti-Chinese animosity in California, explaining to Chinese diplomat Li Hung-Chang that a five-year ban on Chinese immigrants would settle the issue once and for all. Echoing an argument he made regarding Black emigration to the Dominican Republic, Grant believed that whites in California would miss the Chinese laborers when they were gone and, thus, would welcome their return after the five-year ban. Grant argued that African Americans leaving the South would make former Confederates treat them with kindness because they lost a valuable source of labor. With a short five-year ban on Chinese immigration, whites in the West would feel the same way, he argued. Neither proved true. The Page Act led to the Chinese Exclusion Act of 1882 which directly discriminated against Chinese immigrants. The Exclusion Act initially established a twenty-year ban on Chinese immigrants, but President Chester A. Arthur vetoed it—with Grant's approval. Congress reduced the ban to ten years but regularly extended it until making it permanent in 1902. The Page Act and the subsequent Exclusion Act represented political victories for white and Black labor but a loss for republican principles of a race neutral immigration policy.[21]

African Americans' interests did not always align with the interests of immigrants, even if Black Americans supported equal rights for those immigrants regardless of their race or national origin. Black Americans, like many white Americans, did not welcome foreign laborers into the United States even as African Americans were fighting for acceptance as citizens. While some prominent African American leaders supported an end to the exploitation of Chinese contract workers in Cuba, like many white Americans, many Black opinion leaders held strong anti-Chinese views when confronted with these same Chinese workers immigrating to the United States. Chinese workers immigrated into plantations in Louisiana and railroad and mining operations in California, with more than 320,000 laborers supposedly taking jobs from both African Americans and whites between 1850 and 1882. Plantation owners in Louisiana believed hiring Chinese laborers could save them money in the long run. "[W]ith Chinese gangs the planter knew just how many mouths he had to feed," according to one Black editor. "No women, no children, no hogs, no ponies, no forecastle lawyers, and no howling preachers."

Black newspapers covered the influx of Chinese workers into the American South with the same trepidation and xenophobia as white newspapers. With headlines such as "The Heathen Chinee," Black newspapers showcased their American-ness as opposed to the un-American and un-republican Chinese. Editors reported on labor strife throughout the nation, noting the importation of Chinese immigrants in California, Louisiana, and Alabama to inform Black workers of mounting labor competition. The *New National Era* reported in January 1871 that the end of coolie slave labor would inevitably mean an increase of Chinese immigrant labor in the South but claimed it would not influence the overall labor of the region nor become competition to the more industrious Black laborer. The article called the Chinese laborers "slavish and cheap" with "no aspirations above [their] daily routine of duties." The newspaper carried tales of Chinese railroad laborers in Tuscaloosa, Alabama who fled to work on a New Orleans plantation and of Chinese plantation workers in Louisiana who banded together and tied up their Black overseer, marching him up to their employer's house in protest of his harsh treatment. Newspapers also featured stories of the wages that Chinese laborers received ($13 a month in gold, much less than Black wages) on Louisiana plantations, noting that readers should expect an influx of more Chinese laborers in the months to come as plantation owners actively recruited them.[22]

Mississippi Congressman John R. Lynch best exemplified this attitude in an 1876 statement made on the House floor. Lynch, a freedman himself, took to the floor after a white congressman had equated African American Southerners to the Chinese. Admitting that the remark "touched [his] sensitive feeling," Lynch used the occasion not only to point out the racial differences between Black and Chinese men, but also to assert the American-ness of African Americans. "It is certainly known by southern as well as northern men that the colored people of this country are thoroughly American," Lynch told his colleagues, "born and raised upon American soil and under the influence of American institutions." Though newly made citizens, Lynch noted, Black Americans worshipped the same God as their white countrymen and were loyal to the same institutions as they. "For my honorable colleague," Lynch continued, "unwittingly as I believe, to compare this race with the untutored, the uncivilized, the non-Christian, and the un-Americanized Mongolian . . . was unjust, ungenerous, and unfair." Lynch represented many African Americans who had certainly, by the end of Reconstruction, exerted their birthright citizenship and American identity over that of immigrants whom they deemed to be othered and uncivilized.[23]

While competition from the Chinese was certainly a concern for Black laborers considering a move to the West, the more immediate concern was the presence of Native Americans on coveted land in the plains. Many African Americans viewed Native Americans in the same way as did many white Americans, as uncivilized barbarians, but like Grant they believed that they could be taught to be civilized citizens. Frederick Douglass, discussing the potential exodus of African Americans from the United States in the 1850s, noted "there is little reason to hope that any considerable number of the free colored people will ever be induced to leave this country, even if such a thing were desirable. The Black man (unlike the Indian) loves civilization . . . individuals emigrate—nations never." Douglass's views on Native Americans, though, evolved so that by 1867 he saw the nation as a single entity, drawn together by its many nationalities. "A Nation against all ethnological classifications, identities, and differences," Douglass told a crowd in Boston, "Whether all these elements, so apparently opposite, can be freed from antagonism, and rendered homogenous, is the great and all commanding question now remaining to be solved." Douglass acknowledged that Native Americans stood in the middle of the harmonious interactions between whites and Blacks, and he noted that even while they both attempted to civilize and welcome the Indian as "a new candidate for membership in the national family," the Chinese, "knocks for admission." Douglass's speech, delivered two years before Grant's presidency, prefigured an important facet of not only the Grant Doctrine and the Peace Policy, but also the Republican Party's Reconstruction ideology. The republican ideals of liberty, freedom, free labor, and economic stability embodied in the Reconstruction amendments and which Grant hoped to export not only into the Caribbean but also into the American West, called out to peoples around the world. Douglass viewed the United States as "the most perfect national illustration of the unity and dignity of humanity." Welcoming immigrants and civilizing the indigenous people of the continent, he noted, would send a signal to the world that the nation was living up to the promises of Reconstruction.[24]

Native Americans unhappy with settlers encroaching on their land, and Chinese laborers posed potential obstacles to African Americans seeking new opportunities in the West. Black editors discussed not only the increase of Chinese immigrant laborers in the West but also the outrages committed by Native Americans upon new settlers in the region. Black Americans balanced their beliefs in equal rights with the idea that they lived in a Christian and civilized modern world. President Grant had noted in his Peace Policy that his path to citizenship for American Indians was contingent upon their Christianization and civilization. African American leaders expressed similar views about Native Americans and Chinese immigrants when they considered the movement of free Blacks into the western territories. For Black intellectuals, being a civilized American often trumped racial equality, though that did not mean African Americans did not sympathize with the plight of Native Americans or Chinese immigrants. The *New National Era* argued that Democrats and Republicans in California had developed anti-Chinese attitudes because "the trouble is the Chinese are diligent and thrifty. They have no expensive vices and are willing to work cheap," therefore they took labor away from whites and did not spend their wages in the local economy. The newspaper saw the exclusion legislation that California passed in the 1850s and 1860s as decidedly racist and unrepublican and was astounded that members of the Republican Party would continue to support such measures. At the same time, the *Weekly Louisianian* argued that the federal government was spending too much energy promoting "the wholesale immigration of Chinese and other races, which is taxing its energies to civilize the Indian of the plains," thus preventing Black Americans from settling there. Complaints about the increase of Chinese immigrants in the *Louisianian* took a biblical tone when the editors likened them to a plague. "What the grasshopper has done for Kansas, and other eastern sections," the editors wrote, "Coolie labor will do for the Golden State." Once the Chinese had overrun the West, the editors opined, the Chinese would surely move to the South.[25]

The presence of Chinese immigrants in California, though, offered an opportunity for African Americans to test the constitutionality of

Reconstruction laws. Interestingly, the *New National Era* noted that the anti-Chinese sentiment in California presented the first test case for the Enforcement Acts passed in 1870 and 1871. Also known as the "Anti-Ku Klux Klan Acts," Congress intended the Enforcement Acts to protect African Americans in the South from white violence, safeguard their right to vote and hold office, and generally give force to the Fourteenth and Fifteenth Amendments. Chinese immigrants in California sued for the right to testify on their own behalf, a right denied to African Americans in the antebellum era and now protected by the Enforcement Acts. "We are informed that an effort will be made in San Francisco to practically and finally test the question," the *Era* noted, "whether the Federal Constitution and the Congress can be set aside and nullified by the California Supreme Judiciary." The Chinese immigrant in the case settled out of court, but other test cases encountered California courts unwilling to allow Chinese defendants to testify on their own behalf, in violation of the Enforcement Act (and the Burlingame Treaty). The California legislature, though, rescinded its antebellum laws which barred Chinese immigrants from testifying prior to these cases reaching the US Supreme Court, thus eliminating "the ban on Chinese testimony in criminal and civil proceedings." The editors of the *Era* understood that important Reconstruction legislation and case law occurred beyond the South.[26]

While Grant intended the Enforcement Acts as protection of the rights of African Americans against the violent terrorism of white supremacist groups, his Native American Peace Policy had the opposite effect. When Congress refused to support Grant's desire to move the Bureau of Indian Affairs to the War Department, he accepted that reform of the BIA was necessary to implement a fair Peace Policy that, as president, he hoped would transition Native Americans to republican citizens. After Ely S. Parker's resignation as Commissioner of the BIA, Grant then had to rely on an element within the BIA that did not share his views on Native American citizenship. Leaders in Congress, the Congressional Board of Indian Commissioners (BIC), and the US Army all believed that Native Americans were a threat to white men and western settlement and that Grant's Peace Policy, and the BIA, were thus hindering the tide of progress. Native Americans stood in the way of industrial progress, that is, by blocking railroad development, and Congress supported business interests that pushed tribes off coveted land. Inevitably, the army clashed with Western Indian tribes. In 1872 and

1873, the army engaged with Modoc Indians in Oregon, suffering numerous defeats. Throughout 1873 and 1874, Generals Philip Sheridan and William T. Sherman made frequent requests to mount expeditions against Plains Indian tribes in Indian Territory, tribes they deemed hostile. Yet Grant refused to authorize the use of force. Finally, in the summer of 1874, forced off their lands due to the slaughter of the buffalo herds by white hunters, Comanche, Kiowa, and Cheyenne warriors launched raids into Kansas and Texas as revenge against the bison hunters.[27]

These raids in Kansas and Texas were part of several clashes between Native Americans and whites during Grant's second term that ended his Peace Policy and undermined his attempts to "civilize" Native Americans and make them into citizens. The army initially failed in engagements against Modoc warriors due to poor training and lack of resources, but Sheridan's troops that attacked the Plains Indians were better prepared for a longer fight. Whereas Grant's Peace Policy had focused on securing and protecting the supplies and foodstuffs of the Native Americans in Indian Territory, the army now targeted the Indians' food supplies and horse herds to degrade their capability to mount raids against white settlements. This direct challenge to the Peace Policy, which President Grant sanctioned because he argued that he could not allow the Plains Indians to attack white settlements in adjoining states, showed the weakness of Grant's position in terms of sustaining his civilizing policy. He had made efforts to distinguish between peaceful Native Americans and outlaw bands of Indians who acted on their uncivilized nature, when he told Chiefs Red Cloud and Spotted Tail that he hoped "to keep the peace between [Indians] and the whites." However, the army eventually exhausted the supplies of the Plains Indians and those who did not perish had no choice but to accept surrender and forced relocation to reservations in Florida.[28] Grant's Native American policy suffered another blow when white settlers and Northern Pacific Railroad interests violated the Fort Laramie Treaty of 1868 and encroached upon the Lakota Sioux Reservation of South Dakota. Lakota warriors reacted violently to the interlopers and clashes between whites and Lakota escalated toward outright war. Grant's Peace Policy should have honored the treaty and enforced the rights of the Lakota, and members of the BIC implored Grant to halt the use of military force for fear of inflaming a war that would end the Peace Policy for good. Secretary of War William Belknap claimed that US troops were there to "prevent, and not to cause, hostilities. It was supposed that these troops would be used as a protecting, and not as an aggressive, force." When settlers discovered gold in the Black Hills on Lakota hunting grounds in 1874, however, Lieutenant Col. George Armstrong Custer insisted that a fort would be necessary to protect white miners in the region and disregarded the illegality of white incursions into Lakota lands. The Lakota, naturally, attacked the white interlopers and violence escalated as more white fortune-seekers flooded in. All-out war seemed inevitable.[29]

But was war inevitable? Leaders from the Lakota Sioux had petitioned Grant in early 1875 for assistance in dealing with white interlopers on their land. The Fort Laramie Treaty of 1868 had set aside land for a reservation for the Lakota as well as providing vast amounts of "unceded lands" in Montana and Wyoming that the Lakota used for hunting. As one historian notes, "this 'unceded' land was, in effect, an independent state under Indian control. Along with the Black Hills, the unceded land would be a key point of contention" in the Great Sioux War. White settlers, government officials, and military leaders all coveted the unceded lands and, as the nation was still recovering from the Panic of 1873, Grant viewed the prospect of an enormous deposit of gold in this region as too good to pass up.

Historians of the Great Sioux War claim that Grant intentionally sold out the Lakota treaty and instigated a war for acquiring the gold. They argue that Grant held a "secret meeting" to hatch a plan to force the Lakota into a war to take control of the Black Hills. These historians note that the Grant Administration's first act was to leverage the shipment of food to the Lakota to allow white miners into the hills to look for gold. Grant informed the delegation, led by Red Cloud, that "the government's treaty obligation to issue rations had run out and could be revoked; rations continued only because of Washington's kind feelings toward the Lakotas. . . . [T]he Lakotas must either cede the Paha Sapa (the Black Hills) or lose their rations."

On November 3, 1875, Grant held a meeting at the White House that included General Phillip Sheridan (accompanied by his aide General George Crook), Secretary of War William Belknap, new Secretary of the Interior Zachariah Chandler, Assistant Secretary of the Interior Benjamin R. Cowen, and Commissioner of Indian Affairs Edward P. Smith. Rather than a secret meeting, this meeting was widely publicized. The press reported on the meeting and its subject, if not the particulars. If he was planning a conspiratorial cabal with the predetermined purpose of implementing a war against the Lakota, Grant was doing a poor job. "The conferees agreed on a two-phase plan," one historian argues, "The president's edict reaffirming Lakota ownership of the Black Hills would stand, but the army would no longer enforce it. If the Lakotas retaliated against white trespassers, so much the better." The historian noted that "hostilities would help legitimize the secret second phase of the operation. . . . [T]he Indian Bureau was to fabricate complaints against them; and General Sheridan would begin preparations for his favorite form of warfare: a winter campaign against unsuspecting Indian villages."

One historian notes that claims of Indian violence published two weeks later in the press were complete fabrications. He also notes that Crook's aide, Capt. John G. Bourke, wrote in his diary that "General Crook said that at the council General Grant had decided that the Northern Sioux [i.e., the Lakotas] should go upon their reservation or be whipped." That historian, though, fails to mention that Bourke's diary entry was quoting a conversation between Crook and Red Cloud and Little Wound. One can hardly describe a secret conspiracy to dream up a war with the Lakota if one of the conspirators is quoting the content of the secret meeting to the Lakota themselves. While it is certain that Grant was willing to leverage food support to receive concessions from the Lakota, and he was willing to allow the gold miners to enter the Black Hills unmolested, there is not compelling evidence to prove that he intended to deceive the public to start a war with the tribe. He had no need for such deception as most of the public would have supported such an incursion onto Lakota land. In a letter to General Alfred H. Terry, General Sheridan recalled the meeting in the White House, asking Terry to prevent "further resistance by the military . . . to the miners going in" to the Black Hills. Sheridan asked Terry to "quietly cause the Troops in your Department to assume such attitude as will meet the views of the President in this respect?" Some historians have read this letter to mean that Sheridan was ordering Terry to organize his troops against the Lakota, when in fact he was ordering Terry to refrain from using his troops to stop white settlers from entering the Black Hills. The distinction here is slight but important because Grant surely knew by allowing whites into the territory that the Lakota would inevitably clash with them. However, the letter from Sheridan to Terry does not show proof that Grant explicitly ordered American troops to "crush the non-treaty bands" of Sioux. Even so, Grant's decision to allow whites into the territory to mine for gold represents a significant end to any goodwill he had built up with Native Americans. While the decision was self-serving and wrongheaded, it was doubtfully part of a secret cabal manipulating journalists, political leaders, and Native Americans to start a war.

Secretary of State Hamilton Fish was not present for the meeting in question as he was in New York voting. Fish, always wary of the political machinations of fellow cabinet members, makes no note of this supposed secret war. As the president's right-hand man in the cabinet, he would have been aware of any significant decision making and would have written it down in his journals. In his diary, though, he mentions that he arrived back in Washington the next day and on November 5, 1875, attended a cabinet meeting where the only topic of discussion regarding the Indian Bureau and the Department of the Interior was Secretary Chandler mentioning that the office was in possession of $5,000 worth of syphilitic sore medicine purchased by his predecessor.[30]

In early 1876, the US Army went on the offensive against Indian tribes across the West. white settlers continued to encroach upon Indian territories, especially in the Black Hills region of South Dakota as gold mines became more prosperous, and Grant's Bureau of Indian Affairs was ineffective in protecting the lives of the Sioux there. Gone was the Peace Policy and any talk of citizenship, what remained was the army and the reservation. The Great Sioux War in the Black Hills lasted through the end of Grant's presidency, but he began his final year with a moment of hope. Board of Indian Commissioners Chair Clinton Fisk reported to the president in early January 1876 that the Black Hills Lakota Sioux were peaceful, and the Native Americans there were prospering. "There have been those who have cruelly asserted that these Indians should be exterminated to make room for white men," he wrote the president, "Such advocates are found plentifully on the borders of Indian reservations and on the march to the Black Hills. Indeed, wherever the Indian has desirable lands, men of this class can be found looking eagerly for an opportunity to enter in and possess them." Fisk worried that these same men were behind the renewed effort to relocate the Bureau of Indian Affairs to the War Department. "These men to-day are all of the opinion that the Indians should be handed over to the care of the military," Fisk wrote. As far as the commissioner was concerned, in early 1876, the Peace Policy was working, if the president would allow the Bureau, and not the army, to manage interactions with Native Americans.[31]

The Lakota Sioux and the army, however, continued to clash throughout 1876, culminating in the Battle of Little Bighorn. Also known as the Battle of the Greasy Grass, a contingent of Lakota and Cheyenne met Lieutenant Colonel Custer's Seventh Cavalry and decimated the battalion in a major victory for the Plains Indians. Custer's death spurred increased calls for violence and vengeance against the Lakota, and Grant called on Congress to authorize between 2,500 and 5,000 additional troops, the final nail in the coffin for his Peace Policy. In July 1876, the Senate resolved that the president answer "whether the Sioux Indians made any hostile demonstrations prior to the invasion of their treaty reservation by the gold hunters." Senators also wanted Grant to provide information on "whether the present Military operations are conducted for the purpose of protecting said Indians in their rights under the Treaty of Eighteen hundred and sixty-eight, or of punishing them for resisting the violation of that treaty." Grant responded by submitting a statement from General Sherman blaming Sioux warriors, but not the Sioux people, for the violence. Sherman claimed that the discovery of gold was a complication and not a contributing factor in the military expeditions. Grant's new Secretary of War, J. Donald Cameron, endorsed Sherman's views. Grant similarly endorsed the operations when he spent $200,000 for the construction of military posts in the region. By the time Grant left office in March 1877, the army and the Lakota were in a state of constant war, and his Peace Policy of gradual progress toward civilization and citizenship was finished.[32]

CONCLUSION

The promises of Reconstruction were central to Ulysses S. Grant's republican ideology. African American citizenship was one of the most important goals of the Grant administration and the ideas of freedom and equality before the law laid the foundation for the eventual Grant Doctrine. The passage of the Fourteenth Amendment incorporated the millions of formerly enslaved into the citizenry and, for the first time, enshrined equal protection under the laws into the Constitution. Grant genuinely believed in the equality of different races, and he also understood that he was cultivating a political base, understanding that African American men would vote Republican. At the same time, he understood that the only way to reconstruct the American political system after the Civil War was through the implementation of the civil rights legislation of the Fourteenth and Fifteenth Amendments and the exporting of these ideals beyond the South into the new territories which Americans were settling. The Grant Doctrine and the Peace Policy represented Grant's belief in a republican system that championed freedom and equality and pushed forward a civilized republic toward progress and prosperity. By adding new citizens to this civilized republican system, Grant hoped to solidify the gains of the Republican Party for generations to come. His goal was strengthening the Union through the reunification of the states, protecting the rights of African Americans, increasing the nation's economic prosperity, and putting the nation at the forefront of the international system. To do so, he believed, the United States must lead the charge to eradicate slavery in the Western Hemisphere by exporting republicanism and economic growth to the Caribbean and to civilize and make citizens out of Native Americans in the West, and all who lived within its borders.[1]

If Grant was to make his Reconstruction initiatives successful, he needed the enthusiastic support of African Americans. Frederick Douglass recognized that the Republican Party's power grew from being a national party committed to equal rights. "It was from the National Government that the colored men had received all they have," Douglass told African American mechanical students in New Orleans in 1872, arguing that the states had done all they could to limit the rights of African Americans. "The Republican is the national party and the other is the State party." For African American leaders such as Douglass, the alternatives to the Republican Party, be they the Democrats or later the Liberal Republicans, were anathema.[2] Whites, regardless of section, began to view Reconstruction measures that benefitted freedmen as detrimental to their hopes of the full reunification of the nation. Grant was not one of them, yet he did begin to grow weary of constant violence in the Southern states. By 1875, Grant refused to assist the state of Mississippi in its state-wide elections and the Democratic Party again deployed violence and terror to regain control of the legislature. Hiram Revels, the former US Senator and first African American in Congress, wrote a letter to President Grant in November 1875 critical of the Republican Party slate in the Mississippi statewide elections, turning his back on his Republican Party roots. Revels explained the political situation to Grant and his decision-making as to why he had chosen not to support Governor Adelbert Ames and the Republican Party in the 1875 election.[3] Revels noted, "I will premise by saying that I am no politician . . . I never have sought political preferment, nor do I ask it now, but am engaged in my calling—the ministry." Revels stated that he felt "an earnest desire for the welfare of all the people, irrespective of race or color." Revels argued that the Republicans had misled African Americans, "enslaved in mind by unprincipled adventurers, who," he claimed, "caring nothing for country, were willing to stoop to anything, no matter how infamous, to secure power to themselves and perpetuate it." African Americans in Mississippi had realized, he claimed, that they were "being used as mere tools and . . . they determined, by casting their ballots against these unprincipled adventurers, to overthrow them" and in doing so were seeking to coalesce again as Republicans for the national election in 1876. The Republican state administration, ostensibly Adelbert Ames, was "notoriously corrupt and dishonest" and "to defeat [him], at the late election men irrespective of race, color, or party affiliation, united and voted together against men known to be incompetent and dishonest." Revels claimed that "the great masses of the white people have abandoned their hostility toward the General Government and republican principles, and to-day accept as a fact that all men are born free and equal." Mississippians were not at fault, Revels argued. "The bitterness and hate created by the late civil strife has . . . been obliterated in this State, except in some localities, and would have long since been entirely obliterated were it not for some unprincipled men who would keep alive the bitterness of the past." The Republican administration, and not the racial animosity of white Democrats, then, was responsible for any discord in the state.[4]

Revels' assessment of the political situation in Mississippi was, of course, wholly inaccurate. If anything, white Mississippians' virulence toward the Republican Party and the federal government was increasing. The passage of the Civil Rights Bill in 1874 further inflamed the animosity of white Southerners toward African Americans and the hated federal government which intervened on their behalf. However, when the Supreme Court quickly overturned the law as unconstitutional, many white Democrats and Republicans "agreed that there must be no extraordinary legislation on behalf of African Americans who had to work their way up in society like everyone else." This attitude might explain why Revels turned away from the Republican Party. However historian Robert Jenkins has argued that "Revels' support of the Democrats was simply revenge against Ames and the rest of the Republican Party for having ousted him from his presidency at Alcorn College."[5]

Revels' support for Southern whites was nothing new. Revels, as a member of the Senate, introduced petitions on behalf of white Southerners and even supported legislation that would allow former Confederates to regain their political rights. A Methodist preacher, Revels claimed his Christian faith led him to support Grant's Dominican annexation attempt, as he believed that enveloping the Dominicans into the American system would lead them out of poverty. Therefore, Revel's Christian beliefs certainly could have guided him in reconciliation efforts toward white Mississippians. When he offered legislation that asked for magnanimity toward Southern whites, Frederick Douglass surmised that because Revels had been born free, he could not comprehend the feelings of former slaves toward Confederates. "He [Revels] is an amiable man, has always been free," Douglass wrote, "and has, perhaps, not a 'stripe' on his back to forget. Such men are apt to find it easy to forget stripes laid upon other men's backs and can as easily exhort them to forget them."[6]

The Grant administration attempted to secure the rights of Black Americans in the South throughout Reconstruction but the violent backlash from Southern Democrats was widespread and constant. As such, many African Americans hastened to leave the region for better opportunities away from the violence, much as Grant had predicted in his reasoning for annexing the Dominican Republic. Denied opportunity in the Caribbean, many African

Americans chose to move to the West during Reconstruction and, at the turn of the twentieth century, millions more moved North in the Great Migration.[7]

Many Black Southerners believed that the violence in the South would never end once the Democrats regained control of state legislatures. Although the Enforcement Acts had succeeded in driving the Ku Klux Klan underground in many states (specifically South Carolina), they had not stopped the continued violence around election time. Violence and upheaval were part of the daily routine for Black men and women who sought to better their lives in the Palmetto state. The massacre at Hamburg, South Carolina, among many other violent racist attacks, showed that white terrorist groups were not sheepishly leaving the state in droves but were violently overthrowing the duly elected government. Grant decried the "barbarous massacre of innocent men" in Hamburg all while limiting military support for Republicans there. However, he lamented the continued violence in the South and the destruction of republican institutions there noting that a "Government that cannot give protection to the life, property and all guaranteed civil rights (in this country the greatest is an untrammeled ballot,) to the citizen, is in so far a failure."[8]

Grant held similarly fervent views regarding European and Chinese immigration to the United States. The Republican Party encouraged the immigration and naturalization of European and Cuban immigrants, and these immigrants were welcomed as productive members of the body politic and as laborers. Such immigrants accepted republicanism—embracing notions of emancipation, freedom, and liberty. Many of these immigrants exported republican ideology back to their homeland by supporting anti-slavery and anti-monarchical movements. These immigrants, though, were raised in the tenets of Western civilization, were Christians, and were eventually deemed acceptable republican men by Americans. At the same time, Republicans in the West joined with Democrats to vilify the increasing number of Chinese immigrants arriving in the United States. As they took up jobs in cities, mining towns, plantations, and on railroads, American labor groups viewed them as pariahs. The advance of the railroads and industry in the West would have been severely hamstrung without Chinese laborers. Yet their work was viewed not as a benefit, but as a roadblock to white and Black labor. Grant joined his Republican colleagues in decrying Chinese immigration but framed his argument in republican terms of free labor. Arguing against the rise of "coolie" labor, the president supported full Chinese immigration of free labor, but stated that he would exercise his power to stop the importation of Chinese slaves into the Western Hemisphere. Among these coolie slaves were Chinese women who, Grant and Republicans argued, came to the United States as prostitutes. To Grant, this form of slavery was an affront to the republicanism that the Union army and the Republican Party had fought to uphold during the Civil War, and an affront to a civilized Christian society. Reconstruction in the West, then, represented an effort by Grant and his party to complete their work to end the practice of forced labor and the supposed immoral practice of prostitution. It also offered Grant the opportunity to establish his Peace Policy which provided a path to citizenship for Native Americans, a path that would be unattainable in his presidency, but one that reflected his approach to Reconstruction as a race neutral policy based on the acceptance of the tenets of Western civilization.[9]

African American leaders in the Reconstruction era understood that the American Civil War markedly changed the nation and that the Reconstruction amendments had created a new republic for their people. The Grant Doctrine, the attempted annexation of the Dominican Republic, the rebellion in Cuba, the Peace Policy, and the questions of immigration all reflect the Grant administration's attempts to mold this new republic through the process of redefining citizenship rights for non-white Americans and the role that the federal government played in defining these rights. Black leaders supported the Republican Party's platform and, by extension, the platform of President Grant, and sought to challenge those who undermined the Reconstruction of the South. At the same time, African American leaders held widely differing perspectives on foreign and domestic policy. As the Grant administration attempted to annex the Dominican Republic, remain neutral in the Cuban rebellion, implement an Indian Peace Policy, curtail Chinese immigration, or enforce Reconstruction, Black leaders challenged Republican politicians and each other to support the rights of African Americans and to continue to put the integrity of the newly defined Constitution above all else. Many white members of the Republican Party sought only to utilize the new amendments to the Constitution as a means of securing national reunion and strengthening a sense of nationalism through the country. Grant struggled to secure the complete support of the Republican Party, but he knew he could rely on African Americans at the ballot box. By supporting the right to vote for all African American men, the Grant administration earned the near complete support of Black Republicans in his 1872 reelection, but the president could not secure unequivocal Black support for all his foreign and domestic policy initiatives. Black Republicans showed a nuanced understanding of a variety of political issues and supported them accordingly. They supported equal rights for all men, but also understood them through a nineteenth-century concept of civilization. The Grant Doctrine underscored the Grant administration's attempt to make the Reconstruction amendments a reality beyond the confines of the American South, but that did not guarantee support for these policies from African Americans who analyzed each policy on its merits and considered how it affected the lives of Black Americans. Unfortunately for African Americans, many white Republicans prioritized reconciliation with former Confederates and Black Americans would lose the equal rights that they had briefly enjoyed during the Reconstruction era, for nearly a century thereafter.[10]

Grant made the policy of his administration clear in a September 1875 speech delivered in Des Moines, Iowa in which he discussed non-sectarian public education. Grant's words to the gathered Union veterans expressed his beliefs in the ideals of republicanism. Indeed, Grant prefaced his address by telling the crowd, "Let not the results of [our fallen comrade's] sacrifices be destroyed. The Union & free institutions for which they fell should be held more dear for these sacrifices. . . . Let us then begin by guarding against every enemy threatning [sic] the perpetuity of free republican institutions." Harkening back to the sacrifice of his men who fought and died in the Civil War, Grant wondered aloud to the crowd what had they died for. "It is important the sovereign—the people," Grant noted, "should possess intelligence. The free school is the promoter of that intelligence which is to preserve us as a free nation." Grant put his belief in a Protestant, yet sectarian republic, one that put the virtues of equality, freedom, and prosperity over the superstitious beliefs of a Catholic education, Mormonism, or the "barbaric" beliefs of Native Americans and Chinese immigrants. Grant worried that if the nation were to fight a Civil War again it would not be along the lines of North and South but "between patriotism and intelligence on the one side and superstition, ambition and ignorance on the other." To Grant, the ideals of republicanism and civilization were just as important as preserving the Union and eradicating slavery. American citizens, and in Grant's estimation none more so than the citizen-soldiers in the crowd in Iowa that day, understood that the nation's free institutions had been built on sacrifice and those institutions were crucial to its existence. The Grant Doctrine sought to bring new peoples into these national institutions to show that the sacrifices of the Civil War had not been in vain, and the Peace Policy sought to show that Native Americans were capable of being enveloped by the virtues of republicanism and civilization and could be made into upstanding citizens of the United States of America.[11]

The success or failure of the Grant Doctrine was not tied to the fate of Reconstruction as much as it was tied to the fate of the Grant administration. Reconstruction's hugely ambitious goals meant a variety of successes and failures that historians have examined ever since the experiment ended. However, these successes were limiting, as the reunification of the states came at the price of former Confederate "redemption" of Southern legislatures and a return to the status quo. The end of Reconstruction brought about an end to many hard-earned rights for African Americans in the South while many whites, both North and South, Democrat and Republican, embraced a return to normalcy. Had the Grant Doctrine and the Peace Policy succeeded, and the nation added hundreds of thousands of non-white citizens from the Caribbean and from Native American territories into the body politic, would Reconstruction have ended any differently? Probably not, yet Grant's attempts show that had others shared his understanding of the changing nature of citizenship, it might have meant that the American people would not have had to wait nearly a century for the civil rights movement to complete the work of Reconstruction.

NOTES

Introduction

1. March 5, 1869, Benjamin Moran Journal, Library of Congress.
2. Andrew F. Lang, *In the Wake of War: Military Occupation, Emancipation, and Civil War America* (Baton Rouge: Louisiana State University Press, 2017), 3.
3. Kathleen DuVal, "Debating Identity, Sovereignty, and Civilization: The Arkansas Valley after the Louisiana Purchase," *Journal of the Early Republic* 26 (Spring 2006): 26; Andrew F. Lang, *A Contest of Civilizations: Exposing the Crisis of American Exceptionalism in the Civil War Era* (Chapel Hill: University of North Carolina Press, 2021), 11.
4. Martha S. Jones, *Birthright Citizenship: A History of Race and Rights in Antebellum America* (New York: Cambridge University Press, 2018), 4–6.
5. *The* (Washington) *Evening Star*, March 4, 1869; *National Republican*, March 5, 1869; Inaugural Address, March 4, 1869, John Y. Simon, ed. *The Papers of Ulysses S. Grant*, Vol. 19: *July 1, 1868-October 31, 1869* (Carbondale: Southern Illinois University Press, 1994), 139–42.
6. Ron Chernow, *Grant* (New York: Penguin Press, 2017); Ulysses S. Grant, *The Personal Memoirs of Ulysses S. Grant: The Complete Annotated Edition*, ed. John F. Marszalek with David S. Nolen and Louie P. Gallo (Cambridge, MA: Belknap Press of Harvard University Press, 2017), 132–38.
7. Inaugural Address, *PUSG* 19, 139–42.
8. Inaugural Address, *PUSG* 19, 139–42.
9. Inaugural Address, *PUSG* 19, 139–42; See: Robert Winston Mardock, *The Reformers and the American Indian* (Columbia: University of Missouri Press, 1971); Robert L. Whitner, "Grant's Peace Policy on the Yakima Reservation, 1870–1882," *The Western American Indian: Case Studies in Tribal History*, ed. Richard N. Ellis (Lincoln: University of Nebraska Press, 1972), 50–62; Robert H. Keller Jr., *American Protestantism and United States Indian Policy, 1869-1882* (Lincoln: University of Nebraska Press, 1983); Robert Wooster, *The Military and United States Indian Policy, 1865–1903* (New Haven, CT: Yale University Press, 1988); Norman J. Bender, *"New Hope for the Indians": The Grant Peace Policy and the Navajos in the 1870s* (Albuquerque: University of New Mexico Press, 1989); Steve Hahn, "Slave Emancipation,

Indian Peoples, and the Projects of a New American Nation-State," *Journal of the Civil War Era* 3, no. 3 (September 2013): 307–30; Mary Stockwell, *Interrupted Odyssey: Ulysses S. Grant and the American Indians* (Carbondale: Southern Illinois University Press, 2018).

10. Inaugural Address, *PUSG* 19.

11. Ulysses S. Grant, Speech, Republicans from the First Ward, Washington, DC, April 1, 1870, in John Y. Simon, ed., *The Papers of Ulysses S. Grant* (Carbondale: Southern Illinois University Press, 1995), 137–38; The annexation attempt is an example of the global nature of Reconstruction. Historians have recently begun to analyze the pivotal Civil War period in a global context in a variety of essay collections. These include Mark M. Smith, "The Past as a Foreign Country: Reconstruction, Inside and Out," in *Reconstructions: New Perspectives on the Postbellum United States*, ed. Thomas J. Brown (New York: Oxford University Press, 2006), 117–40; David T. Gleeson and Simon Lewis, eds. *The Civil War as Global Conflict: Transnational Meanings of the American Civil War* (Columbia: University of South Carolina Press, 2014); Gregory P. Downs and Kate Masur, eds. *The World the Civil War Made* (Chapel Hill: University of North Carolina Press, 2015); David Prior, ed. *Reconstruction in a Globalizing World* (New York: Fordham University Press, 2018); Gregory P. Downs, *The Second American Revolution: The Civil War-Era Struggle over Cuba and the Rebirth of the American Republic* (Chapel Hill: University of North Carolina Press, 2019); David Prior, *Between Freedom and Progress: The Lost World of Reconstruction Politics* (Baton Rouge: Louisiana State University Press, 2019); and Evan Rothera, *Civil Wars and Reconstructions in the Americas: The United States, Mexico, and Argentina, 1860–1880* (Baton Rouge: Louisiana State University Press, 2022).

12. For the past eighty-five years, the only comprehensive analysis of the Grant administration was historian Allan Nevins's examination of Secretary of State Hamilton Fish's life and career, *Hamilton Fish: The Inner History of the Grant Administration*. Even most modern Grant biographers utilized Nevins's work as the foundation for their discussions of American foreign policy during the Grant administration. While certainly an important contribution to the historiography of the Grant administration, its diplomacy, and the Reconstruction era, the book suffers from several deficiencies. Primarily, Nevins echoes the William Archibald Dunning interpretation of Reconstruction, which examined the era from a white supremacist perspective. Modern historians denounce the Dunning interpretation of Reconstruction, yet they continue to reference Nevins's work as the definitive word on the Grant administration's foreign and domestic policies. A short biography of Hamilton Fish was published in 1918 by A. Elwood Corning, however all modern examinations of the Grant administration utilized Nevins' work exclusively. A. Elwood Corning, *Hamilton Fish* (New York: Lanmere Publishing, 1918); Allan

Nevins, *Hamilton Fish: The Inner History of the Grant Administration* (New York: Dodd, Mead and Company, 1937), 293–94; Ulysses S. Grant (hereafter USG) Speech, April 1, 1870, John Y. Simon, ed., *The Papers of Ulysses S. Grant*, Vol. 20: *November 1, 1869-October 31, 1870* (Carbondale: Southern Illinois University Press, 1995), 137; Lang, *A Contest of Civilizations*23–25; There are a number of excellent biographies of Grant that cover the high points of foreign relations in his administration, including Jean Edward Smith, *Grant* (New York: Simon and Schuster, 2001); Ronald C. White, *American Ulysses: A Life of Ulysses S. Grant* (New York: Random House, 2016), 517; Ron Chernow, *Grant* (New York: Penguin Press, 2017).

13. Inaugural Address, *PUSG* 19.

14. Fifteenth Amendment to the Constitution, No. 10, March 30, 1870, *Statutes at Large and Proclamations of the United States of America from December 1869 to March 1871 . . . Vol. XVI* (Boston: Little Brown and Co. 1871), 1131–32. https://memory.loc.gov.

15. USG to Congress, March 30, 1870; *PUSG* 20, 130–31; Xi Wang, *The Trial of Democracy: Black Suffrage and Northern Republicans, 1860–1910* (Athens: University of Georgia Press, 1997), xvii; Laura F. Edwards, *A Legal History of the Civil War and Reconstruction: A Nation of Rights* (New York: Cambridge University Press, 2015); Jones, *Birthright Citizens*; Garrett Epps, *Democracy Reborn: The Fourteenth Amendment and the Fight for Equal Rights in Post-Civil War America* (New York: Henry Holt and Company, 2006); William A. Link, David Brown, Brian Ward, and Martyn Bone, eds., *Creating Citizenship in the Nineteenth-Century South* (Gainesville: University Press of Florida, 2013); Susanna Michelle Lee, *Claiming the Union: Citizenship in the Post-Civil War South* (New York: Cambridge University Press, 2014), 4; Eric Foner, *The Second Founding: How the Civil War and Reconstruction Remade the Constitution* (New York: W. W. Norton, 2019), xxviii.

16. For more on African American leaders during Reconstruction, see: W. E. B. Du Bois, *Black Reconstruction in America, 1860–1880* (New York: Free Press, 1992); Frederick Douglass, *Life and Times of Frederick Douglass* (New York: Pathway Press, 1941); Philip S. Foner, ed., *The Life and Writings of Frederick Douglass*: Vol. IV, *Reconstruction and After* (New York: International Publishers, 1955); Elizabeth Lawson, *The Gentleman from Mississippi: Our First Negro Congressman, Hiram R. Revels* (New York: Elizabeth Lawson, 1960); Julius E. Thompson, "Hiram Rhodes Revels, 1827–1901: A Reappraisal," *The Journal of Negro History* 79, no. 3 (Summer 1994): 297–303; Ryan P. Semmes, "Hiram R. Revels, Ulysses S. Grant, Party Politics, and the Annexation of Santo Domingo," *Journal of Mississippi History* LXXX, no. 1–2 (Spring-Summer 2018): 49–65; Robert L. Jenkins, "Black Voices in Reconstruction: The Senate Careers of Hiram R. Revels and Blanch K. Bruce" (PhD diss., Mississippi State University, 1975); James Haskin, *Pinckney Benton Stewart Pinchback* (New York: Macmillan, 1973); Earl Ofari, *"Let Your Motto Be Resistance:" The Life and*

Thought of Henry Highland Garnet (Boston: Beacon Press, 1972); Joel Schor, *Henry Highland Garnet: A Voice of Black Radicalism in the Nineteenth Century* (Westport, CT: Greenwood Press, 1977); John Mercer Langston, *From the Virginia Plantation to the National Capitol* (New York: Arno Press, 1969); John Hope Franklin, ed. *Reminiscences of an Active Life: The Autobiography of John Roy Lynch* (Chicago: University of Chicago Press, 1970); John Hope Franklin, *George Washington Williams: A Biography* (Chicago: University of Chicago Press, 1985); Edward A. Miller, Jr., *Gullah Statesman: Robert Smalls From Slavery to Congress, 1839–1915* (Columbia: University of South Carolina Press, 1995); Carlton Mabee and Susan Mabee Newhouse, *Sojourner Truth: Slave, Prophet, Legend* (New York: New York University Press, 1993); Nell Irvin Painter, *Sojourner Truth: A Life, A Symbol* (New York: W. W. Norton, 1996); Shawn Leigh Alexander, ed., *T. Thomas Fortune the Afro-American Agitator: A Collection of Writings, 1880–1928* (Gainesville: University Press of Florida, 2008); Philip Dray, *Capitol Men: The Epic Story of Reconstruction Through the Lives of the First Black Congressmen* (Boston: Houghton Mifflin Company, 2008).

17. Other biographies of Grant worth examining are: William S. McFeely, *Grant: A Biography* (New York: W. W. Norton, 1982); Geoffrey Perret, *Ulysses S. Grant: Soldier and President* (New York: Random House, 1997); Joan Waugh, *U. S. Grant: American Hero, American Myth* (Chapel Hill: University of North Carolina Press, 2009); H. W. Brands, *The Man Who Saved the Union: Ulysses Grant in War and Peace* (New York: Anchor Books, 2012); For further reading on Reconstruction see: W. E. B. Du Bois, *Black Reconstruction in America, 1860–1880* (New York: The Free Press, 1992); Kenneth Stampp, *The Era of Reconstruction, 1865–1877* (New York: Alfred A. Knopf, 1966); John Hope Franklin, *Reconstruction after the Civil War*, 3rd. ed. (Chicago: University of Chicago Press 2012); Eric Foner, *Reconstruction: America's Unfinished Revolution, 1863–1877* (New York: Perennial Classics, 1988); Michael W. Fitzgerald, "Reconstruction Politics and the Politics of Reconstruction," in Thomas J. Brown, ed., *Reconstructions: New Perspectives on the Postbellum United States* (New York: Oxford University Press, 2006), 92–99; William Gillette, *Retreat from Reconstruction, 1869–1879* (Baton Rouge: Louisiana State University Press, 1979), 361, quoted in Fitzgerald; Michael W. Fitzgerald, *Splendid Failure: Postwar Reconstruction in the American South* (Chicago: Ivan R. Dee, 2007); Forrest A. Nabors, *From Oligarchy to Republicanism: The Great Task of Reconstruction* (Columbia: University of Missouri Press, 2017); Mark Wahlgren Summers, *The Ordeal of the Reunion: A New History of Reconstruction* (Chapel Hill: University of North Carolina Press, 2014), 4; Allen C. Guelzo, *Reconstruction: A Concise History* (New York: Oxford University Press, 2018), 11–12; See also: William Gillette, *Retreat from Reconstruction, 1869–1879* (Baton Rouge: Louisiana State University Press, 1979); Ted Tunnell, *Crucible of Reconstruction: War, Radicalism and Race in Louisiana, 1862–1877* (Baton Rouge: LSU Press, 1984); Bruce E. Baker, *What Reconstruction Meant: Historical Memory in the American South* (Charlottesville: University of Virginia Press, 2007).

18. Nearly eighty years after Allen Nevins' analysis, historian Charles W. Calhoun published the first comprehensive reexamination of the Grant presidency. Calhoun was able to utilize the complete run of *The Papers of Ulysses S. Grant*, and thus a more complex picture of the Grant presidency emerges. Charles W. Calhoun, *The Presidency of Ulysses S. Grant* (Lawrence: University Press of Kansas, 2017), 152; The only other examination of the Grant presidency is Brooks D. Simpson, *The Reconstruction Presidents* (Lawrence: University Press of Kansas, 1998), which examined Reconstruction from Lincoln's through Hayes' presidencies. Simpson noted that Grant's Reconstruction policies struggled due to a lack of presidential power in the face of a powerful Congress and economic and political circumstances that were out of his control. Though he analyzed the Dominican scheme, Simpson did not focus on any other foreign policy issues. For an examination of the Greater Reconstruction of the American West see: Elliott West, *The Last Indian War: The Nez Perce Story* (New York: Oxford University Press, 2009).

19. Foner, *The Second Founding*, 67; Stacey L. Smith, "Beyond North and South: Putting the West in the Civil War and Reconstruction," *Journal of the Civil War Era* 6, no. 4 (December 2016): 570; Summers, *The Ordeal of the Reunion*, 13, 396; West, *The Last Indian War*, xxii; David Prior, "Reconstruction, from Transatlantic Polyseme to Historiographical Quandary," in *Reconstruction in a Globalizing World*, ed. David Prior (New York: Fordham University Press, 2018), 172.

20. Gregory P. Downs and Kate Masur, eds., *The World the Civil War Made* (Chapel Hill: University of North Carolina Press, 2015), 4–6; Jay Sexton, *Debtor Diplomacy: Finance and American Foreign Relations in the Civil War Era, 1837–1873* (New York: Oxford University Press, 2005), 190; Jay Sexton, *The Monroe Doctrine: Empire and Nation in Nineteenth-Century America* (New York: Hill and Wang, 2011) 160–61; Mark M. Smith, "The Past as a Foreign Country: Reconstruction, Inside and Out," in *Reconstructions: New Perspectives on the Postbellum United States*, ed. Thomas J. Brown (New York: Oxford University Press, 2006): 117–40; David Prior, ed., *Reconstruction in a Globalizing World* (New York: Fordham University Press, 2018) 1–2, 94–120; Heather Cox Richardson, *The Death of Reconstruction: Race, Labor, and Politics in the Post-Civil War North, 1865–1901* (Cambridge, MA: Harvard University Press, 2001), 143; Heather Cox Richardson, "North and West of Reconstruction: Studies in political Economy," in *Reconstructions: New Perspectives on the Postbellum United States*, ed. Thomas J. Brown (New York: Oxford University Press, 2006), 69.

21. For more analyses on Reconstruction see: Du Bois, *Black Reconstruction in America*; Stampp, *The Era of Reconstruction*, 206–207; Franklin, *Reconstruction after the Civil War*; Elliott West, "Reconstructing Race," *Western Historical Quarterly* 34 (Spring 2003): 7–26; West, *The Last Indian War: The Nez Perce Story* (New York: Oxford University Press, 2009), xiv–xxii; Summers, *Ordeal*; Heather Cox Richardson, *West from Appomattox: The Reconstruction of America after the Civil War* (New Haven, CT: Yale University Press, 2007); Gregory Downs, *Declarations*

of Dependence: The Long Reconstruction of Popular Politics in the South, 1861–1908 (Chapel Hill: University of North Carolina Press, 2011); Lang, *In the Wake of War*; Guelzo, *Reconstruction*.

22. "Reasons why San Domingo should be Annexed to the United States," [1869–1870], Series 3: Speeches, Reports, Messages, 1863–1876, Ulysses S. Grant Papers, Library of Congress; The no-transfer principle was rarely enforced from the 1830s until Fish instituted it in 1870. Jay Sexton, "The United States, the Cuban Rebellion, and the Multilateral Initiative of 1875," *Diplomatic History* 30, no. 3 (June 2006): 335–65; Jay Sexton, *The Monroe Doctrine: Empire and Nation in Nineteenth-Century America* (New York: Hill and Wang, 2011), 4.

23. "Reasons why" memo, USG, LC; Though Grant's internal memo mentions African Americans moving to the Dominican Republic he never mentions this in his message to Congress related to annexation. Eric T. L. Love, *Race over Empire: Racism and U. S. Imperialism, 1865–1900* (Chapel Hill: University of North Carolina Press, 2004), 31–32; Simpson, *The Reconstruction Presidents*, 146.

24. A note on my choice to capitalize "Blacks" throughout this book: I decided to follow the style guidelines of the Brookings Institution which decided, in September 2019, to capitalize Black and Blacks, "when used to reference census-defined black or African American people." https://www.brookings.edu; Jones, *Birthright Citizens*, 28.

25. Heather Cox Richardson, "North and West of Reconstruction: Studies in Political Economy," in *Reconstructions: New Perspectives on the Postbellum United States*, ed. Thomas J. Brown (New York: Oxford University Press, 2006), 69.

26. Summers, *Ordeal*, 4–5; Gregory P. Down and Kate Masur, eds, *The World the Civil War Made* (Chapel Hill: University of North Carolina Press, 2015), 3.

27. Love, *Race over Empire*, 33.

Chapter 1: Exporting Republicanism beyond the South

1. Hamilton Fish Diaries, April 5, 1869, Hamilton Fish Papers, Library of Congress. For an examination of public education in Virginia and Alabama, see Hilary Green, *Educational Reconstruction: African American Schools in the Urban South, 1865–1890* (New York: Fordham University Press, 2016); For an analysis of Fish's relationship with Spain see Gregg French, "Domestic Stability and Imperial Continuities: U.S.-Spanish Relations in the Reconstruction Era," in David Prior, ed., *Reconstruction and Empire: The Legacies of Abolition and Union Victory for an Imperial Age* (New York: Fordham University Press, 2022); For information on the *Mary Lowell*, see House of Commons, United Kingdom Parliament, "Spain—Case of Mary Lowell," Vol. 199, March 14, 1870, https://hansard.parliament.uk.

2. April 5, 1869; April 6, 1869, Hamilton Fish diary, Hamilton Fish papers, Library of Congress.

3. Jay Sexton argued that Grant turned to the Monroe Doctrine as a last resort to gain support in the Senate. However, an examination of Grant's December

1869 memorandum shows that Grant was considering the implications of annexation as an outgrowth of the Monroe Doctrine before the annexation treaty had even been made public; Jay Sexton, *The Monroe Doctrine: Empire and Nation in Nineteenth-Century America* (New York: Hill and Wang, 2011), 164–65; For an analysis of Seward see Walther Stahr, *Seward: Lincoln's Indispensable Man* (New York: Simon and Schuster, 2012) and Daniel J. Burge, *A Failed Empire: The Collapse of Manifest Destiny, 1845–1872* (Lincoln: University of Nebraska Press, 2022), 129–49.

4. March 12, 1869, April 6, 1869, 41st Congress 1st Session, *Congressional Globe* (Washington, DC: Government Printing Office, 1870), 59, 523–24.

5. April 6, 1869, *The Congressional Globe*, 523–24; According to Andrew Lang, "Napoleon considered the Confederacy essential to his "Grand Design" of reestablishing France's North American empire." Lang notes, for many immigrants and those aligned with their beliefs, "slave-holding oligarchs who waged war against a liberal republic personified the European despots." Andrew F. Lang, *A Contest of Civilizations: Exposing the Crisis of American Exceptionalism in the Civil War Era* (Chapel Hill: University of North Carolina Press, 2021), 150, 190.

6. April 6, 1869, *The Congressional Globe*, 524–26.

7. April 6, 1869, *The Congressional Globe*, 526–27; Burge, *A Failed Vision of Empire*, 138; Joseph W. Fabens, *Resources of Santo Domingo: From a Paper read before the American Geographical and Statistical Society of New York, 1862* (Washington, DC: Gibson Brothers, Printers, 1869), 9; For more on olfactory and visual stereotypes of Black people see Mark M. Smith, *How Race is Made: Slavery, Segregation, and the Senses* (Chapel Hill: University of North Carolina Press, 2006), 12–16.

8. April 6, 1869, *The Congressional Globe*, 527.

9. For analysis of abolition in Latin America see: Rafael Marquese, "The Civil War in the United States and the Crisis of Slavery in Brazil," *American Civil Wars: The United States, Latin America, Europe, and the Crisis of the 1860s*, ed. Don H. Doyle (Chapel Hill: University of North Carolina Press, 2017), 222–45; Andrew F. Lang, *In the Wake of War: Military Occupation, Emancipation, and Civil War America* (Baton Rouge: Louisiana State University Press, 2017), 3; Timothy Mason Roberts examined ideas of republicanism and citizenship in both the American South and French Algeria in his article "Republican Citizenship in the post-Civil War South and French Algeria, 1865–1900," *American Nineteenth Century History* 19 (March 2018): 81–104; Mark Wahlgren Summers, *The Ordeal of the Reunion: A New History of Reconstruction* (Chapel Hill: University of North Carolina, 2014), 3.

10. John Y. Simon, ed., *The Papers of Ulysses S. Grant*, Vol. 19: *July 1, 1868-October 31, 1869* (Carbondale: Southern Illinois University Press, 1995), 142; David Prior, *Between Freedom and Progress: The Lost World of Reconstruction Politics* (Baton Rouge: Louisiana State University Press, 2019), 7–9; Burge, *A Failed Vision of Empire*, 160–61; For more on Native American citizenship see Stephen Kantrowitz,

"'Not Quite Constitutionalized': The Meanings of 'Civilization' and the Limits of Native American Citizenship," *The World the Civil War Made*, eds. Gregory P. Downs and Kate Masur (Chapel Hill: University of North Carolina Press, 2015), 75-105; Slap identified the ideology of liberal republicanism as being separate from the Liberal Republican political party founded by the same men in 1870; Andrew L. Slap, *The Doom of Reconstruction: The Liberal Republicans in the Civil War Era* (New York: Fordham University Press, 2006), xi-xxv; See also Heather Cox Richardson, *The Death of Reconstruction: Race Labor, and Politics in the Post-Civil War North, 1865-1901* (Cambridge, MA: Harvard University Press, 2001).

11. See Robert E. May, *The Southern Dream of a Caribbean Empire, 1854-1861* (Athens: University of Georgia Press, 1989), 1-20; Eric T. L. Love, *Race over Empire: Racism and U. S. Imperialism, 1865-1900* (Chapel Hill: University of North Carolina Press, 2004), 20-25.

12. John Y. Simon, ed., *The Papers of Ulysses S. Grant*, Vol. 21: *November 1, 1870–May 31, 1871* (Carbondale: Southern Illinois University Press, 1998), 53.

13. Orders to Orville E. Babcock from Hamilton Fish, No Date, Orville E. Babcock Collection, Ulysses S. Grant Presidential Library (USGPL), Mississippi State University.

14. Orders to Orville E. Babcock; *Report of the Select Committee Appointed to Investigate the Memorial of Davis Hatch*, SR 234, June 1870, 189; Walter LaFeber, *The New Empire: An Interpretation of American Expansion, 1860-1868* (Ithaca, NY: Cornell University Press, 1963), 36-37.

15. Charles W. Calhoun, *The Presidency of Ulysses S. Grant* (Lawrence: University Press of Kansas, 2017), 206-210; See also Ryan P. Semmes, "Hiram R. Revels, Ulysses S. Grant, Party Politics, and the Annexation of Santo Domingo," *Journal of Mississippi History* LXXX, no. 1-2 (Spring-Summer 2018): 49-65.

16. Allan Nevins, *Hamilton Fish: The Inner History of the Grant Administration* (New York: Dodd, Mead and Company, 1937), 265-72; *Report of the Select Committee to Investigate the Memorial of Davis Hatch*, 36; Eric Foner, *Reconstruction: America's Unfinished Revolution, 1863-1877* (New York: Perennial Classic, 1988), 494-95; Love, *Race over Empire*, 38; Stephen McCullough claimed that Babcock not only exceeded his instructions but "that Babcock conspired with Baez to secure annexation is beyond question." McCullough cited Babcock's diaries and notes in reaching his conclusion. Stephen McCullough, *The Caribbean Policy of the Ulysses S. Grant Administration: Foreshadowing an Informal Empire* (Lanham, MD: Lexington Books, 2018), 56; Ron Chernow echoes the Nevins claim. Ron Chernow, *Grant* (New York: Penguin Press, 2017), 664.

17. Prior, *Between Freedom and Progress*, 160-61; Eric Foner, *Free Soil, Free Labor, Free Men: The Ideology of the Republican Party before the Civil War* (New York: Oxford University Press, 1995), 18-19.

18. Frank Moya Pons, *The Dominican Republic: A National History* (Princeton, NJ: Markus Wiener, 1995), 143–96; Anne Eller notes that historically Europeans, Haitians, and Dominicans rallied against US plans to establish leases in Samana Bay, including a plan hatched by Williams Cazneau and his wife, See: Anne Eller, *We Dream Together: Dominican Independence, Haiti, and the Fight for Caribbean Freedom* (Durham, NC: Duke University Press, 2016), 51–53.

19. Pons, *The Dominican Republic*, 200–218; William Javier Nelson, *Almost a Territory: America's Attempt to Annex the Dominican Republic* (Newark: University of Delaware Press, 1990), 46–47.

20. Christopher Wilkins, "'They had heard of emancipation and the enfranchisement of their race': The African American Colonists of Samaná, Reconstruction, and the State of Santo Domingo," *The Civil War as Global Conflict: Transnational Meanings of the American Civil War*, eds. David T. Gleeson and Simon Lewis (Columbia: University of South Carolina Press, 2014), 211–34.

21. Wilkins, "'They had heard of emancipation,'" 211–34; Richardson, *The Death of Reconstruction*, 143; Summers, *The Ordeal of the Reunion*, 221–22, 305–6.

22. April 6, 1869, HF diary, HF papers, LC; June 21, 1869, HF diary, HF papers, LC; Andrew Priest, "Thinking about Empire: The Administration of Ulysses S. Grant, Spanish Colonialism and the Ten Years' War in Cuba," *Journal of American Studies* 48, no. 2 (May 2014): 547–48.

23. October 19, 1869, HF diary, HF papers, LC.

24. John F. Marszalek, *Sherman: A Soldier's Passion for Order* (Carbondale: Southern Illinois University Press, 1993), 365–72; Summer, *Ordeal of the Reunion*, 221; October 25, 1869, HF diary, HF papers, LC; See Christina Cecelia Davidson, "Black Protestants in a Catholic Land: The AME Church in the Dominican Republic, 1899–1916," *New West Indian Guide* 89, no. 3/4 (2015): 258–88, Davidson, "Disruptive Silences: The AME Church and Dominican-Haitian Relations," *Journal of Africana Religions* 5, no. 1 (2017): 1–25 and Yingling, *Siblings of Soil*, 209–15, for examinations of the racial undertones of the Catholic-Protestant divide in the Dominican Republic.

25. Howard Jones, *Blue and Gray Diplomacy: A History of Union and Confederate Foreign Relations* (Chapel Hill: University of North Carolina Press, 2010), 192–93; Frank J. Merli, *The Alabama, British Neutrality, and the American Civil War* (Bloomington: Indiana University Press, 2004), 63–66; Phillip E. Myers, *Dissolving Tensions: Rapprochement and Resolution in British-American-Canadian Relations in the Treaty of Washington Era, 1865–1914* (Kent, OH: Kent State University Press, 2015), 21, 77.

26. Jones, *Blue and Gray Diplomacy*, 56–63; Stahr, *Seward*, 522–23; March 5, 1869, Benjamin Moran Journals, LC.

27. Adrian Cook, *The Alabama Claims: American Politics and Anglo-American Relations, 1865–1872* (Ithaca, NY: Cornell University Press, 1975), 73–102; "The

Alabama Claims" Speech by the Honorable Charles Sumner, Delivered in Executive Session of the United States Senate, Delivered on Tuesday, April 13, 1869, Against the Ratification of the Johnson-Clarendon Treaty for the Settlement of the Alabama and other Claims (London: Stevens Brothers, 1869). See also Nevins, *Hamilton Fish*.

28. Lucy E. Salyer, *Under the Starry Flag: How a Band of Irish Americans Joined the Fenian Revolt and Sparked a Crisis over Citizenship* (Cambridge, MA: Belknap Press of Harvard University Press, 2018), 70–71; See also Christian G. Samito, *Becoming American Under Fire: Irish Americans, African Americans, and the Politics of Citizenship during the Civil War Era* (Ithaca, NY: Cornell University Press, 2009), 196–99.

29. Calhoun, *The Presidency of Ulysses S. Grant*, 160–61, 181–86; Andre Fleche, "The Last Filibuster: The Ten Years' War in Cuba and the Legacy of the American Civil War," in David Prior, ed. *Reconstruction and Empire: The Legacies of Abolition and Union Victory for an Imperial Age* (New York: Fordham University Press, 2022), 46–47; For more on Daniel Sickles Ministry to Madrid see Gregory P. Downs, *The Second American Revolution: The Civil War-Era Struggle over Cuba and the Rebirth of the American Republic* (Chapel Hill: University of North Carolina Press, 2019), 113–21.

30. Franklin W. Knight, *Slave Society in Cuba during the Nineteenth Century* (Madison: University of Wisconsin Press, 1970), 6, 22, 188–89; José Alvarez Junco and Adrian Shubert, eds., *Spanish History Since 1808* (London: Arnold Publishers, 2000), 79–89; For more on the racial and class makeup of Cuban nationalism in the Cuban rebellion see Ada Ferrer, *Insurgent Cuba: Race, Nation, and Revolution, 1868–1898* (Chapel Hill: University of North Carolina Press, 1999), 1–12.

31. "Reasons why San Domingo should be Annexed to the United States," [1869–1870], Series 3: Speeches, Reports, Messages, 1863–1876, Ulysses S. Grant Papers, LC; For more on the United States' support of slavery in Cuba through importing tropical goods see Louis A. Perez, Jr., *Cuba and the United States: Ties of Singular Intimacy* (Athens: University of Georgia Press, 1997), 55–65; Gerald Horne, *Race to Revolution: The United States and Cuba during Slavery and Jim Crow* (New York: Monthly Review Press, 2014), 115–16; Ada Ferrer, *Cuba: An American History* (New York: Scribner, 2022), 109–11.

32. December 13, 1869, HF diary, HF papers, LC; See also Ryan P. Semmes, "Counselor not Savior: Hamilton Fish and Foreign Policy Decision-Making during the Grant Administration," *American Nineteenth Century History* (December 2022).

33. Aaron Sheehan-Dean, *The Calculus of Violence: How Americans Fought the Civil War* (Cambridge, MA: Harvard University Press, 2018), 27.

34. *The* (New York) *Sun*, March 17, 1869.

35. *The* (New York) *Sun*, March 26, 1869.

36. Richard Gott, *Cuba: A New History* (New Haven, CT: Yale University Press, 2004), 72–73; Ada Ferrer, *Insurgent Cuba: Race, Nation, and Revolution, 1868–1898* (Chapel Hill: University of North Carolina Press, 1999), 4–7.

37. Order, July 14, 1869, Simon, ed. *Papers of Ulysses S. Grant*, Vol. 19, 210–11; HF to J. C. B. Davis, July 23, 1869; HF to Daniel Sickles, July 29, 1869; Sickles to HF, August 1, 1869; Sickles to HF, August 13, 1869; USG to HF, August 14, 1869, HF papers, LC; See Fleche, "The Last Filibuster," 32.

38. Stephen McCullough, *The Caribbean Policy of the Ulysses S. Grant Administration: Foreshadowing an Informal Empire* (Lanham, MD: Lexington Books, 2018), 2–9; HF to J. C. B. Davis, August 16, 1869 and USG Memorandum, [August 31], 1869, HF papers, LC; Allen Ottens, *General John A. Rawlins: No Ordinary Man* (Bloomington: Indiana University Press, 2021), 504–7, 512–13.

39. J. C. B. Davis to HF, August 22, 1869, HF papers, LC.

40. No. 6 Gabriel Suarez Del Villar, Cuban Claims, HF papers, LC.

Chapter 2: Challenges to Annexation

1. *Report of the Select Committee Appointed to Investigate the Memorial of Davis Hatch*, SR 234, June 1870, 137; November 10, 1869, Orville E. Babcock Diary, Orville E. Babcock collection (hereafter OEB), Ulysses S. Grant Presidential Library (hereafter USGPL), Mississippi State University.

2. *Davis Hatch*, 51; November 18–29, 1869, Babcock Diary, OEB collection, USGPL.

3. The *Evening Star*, December 24, 1869; *Alexandria Gazette and Virginia Advertiser*, December 30, 1869.

4. A recent study by Stephen McCullough examining the Grant administration's policy in the Caribbean posits that Grant and Fish laid the groundwork for future economic expansion into the region that would be borne out in the late nineteenth century. Stephen McCullough, *The Caribbean Policy of the Ulysses S. Grant Administration: Foreshadowing an Informal Empire* (Lanham, MD: Lexington Books, 2018), 183; Walter F. LaFeber, *Cambridge History of American Foreign Relations* Vol. II: *The American Search for Opportunity, 1865–1913* (Cambridge: Cambridge University Press, 1993), 66–67.

5. Mark Wahlgren Summers, *The Ordeal of the Reunion: A History of Reconstruction* (Chapel Hill: University of North Carolina Press, 2014), 13; Historian Gregg French notes that Secretary of State Hamilton Fish believed that American intervention in the Caribbean and the introduction of non-white people into the citizenry of the United States created instability both domestically and internationally. See French, "Domestic Stability and Imperial Continuities: U.S.-Spanish Relations in the Reconstruction Era," in David Prior, ed., *Reconstruction and Empire: The Legacies of Abolition and Union Victory for an Imperial Age* (New York: Fordham University Press, 2022), 79–104.

6. For more on the growing scholarship of the Civil War-era in a global context, see: C. A. Bayly, *The Birth of the Modern World, 1780–1914: Global Connections and Comparisons* (Malden, MA: Blackwell Publishing, 2004), 161–64; Amanda

Foreman, *A World on Fire: Britain's Crucial Role in the American Civil War* (New York: Random House, 2012); Howard Jones, *Union in Peril: The Crisis over British Intervention in the Civil War* (Chapel Hill: University of North Carolina Press, 1992); Jones, *Blue and Gray Diplomacy* (Chapel Hill: University of North Carolina Press, 2010); Doyle, *The Cause of All Nations*; David T. Gleeson and Simon Lewis, eds., *The Civil War as Global Conflict*; David Armitage, et al., "Interchange: Nationalism and Internationalism in the Era of the Civil War," *The Journal of American History* 98, no. 2 (September 2011): 455–89; Jay Sexton, "Toward a Synthesis of Foreign Relations in the Civil War Era, 1848–77," *American Nineteenth Century History* 5, no. 3 (Fall 2004): 50–73; Patrick J. Kelly, "The European Revolutions of 1848 and the Transnational Turn in Civil War History," *Journal of the Civil War Era* 4, no. 3 (September 2014): 431–43; Thomas Bender *A Nation Among Nations: America's Place in World History* (New York: Hill and Wang, 2006); USG to United States House of Representatives, March 30, 1870, Series 3: Speeches, Reports, Messages, 1863–1876, Ulysses S. Grant Papers, LC.

7. Eric T. L. Love examined the ways in which race was used to defeat the annexation of the Dominican Republic in his book *Race over Empire*. He argued that Grant kept the racial motivation for annexation—possible African American migration to the territory—a secret because he understood that it would ruin the chances of Senate approval of the treaty. Love noted that all of Grant's messages to Congress on annexation left out the migration (or as Love calls it, colonization) of African Americans which Grant mentioned in his memorandum and he faults Grant for failing to come up with a better solution to the racial strife of the Reconstruction South than the mass removal of African Americans. Eric T. L. Love, *Race over Empire: Racism and U. S. Imperialism, 1865–1900* (Chapel Hill: University of North Carolina Press, 2004), 27–72; Sexton, *The Monroe Doctrine*, 164–65.

8. "Reasons why San Domingo should be Annexed to the United States," [1869–1870], Series 3: Speeches, Reports, Messages, 1863–1876, Ulysses S. Grant Papers, LC. Bracketed materials added by Hamilton Fish or his clerk; Grant commissioned seven surveys of Nicaragua during his presidency as his preferred location for a route across Central America. For a look at the attempts at a Nicaraguan Canal see Lawrence A. Clayton, "The Nicaragua Canal in the Nineteenth Century: Prelude to American Empire in the Caribbean," *Journal of Latin American Studies* 19, no. 2 (November 1987): 323–52; For an overview of steam powered transportation in this era see Jay Sexton, "Steam Transport, Sovereignty, and Empire in North America, circa 1850–1854," *Journal of the Civil War Era* 7, no. 4 (December 2017): 620–47.

9. "Reasons why" memo; See Christina Cecelia Davidson, "Black Protestants in a Catholic Land: The AME Church in the Dominican Republic, 1899–1916," *New West Indian Guide* 89, no. 3/4 (2015): 258–88 and Davidson, "Disruptive Silences:

The AME Church and Dominican-Haitian Relations," *Journal of Africana Religions* 5, no. 1 (2017): 1–25.

10. "Reasons why" memo; Love, *Race over Empire*, 45–47; For an interesting analysis of pre-Civil War African American immigration to the Dominican Republic see Christopher Wilkins, "'They had heard of emancipation and the enfranchisement of their race': The African American Colonists of Samana, Reconstruction, and the State of Santo Domingo," in Gleeson and Lewis, eds. *The Civil War as Global Conflict*, 211–34; Prior to the Great Migration, 90 percent of African Americans lived in the South; following the Great Migration, 47 percent of all African Americans were then living in the North and West; See Isabel Wilkerson, "The Great Migration, 1914–1919," in *Four Hundred Souls: A Community History of African America, 1619–2019*, eds. Ibram X. Kendi and Keisha N. Blain (New York: OneWorld, 2021), 278–82.

11. Nathan Miller, *The U.S. Navy: A History*, 3rd ed. (Annapolis, MD: Naval Institute Press, 1997), 143–44.

12. "Reasons why" memo; Charles Sumner, *The Alabama Claims Speech of the Honourable Charles Sumner, Delivered in Executive Session of the United States Senate, On Tuesday, April 13th, 1869, Against the ratification of the Johnson-Clarendon Treaty for the Settlement of the Alabama and Other Claims* (London: Stevens Brothers, 1869), 24–25.

13. "A Good Margin," *Birmingham Daily Post*, April 30, 1869, 3; "Quiet people . . . ," *Gloucester Journal*, May 15, 1869, 5; "Our London Correspondent," *The Grantham Journal*, May 15, 1869, 3; "Our American Quarrel," *The Manchester Courier and Lancashire General Advertiser*, May 1, 1869, 7; Two interesting analyses of the differences between the United States and Great Britain that examine the *Alabama* Claims are: Frank J. Merli, *The Alabama, British Neutrality, and the American Civil War* (Bloomington: Indiana University Press, 2004) and Philip E. Myers, *Dissolving Tensions: Rapprochement and Resolution in British-American-Canadian Relations in the Treaty of Washington Era, 1865–1914* (Kent, OH: The Kent State University Press, 2015).

14. "Reasons why San Domingo . . ."; For more on exports and imports from the Caribbean see Bayly, *The Birth of the Modern World*, 129–169; Summers, *Ordeal*, 396.

15. "Reasons why San Domingo . . ."; For more on Spain, Cuba, and slavery see Bayly, *The Birth of the Modern World*, 404–405; H. L. Wessling, *The European Colonial Empires, 1815–1919*, trans. Diane Webb (Harlow, England: Pearson Longman, 2004), 82–84; Don H. Doyle, ed., *American Civil Wars: The United States, Latin American, Europe, and the Crisis of the 1860s* (Chapel Hill: University of North Carolina Press, 2017); McCullough, *The Caribbean Policy of the Ulysses S. Grant Administration*, 95–96; For an excellent analysis of the legacy of the Monroe Doctrine by historians Konstantin Dierks, Juan Pablo Scarfi, Marixa Lasso, Paolo Riguzzi,

Caitlin Fitz, Nicholas Guyatt, and Jay Sexton, see "Forum: The Monroe Doctrine at 200," *Diplomatic History* 47, no. 5 (November 2023); Rafael Marquese, "The Legacies of the Second Slavery: The Cotton and Coffee Economies of the United States and Brazil during the Reconstruction Era, 1865–1904," in *United States across the Americas*, ed. William Link (Gainesville: University Press of Florida, 2019), 11–46.

16. "Reasons why" memo; For more on Manifest Destiny and the purchase of Alaska see LaFeber, *The Cambridge History of American Foreign Relations*, 12–20 and 42–58; Anders Stephanson, *Manifest Destiny: American Expansion and the Empire of Right* (New York: Hill and Wang, 1995); Linda S. Hudson, *Mistress of Manifest Destiny: A Biography of Jane McManus Storm Cazneau, 1807–1878* (Austin: Texas State Historical Commission, 2001), Jane Cazneau was the wife of William Cazneau, the land speculator behind the annexation scheme and confidante of Grant's private secretary Orville Babcock; Thomas R. Hietala, *Manifest Design: American Exceptionalism and Empire* (Ithaca, NY: Cornell University Press, 2002); Amy S. Greenberg, *Manifest Manhood and the Antebellum American Empire* (New York: Cambridge University Press, 2005); Walter Stahr, *Seward: Lincoln's Indispensable Man* (New York: Simon and Schuster, 2013), 482–507; Daniel J. Burge, *A Failed Vision of Empire: The Collapse of Manifest Destiny, 1845–1872* (Lincoln: University of Nebraska Press, 2022), 151–70; For more on Seward and Grant's disagreements over how to handle the alliance between France and Mexico after the Civil War see Don H. Doyle, "Reconstruction and Anti-Imperialism: The United States and Mexico," in *United States Reconstruction across the Americas*, ed. William Link (Gainesville: University Press of Florida, 2019), 47–80.

17. For analyses of this meeting, see William S. McFeely, *Grant: A Biography* (New York: W. W. Norton and Co., 1981), 340–41; Eric Foner, *Reconstruction: America's Unfinished Revolution, 1863–1877* (New York: Harper and Row, 1988), 494–97; Geoffrey Perret, *Ulysses S. Grant: Soldier and President* (New York: Random House, 1997), 396–97; David Donald, *Charles Sumner* (New York: De Capo Press, 1996), Part II, 434–39; Jean Edward Smith, *Grant* (New York: Simon and Schuster, 2001), 503–4; Ronald C. White, *American Ulysses: A Life of Ulysses S. Grant* (New York: Random House, 2016), 509–11; Ron Chernow, *Grant* (New York: Penguin Press, 2017), 691–92; Charles W. Calhoun, *The Presidency of Ulysses S. Grant* (Lawrence: University of Press of Kansas, 2017), 230–32.

18. USG to Untied States Senate, May 31, 1870, Series 3: Speeches, Reports, Messages, 1863–1876, Ulysses S. Grant Papers, LC. Parenthetical additions are edits made to the original document by either Ulysses S. Grant, Hamilton Fish, or Fish's clerk. In his diary, Fish recorded that Grant had written the message three days prior to sending it to Congress, noting that he had left the President with the vote count for annexation from the Dominican Republic in the same cabinet meeting. See May 28, 1870, HF diary, HF papers, LC. Eric T. L. Love focuses his analysis not on the idea of emancipation but on the colonization of African Americans to the Dominican

Republic: *Race over Empire*, 44–45. For more on the Grant corollary see Alan Nevins *Hamilton Fish: The Inner History of the Grant Administration* (New York: Dodd, Mead, and Company, 1937), 328–29; LaFeber, *Cambridge History of American Foreign Relations*, 67–68; Brian Loveman, *No Higher Law: American Foreign Policy and the Western Hemisphere Since 1776* (Chapel Hill: University of North Carolina Press, 2010), 80–81.

19. May 21, 1871, HF diary, HF papers, LC; USG to United States Senate, May 31, 1870, USG, LC.

20. USG to United States Senate, May 31, 1870, USG, LC.

21. USG to United States Senate, May 31, 1870, USG, LC.

22. USG to United States Senate, May 31, 1870, USG, LC. For more on Emancipation in Cuba see Wesseling, *The European Colonial Empires*, 82–84; for more on Republican antagonism to African American rights see Richardson, *The Death of Reconstruction*, 143–46.

23. USG to United States Senate, May 31, 1870, USG, LC.

24. USG to United States Senate, May 31, 1870, USG, LC; Jay Sexton, *Debtor Diplomacy: Finance and American Foreign Relations in the Civil War Era, 1837–1873* (New York: Oxford University Press, 2005), 10–19.

25. USG to United States Senate, May 31, 1870, USG, LC.

26. Sexton, *The Monroe Doctrine*, 108–11.

27. See news clippings: "Cuba and the United States," *Evening Post*; "Spain Bullying the United States," September 21, 1869; "Afraid of the People"; "Discouraging Accounts from the Cuban Patriots," January 6, 1870; "The Republican Party and Cuba," (Newspaper names not given), Hamilton Fish Papers, LC.

28. Myers, *Dissolving Tensions*, 84–85; Lester Burrell Shippee, *Canadian American Relations, 1849–1874* (New Haven, CT: Yale University Press, 1939), 204–5.

29. See: Shippee, *Canadian American Relations*, 213–39 and 262–87; Robert E. Ankli, "The Reciprocity Treaty of 1854," *The Canadian Journal of Economics* 4, no. 1 (February 1971): 1–3; David T. Gleeson, *The Irish in the South, 1815–1877* (Chapel Hill: University of North Carolina Press, 2001); Mitchell Snay, *Fenians, Freedmen, and Southern Whites: Race and Nationality in the Era of Reconstruction* (Baton Rouge: Louisiana State University Press, 2007); Sexton, *The Monroe Doctrine*, 129; Caleb Richardson, "'The Failure of the Men to Come Up': The Reinvention of Irish-American Nationalism," *Reconstruction in a Globalizing World*, ed. David Prior (New York: Fordham University Press, 2018), 121–44.

30. November 11, 1870, December 20, 1870, HF diary, HF papers, LC; Box 57, G. Kemble to HF, March 15, 1869; Box 61, Francis Lieber to HF, June 8, 1869, HF papers, LC; George S. Boutwell to USG, July 29, 1870, *PUSG* Vol. 20, 256.

31. See William Glade, "Latin America and the International Economy," *The Cambridge History of Latin America, Vol. IV, 1870 to 1930*, ed. Leslie Bethell (New York: Cambridge University Press, 1986), 1–56; Ada Ferrer, *Insurgent Cuba: Race,*

Nation, and Revolution, 1868–1898 (Chapel Hill: University of North Carolina Press, 1999), 3; Richard Gott, *Cuba: A New History* (New Haven, CT: Yale University Press, 2004), 71–112; Rebecca J. Scott, *Degrees of Freedom: Louisiana and Cuba After Slavery* (Cambridge, MA: Harvard University Press, 2005), 94–128; Jay Sexton, "The United States, the Cuban Rebellion, and the Multilateral Initiative of 1875," *Diplomatic History* 30, no. 3 (June 2006): 335–65; Lisandro Pérez, *Sugar, Cigars, and Revolution: The Making of Cuban New York* (New York: New York University Press, 2018); Gregory P. Downs, *The Second American Revolution: The Civil War-Era Struggle over Cuba and the Rebirth of the American Republic* (Chapel Hill: University of North Carolina Press, 2019).

32. Allison Clark Efford, "The Arms Scandal of 1870–1872: Immigrant Liberal Republicans and America's Place in the World," *Reconstruction in a Globalizing World*, ed. David Prior (New York: Fordham University Press, 2018), 94–120; Philip M. Katz, *From Appomattox to Montmartre: Americans and the Paris Commune* (Cambridge, MA: Harvard University Press, 1998), 138–40; Richardson, *The Death of Reconstruction*, 83–117.

33. USG to Edwards Pierrepont, September 13, 1875, John Y. Simon, ed., *The Papers of Ulysses S. Grant*: Vol. 26: 1875 (Carbondale: Southern Illinois University Press, 2003), 312; *New York Herald*, June 22, 1879; Heather Cox Richardson, "North and West of Reconstruction: Studies in Political Economy," *Reconstructions: New Perspectives on the Postbellum United States*, ed. Thomas J. Brown (New York: Oxford University Press, 2006), 66–90; Martha S. Jones, *Birthright Citizens: A History of Race and Rights in Antebellum America* (New York: Cambridge University Press, 2018), 146–53.

Chapter 3: Annexation's Failure

1. While it was the case that the president and the secretary of state were of one mind on foreign policy, what most concerned Fish was the rumors in the press that the two were constantly at odds. The *Nashville Union and American* published a report from the *New York Sun* that Grant would replace Fish with Senator Justice Smith Morrill. A few weeks later, the same newspaper reported that Fish would replace the American minister to Great Britain; May 31, 1870, Hamilton Fish diary, Hamilton Fish papers, LC; USG to Adam Badeau, October 23, 1870, John Y. Simon, ed., *The Papers of Ulysses S. Grant*, Vol. 20: *November 1, 1869-October 31, 1870* (Carbondale: Southern Illinois University Press, 1995), 318; *Nashville Union and American*, June 7, 1870; June 25, 1870.

2. June 13, 1870, July 10, 1870, HF diary, HF papers, LC; See: Ryan P. Semmes, "Counselor not Savior: Hamilton Fish and Foreign Policy Decision-Making during the Grant Administration," *American Nineteenth Century History* (December 2022).

3. Charles W. Calhoun, *The Presidency of Ulysses S. Grant* (Lawrence: University Press of Kansas, 2017), 194–195; June 17, 1870, HF Diary, HF papers, LC.

4. Francis Lieber to Ulysses S. Grant, October 26, 1868, John Y. Simon, ed., *The Papers of Ulysses S. Grant*, Vol. 19 (Carbondale: Southern Illinois University Press, 1995), 55. Emphasis in original.

5. Lucy E. Salyer, "Reconstructing the Immigrant: The Naturalization Act of 1870 in Global Perspective," *Journal of the Civil War Era* 11, no. 3 (September 2021): 388–95; See also Lucy E. Salyer, *Under the Starry Flag: How a Band of Irish Americans Joined the Fenian Revolt and Sparked a Crisis over Citizenship* (Cambridge, MA: Belknap Press, 2018).

6. Salyer, "Reconstructing the Immigrant," 388–95; "An Act concerning the Rights of American Citizen in foreign States," 15th Statutes at Large 223: 40th Congress, 2nd Session, Chapter 249, 1868, 223–24; Moon-Ho Jung, *Coolies and Cane: Race, Labor and Sugar in the Age of Emancipation* (Baltimore, MD: Johns Hopkins University Press, 2006), 138–45.

7. Jeff Diamond, "African American Attitudes toward United States Immigration Policy," *International Migration Review* 32, no. 2 (Summer 1998): 453; Rick Halpern, "Solving the 'Labour Problem': Race, Work and the State in the Sugar Industries of Louisiana and Natal, 1870–1910," *Journal of Southern African Studies* 30, no. 1, (March 2004): 29; Frederick Douglass to Charles Sumner, July 6, 1870, Philip S. Foner, ed., *The Life and Writings of Frederick Douglass*: Vol. IV, *Reconstruction and After* (New York: International Publishers, 1955), 222–23; Sumner "Naturalization Laws: No Discrimination on Account of Color. Remarks in Senate, July 2 and 4 1870," in *Charles Sumner: His Complete Works*, Vol. XVIII, ed. George F. Hoar (Boston: Lee and Shepherd, 1900), 144–68, http://www.gutenberg.org; *New National Era*, August 10, 1871.

8. Jung, *Coolies and Cane*, 107–9, 138–45; *New National Era*, March 9, 1871; March 30, 1871; Frederick Rudolph, "Chinamen in Yankeedom: Anti-Unionism in Massachusetts in 1870," *American Historical Review* 53, no. 1 (October 1947): 1–29; Joshua Paddison, *American Heathens: Religion, Race, and Reconstruction in California* (San Marino, CA: Huntington Library Press & University of California Press, 2012), 20–21.

9. HF to USG, August 16, 1870, HF papers, LC; October 7, 1870, HF diary, HF papers, LC.

10. *Semi-Weekly Louisianian*, August 24, 1871; David W. Blight, *Frederick Douglass: Prophet of Freedom* (New York: Simon and Schuster, 2018), 537; Calhoun, *Presidency*, 187–197; See: Summers, *Ordeal*, 209–19; USG to HF, September 17, 1869, HF papers, LC; Rebecca J. Scott showed that calls of violence from the Cuban Junta in New York had mixed results in the actual rebellion in Cuba. A December 1869 call by the New York Junta on the free workers of Cuba to set fire to the cane fields resulted in very few burning incidents. In fact, she notes, that year posted a record harvest. See Scott, *Slave Emancipation in Cuba*, 62–63; *Slavery in Cuba: A Report of the Proceedings of the Meeting held at Cooper Institute, New York City, December 13, 1872* (New York: Powers, MacGowan, and Slipper Printers, 1872), 16–17; Earl Ofari,

"Let Your Motto Be Resistance": The Life and Thought of Henry Highland Garnet (Boston: Beacon Press, 1972), 121.

11. Frederick Douglass to S. R. Scottron, March 29, 1873, Frederick Douglass papers, LC.

12. Charles Callan Tansill, *The United States and Santo Domingo, 1798–1873* (Baltimore, MD: Johns Hopkins University Press, 1938), 383–89; See also David Donald, *Charles Sumner* (New York: De Capo Press, 1996), II, 435.

13. Fish quoted in Donald, *Charles Sumner* II, 439; Tansill, *The U.S. and Santo Domingo*, 389; "Speech of Gerrit Smith to his Neighbors, in Petersboro, N. Y., June 22, 1872," 3, Broadsides and Ephemera Collection, David M. Rubenstein Rare Book & Manuscript Library, Duke University Libraries https://idn.duke.edu; Beverly Wilson Palmer, ed., *The Selected Letters of Charles Sumner*, Vol. Two (Boston, MA: Northeastern University Press, 1990), 597–601; See also Charles Sumner, "Republicanism vs. Grantism: Speech of the Honorable Charles E. Sumner of Massachusetts, delivered in the Senate, May 31, 1872," (Washington, DC: F. and J. Rives and George A. Bailey, 1872), 22–25, Pamphlet collection, Ulysses S. Grant Presidential Library.

14. Mark Wahlgren Summers, *The Era of Good Stealings* (New York: Oxford University Press, 1993), vii–xi; August 20, 1869, Diary: The First Journey to Santo Domingo, July 17 to September 4, 1869, Orville E. Babcock Papers, Ulysses S. Grant Presidential Library; See also Mark Wahlgren Summers, *The Press Gang: Newspapers and Politics, 1865–1878* (Chapel Hill: University of North Carolina Press, 1994).

15. Simon, *Papers of Ulysses S. Grant*, Vol. 20, 180n; *Report of the Commission of inquiry to Santo Domingo, with the introductory message of the President, special reports made to the commission, state papers furnished by the Dominican government, and the statements of over seventy witnesses* (Washington: Government Printing Office, 1871), xxxix, xlvi.

16. April 4, 1870; May 21, 1870, HF diary HF Papers, LC; *New York Herald* quoted in Eric T. L. Love, *Race over Empire: Racism and U. S. Imperialism, 1865–1900* (Chapel Hill: University of North Carolina Press, 2004), 56–58; *New York Herald*, March 25, 1870; March 26, 1870; March 28, 1870.

17. December 23, 1870, HF diary, HF papers, LC; David Donald cheekily suggests that Fish was not an expert in psychology and that Sumner was not acting any different or out of the ordinary compared to previous Congressional fights; See David Herbert Donald, *Charles Sumner and the Rights of Man* (Open Road Media, 2016), 66, Google Books.

18. USG to HF, March 22, 1870, HF papers, LC; Love, *Race over Empire*, 52.

19. Love, *Race over Empire*, 52–55; "Annexation of San Domingo," Speech of the Honorable Carl Schurz, of Missouri, in the United States Senate, January 11, 1871, *Speeches, correspondence and political papers of Carl Schurz*, Vol. II, ed. Frederic Bancroft (New York: G. P. Putnam Sons, 1913), 71–122.

20. Mark Wahlgren Summers, *The Ordeal of the Reunion: A New History of Reconstruction* (Chapel Hill; University of North Carolina Press, 2014), 220–24.

21. OEB to Adam Badeau, June 18, 1870, *Papers of Ulysses S. Grant*, Vol. 20, 163–164n; J. C. B. Davis to OEB, February 28, 1870, Orville E. Babcock papers, Newberry Library; Love, *Race over Empire,* 64; Babcock was referring to Sumner's highly publicized divorce from Alice Hooper where, rumor had it, she left Sumner on the grounds of impotency. The marriage most likely failed due in large part to the wide age difference between the two. Hooper left the United States for Europe and Sumner sued for divorce on the grounds of desertion. Donald, *Charles Sumner* II, 313–14.

22. *New Era*, February 24, 1870; George C. Rable, *But There Was No Peace: The Role of Violence in the Politics of Reconstruction* (Athens: University of Georgia Press, 2007), xiii–xvi; Carole Emberton, *Beyond Redemption: Race, Violence, and the American South after the Civil War* (Chicago: University of Chicago Press, 2013), 5–7.

23. Calhoun, *Presidency*, 236; David Donald, *Charles Sumner* II, 443.

24. Knoxville *Daily Chronicle*, March 28, 1870.

25. Quoted in Calhoun, *Presidency,* 238.

26. See Ofari, 121; Love, *Race over Empire: Racism*, 27–72; Merline Pitre, "Frederick Douglass and the Annexation of Santo Domingo," *Journal of Negro History* 62, no. 4 (October 1972): 390–400; Merline Pitre, "Frederick Douglass and American Diplomacy in the Caribbean," *Journal of Black Studies* 13, no. 4 (June 1983): 457–475; Nicholas Guyatt, "America's Conservatory: Race, Reconstruction, and the Santo Domingo Debate," *Journal of American History* 97, no. 4 (March 2011): 974–1000.

27. John R. McKivigan, "Stalwart Douglass: *Life and Times* as Political Manifesto," *Journal of African American History* 99, no. 1-2 (Winter-Spring 2014): 46–55; FD to OEB, May 31, 1875, John Y. Simon, ed., *The Papers of Ulysses S. Grant*, Vol. 26: *1875* (Carbondale: Southern Illinois University Press, 2003), 135; Eric Foner, *Reconstruction: America's Unfinished Revolution* (New York: Perennial Classics, 1988), 291.

28. David Blight, *Frederick Douglass: Prophet of Freedom* (New York: Simon and Schuster, 2018), 525, 532–36.

29. Pitre, "Frederick Douglass and the Annexation of Santo Domingo," 390–393; January 3, 1871, HF diary, HF papers, LC; African Americans and White abolitionists were unhappy with Douglass's appointment as an assistant secretary. Many saw the appointment as subordinate to the commissioners; however, Douglass was happy to accept the post. Blight, *Frederick Douglass*, 538.

30. Charles Sumner, "Naboth's Vineyard: Speech of Hon. Charles Sumner, of Massachusetts, on the Proposed Annexation of 'The Island of San Domingo,' December 21, 1870," (Washington, DC: F. and J. Rives and George A. Bailey, 1870).

31. *Report of the Commission of inquiry to Santo Domingo, with the introductory message of the President, special reports made to the commission, state papers*

furnished by the Dominican government, and the statements of over seventy witnesses (Washington, DC: Government Printing Office, 1871), 32.

32. Quoted in Pitre, "Frederick Douglass and the Annexation of Santo Domingo," 398; Frederick Douglass, *Life and Times of Frederick Douglass His Early Life as a Slave, His Escape from Bondage, and His Complete History to the Present Time: Electronic Edition*. 416 https://docsouth.unc.edu/neh/douglasslife/douglass.html [accessed 17 April 2024].

33. *New National Era*, January 12, 1871; "Santo Domingo: An Address Delivered in St. Louis, Missouri, on 13 January 1873," In *The Frederick Douglass Papers, Series One: Speeches, Debates, and Interviews*, Vol. 4: *1864–80*, eds. John W. Blassingame and John R. McKivigan (New Haven, CT: Yale University Press, 1991), 354–55.

34. Foner, *Reconstruction*, 496; Charles W. Calhoun, *Conceiving a New Republic: The Republican Party and the Southern Question, 1869–1900* (Lawrence: University Press of Kansas, 2006), 40; Summers, *Ordeal*, 221, 305.

35. *New National Era*, January 25, 1872; July 18, 1872; August 29, 1872; Blight, *Frederick Douglass*, 542; William S. McFeely, *Frederick Douglass* (New York: W. W. Norton, 1991), 277.

36. *New York Times*, March 30, 1871, quoted in H. W. Brands, *The Man Who Saved the Union: Ulysses Grant in War and Peace* (New York: Doubleday, 2012.), 462; Blight, *Frederick Douglass*, 542; Palmer, ed., *The Selected Letters of Charles Sumner*, 597–601; "Speech of Gerrit Smith," 3, https://idn.duke.edu, "Republican vs. Grantism," 5, 24, USGPL; Walter Stahr, *Stanton: Lincoln's War Secretary* (New York: Simon and Schuster, 2017), 532, 538–39; Edwin Stanton to USG, December 21, 1869, Simon, *PUSG* 20, 79–80.

37. February 3, 1871; March 31, 1871; October 27, 1871, HF diary, HF papers, LC.

38. *Semi-Weekly Louisianian*, May 4, 1871, August 20, 1871; *New National Era*, January 12, 1871; Foner, *Reconstruction*, 497–99.

39. June 25, 1870, HF diary, HF papers, LC.

40. Donald, *Charles Sumner* II, 9; 242–48; 352–54; 467–80; March 21, 1871, HF diary, HF papers, LC.

41. Donald, *Charles Sumner* II, 467–80; Calhoun, *Presidency*, 302–5.

42. Second Inaugural, March 4, 1873, John Y. Simon, ed. *The Papers of Ulysses S. Grant*, Vol. 24, *1873* (Carbondale: Southern Illinois University, 2000), 62; Draft Annual Message, December 5, 1876, John Y. Simon, ed. *The Papers of Ulysses S. Grant*, Vol. 28, *November 1, 1876-September 30, 1878* (Carbondale: Southern Illinois University, 2005), 68; John F. Marszalek, et al., *The Personal Memoirs of Ulysses S. Grant: The Complete Annotated Edition* (Cambridge, MA: Belknap Press of the Harvard University Press, 2017), 760–61.

43. John Hope Franklin, ed. *Reminiscences of an Active Life: The Autobiography of John Roy Lynch* (Chicago: University of Chicago Press, 1970), 248.

Chapter 4: Reconstructing the "Uncivilized"

1. William H. Armstrong, *Warrior in Two Camps: Ely S. Parker Union General and Seneca Chief* (Syracuse, NY: Syracuse University Press, 1978), 151; C. Joseph Genetin-Pilawa, *Crooked Paths of Allotment: The Fight over Federal Indian Policy after the Civil War* (Chapel Hill: University of North Carolina Press, 2012), 99–100; Alaina E. Roberts, *I've Been Here All the While: Black Freedom on Native Land* (Philadelphia: University of Pennsylvania Press, 2021), 2; *National Republican*, March 6, 1869.

2. See Heather Cox Richardson, *West from Appomattox: The Reconstruction of America after the Civil War* (New Haven, CT: Yale University Press, 2007); David Prior, "Civilization, Republic, Nation: Contested Keywords, Northern Republicans, and the Forgotten Reconstruction of Mormon Utah," *Civil War History* 56, no. 3 (September 2010): 283–310; Stacey L. Smith, "Beyond North and South: Putting the West in the Civil War and Reconstruction," *Journal of the Civil War Era* 6, no. 4 (December 2016): 566–91.

3. Inaugural Address, March 4, 1869, *The Papers of Ulysses S. Grant Digital Edition*. Charlottesville: University of Virginia Press. Rotunda, 2018. Vol. 19: July 1, 1868-October 31, 1869. http://rotunda.upress.virginia.edu; Francis Paul Prucha, *American Indian Policy in Crisis: Christian Reformers and the Indian, 1865–1900* (Norman: University of Oklahoma Press, 1976), 30–71; Robert H. Keller, Jr., *American Protestantism and United States Indian Policy, 1869-82* (Lincoln: University of Nebraska Press, 1983), 17–19; Norman J. Bender, *"New Hope for the Indians": The Grant Peace Policy and the Navajos in the 1870s* (Albuquerque: University of New Mexico Press, 1989), 1–8; C. Joseph Genetin-Pilawa, "Ely Parker and the Contentious Peace Policy," *Western Historical Quarterly* 41, no. 2 (Summer 2010): 196–217; C. Joseph Genetin-Pilawa, "Ely S. Parker and the Paradox of Reconstruction Politics in Indian Country," in *The World the Civil War Made*, eds. Gregory P. Downs and Kate Masur (Chapel Hill: University of North Carolina Press, 2015), 183–205; Mary Stockwell, *Interrupted Odyssey: Ulysses S. Grant and the American Indians* (Carbondale: Southern Illinois University Press, 2018), 47–49; Elliott West, *The Last Indian War: The Nez Perce Story* (New York: Oxford University Press, 2009), xxi–xxii.

4. Genetin-Pilawa, "Ely S. Parker and the Paradox of Reconstruction," 185; Parucha, *American Indian Policy in Crisis*, 48–49.

5. Stephen Kantrowitz, "'Not Quite Constitutionalized': The Meanings of 'Civilization' and the Limits of Native American Citizenship," in *The World the Civil War Made*, eds. Gregory P. Downs and Kate Masur (Chapel Hill: University of North Carolina Press, 2015), 75–77; Megan Kate Nelson, *Saving Yellowstone: Exploration and Preservation in Reconstruction America* (New York: Scribner, 2022), 74; Genetin-Pilawa, *Crooked Paths*, 88–89.

6. Genetin-Pilawa, *Crooked Paths*, 43; Armstrong, *Warrior in Two Camps*, 62–74; Ely S. Parker to Secretary of the Treasury Howell Cobb, April 11, 1857; Ely S.

Parker to F. Martindale, January 25, 1858, Ely Samuel Parker Papers, A.P24, Rare Books, Special Collections, and Preservation, River Campus Libraries, University of Rochester.

7. Nathaniel G. Taylor to USG, March 23, 1869; John M. Thayer to USG, March 6, 1869; Ebenezer R. Hoar to Jacob Cox, April 12, 1869; Jacob Cox to USG, April 13, 1869, *The Papers of Ulysses S. Grant Digital Edition*. Charlottesville: University of Virginia Press, Rotunda, 2018. Vol. 19: July 1, 1868—October 31, 1869. http://rotunda.upress.virginia.edu; Mary Stockwell, *Interrupted Odyssey: Ulysses S. Grant and the American Indians* (Carbondale: Southern Illinois University Press, 2018), 65–66; Fourteenth Amendment to the United States Constitution, https://www.law.cornell.edu.

8. *New York Herald*, December 9, 1870; *Yorkville (SC) Enquirer*, April 22, 1869.

9. Genetin-Pilawa, *Crooked Paths*, 78–81.

10. Richardson, *West from Appomattox*, 3–4; Andrew F. Lang, *In the Wake of War: Military Occupation, Emancipation, and Civil War America* (Baton Rouge: Louisiana State University Press, 2017), 222–23.

11. Stockwell, *Interrupted Odyssey*, 55–57; "Report to the President of the Indian Peace Commission, January 7, 1868," *Annual Report of the Commissioner of Indian Affairs for the Year 1868* (Washington, DC: Government Printing Office, 1868), 26–50.

12. Stockwell, *Interrupted Odyssey*, 73; Robert Wooster, *The Military and United States Indian Policy, 1865–1903*. (Lincoln: University of Nebraska Press, 1988), 81–83; See also John F. Marszalek, *Sherman: A Soldier's Passion for Order* (Carbondale: Southern Illinois University, 1993), 377–83.

13. Genetin-Pilawa, *Crooked Paths*, 25; See also Francis Paul Prucha, *American Indian Treaties: The History of a Political Anomaly* (Berkeley: University of California Press, 1994), 305–10; Speech, *New York Times*, January 26, 1870; Mark Wahlgren Summers, *The Ordeal of the Reunion: A New History of Reconstruction* (Chapel Hill: University of North Carolina Press, 2014) 181–183.

14. Genetin-Pilawa, 46–49; Armstrong, *Warrior in Two Camps*, 16–18, 25–31.

15. USG Message to Congress, January 30, 1871, *The Papers of Ulysses S. Grant Digital Edition*. Charlottesville: University of Virginia Press, Rotunda, 2018. Vol. 21: November 1, 1870–May 31, 1871. http://rotunda.upress.virginia.edu. Bracketed words are insertions to the document not in Grant's handwriting; Jean Edward Smith, *Grant* (New York: Simon and Schuster, 2001), 540; H. W. Brands, *The Man Who Saved the Union: Ulysses Grant in War and Peace* (New York: Anchor Books, 2012), 561.

16. Genetin-Pilawa, 88–89; Samuel Checote, et al. to USG, March 14, 1871, *The Papers of Ulysses S. Grant Digital Edition*. Charlottesville: University of Virginia Press, Rotunda, 2018. Vol. 21: November 1, 1870–May 31, 1871. http://rotunda.upress.virginia.edu.

17. Nag-ga-rash, et al. to USG, Columbus Delano, and Ely S. Parker, February 27, 1871; Nag-ga-rash, et al. to USG and Congress, December 8, 1871, *The Papers of Ulysses S. Grant Digital Edition*. Charlottesville: University of Virginia Press, Rotunda, 2018. Vol. 21: November 1, 1870–May 31, 1871. http://rotunda.upress.virginia.edu.

18. USG Executive Order, June 3, 1869, Record Group 130, Executive Orders and Proclamations, National Archives; Jacob Cox to William Welsh, July 5, 1869, *The Papers of Ulysses S. Grant Digital Edition*. Charlottesville: University of Virginia Press, Rotunda, 2018. Vol. 19: July 1, 1868–October 31, 1869. http://rotunda.upress.virginia.edu; Genetin-Pilawa, 92–93.

19. *New York Herald*, December 30, 1870; December 9, 1870.

20. Armstrong, *Warrior in Two Camps*, 154; Ely S. Parker to USG, June 29, 1871; Ely S. Parker to Columbus Delano, January 12, 1871, *The Papers of Ulysses S. Grant Digital Edition*. Charlottesville: University of Virginia Press, Rotunda, 2018. Vol. 22: June 1, 1871–January 31, 1872. http://rotunda.upress.virginia.edu; Stockwell, *Interrupted Odyssey*, 181–82; For an analysis on Quaker influence on Indian affairs see Jennifer Graber, "'If a War it May Be Called': The Peace Policy with American Indians," *Religion and American Culture: A Journal of Interpretation* 24, no. 1 (Winter 2014): 36–69.

21. Stockwell, *Interrupted Odyssey*, 98–99; Armstrong, *Warrior in Two Camps*, 154–55; Genetin-Pilawa, *Crooked Paths*, 100–101; *Affairs in the Indian Department*, House of Representatives, Report No. 39, 41st Congress, 3rd Session, Committee on Appropriations, February 25, 1871, 62–63, 106–7; Keller, Jr., *American Protestantism*, 83–85.

22. *Affairs in the Indian Department*, 62–65.

23. Stockwell, *Interrupted Odyssey*, 104; July 1, 1870, Charles Richard Williams, ed., *Diary and Letters of Rutherford B. Hayes: Nineteenth President of the United States, Vol. III, 1865–1881* (Columbus: Ohio State Archaeological and Historical Society, 1924), 112.

24. The transcripts totaled nearly three hundred pages of testimony and evidence, as well as an additional ten-page report of findings from the Committee. Generals Chipman and Parker also released a one-hundred-twenty-one-page version of the investigation testimony that featured Chipman's argument on behalf of Parker as well as evidence submitted on his behalf. See *Affairs in the Indian Department* no. 39. 41 (3), I-X, and *Investigations into Indian Affairs before the Committee on Appropriations of the House of Representatives, Argument of N. P. Chapman on Behalf of Hon. E. S. Parker, Commissioner of Indian Affairs* (Washington: Powell, Ginck, and Co., 1871).

25. Ely S. Parker to USG, June 29, 1871; USG to Ely S. Parker, July 13, 1871, *The Papers of Ulysses S. Grant Digital Edition*. Charlottesville: University of Virginia Press,

Rotunda, 2018. Vol. 22: June 1, 1871–January 31, 1872. http://rotunda.upress.virginia.edu; *Investigations into Indian Affairs*, 1–3.

26. See Loring Benson Priest, *Uncle Sam's Stepchildren: The Reformation of United States Indian Policy, 1865–1887* (New York: Octagon Books, 1969), 28–41; Norman J. Bender, *"New Hope for the Indians": The Grant Peace Policy and the Navajos in the 1870s* (Albuquerque: University of New Mexico Press, 1989), 57–59; Keller, Jr., *American Protestantism*, 84.

27. Ely S. Parker to Harriet Maxwell Converse (Gayaneshaoh), Ely Parker Papers, Newberry Library; Armstrong, *Warrior in Two Camps*, 174–78; C. Joseph Genetin-Pilawa, "Ely Parker and the Contentious Peace Policy," 197.

Chapter 5: Native Americans, Chinese Immigrants, and Civilization

1. *Report of the Secretary of the Interior*; being part of the message and documents communicated to the two Houses of Congress at the beginning of the second session of the Forty-third Congress, 1874, Vol. 1, (Washington, DC: Government Printing Office, 1874), v–vi; Brands, *The Man Who Saved the Union*, 564.

2. *Report of the Secretary of the Interior*, vi–vii; Delano noted that tribal sovereignty "has been several times recognized by the courts."

3. *Report of the Secretary of the Interior*, vi–vii.

4. *Report of the Secretary of the Interior*, vii–ix; Heather Cox Richardson, *The Death of Reconstruction: Race, Labor, and Politics in the Post-Civil War North, 1865–1901* (Cambridge, MA: Harvard University Press, 2001), 31; Richardson, *West from Appomattox*, 25–28; For more on the destruction of the bison herd and on Delano's resignation see C. Joseph Genetin-Pilawa, *Crooked Paths to Allotment: The Fight over Federal Indian Policy after the Civil War* (Chapel Hill: University of North Carolina Press, 2012), 107–8; Mary Stockwell, *Interrupted Odyssey: Ulysses S. Grant and the American Indians* (Carbondale: Southern Illinois University Press, 2018), 128–30, 169–70; Nelson, *Saving Yellowstone*, 104–10.

5. Alaina E. Roberts, *I've Been Here All the While: Black Freedom on Native Land* (Philadelphia: University of Pennsylvania Press, 2021), 4, 50.

6. Report of the Secretary of the Interior, viii; Intercourse Act, June 30, 1834, c h. 161, 4 Stat. 729; "Speech of the Honorable Columbus Delano delivered at Raleigh, North Carolina, July 24, 1872, 5. https://archive.org.

7. Report of the Secretary of the Interior, viii.

8. Interview with USG, *New York Times*, February 21, 1874; USG to Senate, January 13, 1875, *Journal of the Senate of the United States of America, Being the second session of the forty-third Congress, December 7, 1874* (Washington, DC: Government Printing Office, 1874), 104–5; USG to D. H. Chamberlain, July 26, 1876, John Y. Simon, ed., *The Papers of Ulysses S. Grant*, Vol. 27, *January 1–October 31, 1876*, (Carbondale: Southern Illinois University Press, 2005), 199.

9. *Report of the Secretary of the Interior*, ix; "Treaty of Guadalupe Hidalgo," Article VIII, National Archives and Records Administration, Milestone Documents, https://www.archives.gov.

10. Ulysses S. Grant, Draft Annual Message, December 7, 1874, John Y. Simon, ed, *The Papers of Ulysses S. Grant*, Vol. 25, *1874* (Carbondale: Southern Illinois University Press, 2003), 282.

11. Parker's bill to organize the Oklahoma territory met with resistance not only from fellow members of Congress but also from Native Americans in the Oklahoma territory; Congressional Record: Containing the Proceedings and Debates of the Forty-Third Congress, Second Session, Vol. III (Washington, DC: Government Printing Office, 1875), 19; Maty M. Stolberg, "Politician, Populist, Reformer: A Reexamination of 'Hanging Judge' Isaac C. Parker," *The Arkansas Historical Quarterly* 47, no. 1 (Spring 1988): 6–7 (3–28); Michael J. Broadhead, *Isaac C. Parker: Federal Justice on the Frontier* (Norman: University of Oklahoma Press, 2003), 22.

12. On July 1, 1862, Congress passed the Morrill Anti-Bigamy Act which banned polygamy in all territories of the United States, making special mention of Utah and the Latter-Day Saints. However, with the Civil War underway, enforcement of the law remained a low priority. See Laurel Thatcher Ulrich, *A House Full of Females: Plural Marriage and Women's Rights in Early Mormonism, 1835–1870* (New York: Alfred A. Knopf, 2017), xi, 385; United States Statutes at Large, 37th Congress, 2nd Session 501–2; USG Annual Message, December 7, 1875, The Papers of Ulysses S. Grant Digital Edition. Charlottesville: University of Virginia Press, Rotunda, 2018. Vol. 26: 1875. http://rotunda.upress.virginia.edu.

13. United States Statutes at Large, 501-502; This wasn't the first time the Grant administration admonished the importation of Chinese workers as a form of slavery. Hamilton Fish accused the British of supporting the "coolie" or Chinese immigrant trade, arguing that it was just another form of slavery, November 7, 1873, Hamilton Fish diary, Hamilton Fish papers, LC.

14. John R. Hadad, *America's First Adventure in China: Trade, Treaties, Opium, and Salvation* (Philadelphia: Temple University Press, 2013), 220–24; "Burlingame Treaty, July 28, 1868: Additional Article to the Treaty Between the United States and the Ta-Tsing Empire of the 18th of June 1858," https://iowaculture.gov; Manu Karuka, *Empire's Tracks: Indigenous Nations, Chinese Workers, and the Transcontinental Railroad* (Berkeley: University of California Press, 2019), 83.

15. See Beth Lew-Williams, *The Chinese Must Go: Violence, Exclusion, and the Making of the Alien in America* (Cambridge, MA: Harvard University Press, 2018), 44–46.

16. Henry G. Blasdel to USG, June 17, 1869, The Papers of Ulysses S. Grant Digital Edition. Charlottesville: University of Virginia Press, Rotunda, 2018. Vol. 19: July 1, 1868–October 31, 1869. http://rotunda.upress.virginia.edu.

17. *Chinese Emigration, The Cuba Commission: Report of the Commission Sent by China to Ascertain the Condition of Chinese Coolies in Cuba* (Shanghai: Imperial Maritime Customs Press, 1877), 8.

18. Andrew Gyory, *Closing the Gate: Race, Politics, and the Chinese Exclusion Act* (Chapel Hill: University of North Carolina, 1998), 54–59; George Anthony Peffer, *If They Don't Bring Their Women Here: Chinese Female Immigration before Exclusion* (Urbana: University of Illinois Press, 1999), 33–34; Amos T. Akerman to USG, July 29, 1870, The Papers of Ulysses S. Grant Digital Edition. Charlottesville: University of Virginia Press, Rotunda, 2018. Vol. 20: November 1, 1869–October 31, 1870. http://rotunda.upress.virginia.edu; For more on Irish Americans, whiteness, and anti-Chinese movements see David R. Roediger, *The Wages of Whiteness: Race and the Making of the American Working Class* (London: Verso, 2007), 189; Noel Ignatiev *How the Irish Became White* (New York: Routledge, 1995), 2–3; Matthew Frye Jacobson, *Whiteness of a Different Color: European Immigrants and the Alchemy of Race* (Cambridge, MA: Harvard University Press, 1998), 144–46; see also: David R. Roediger, *Working Toward Whiteness: How America's Immigrants Became White: The Strange Journey from Ellis Island to the Suburbs* (New York: Basic Books, 2018).

19. Annual Message, December 7, 1874, The Papers of Ulysses S. Grant Digital Edition. Charlottesville: University of Virginia Press, Rotunda, 2018. Vol. 25: 1874. http://rotunda.upress.virginia.edu; Peffer, *If They Don't Bring Their Women Here*, 11.

20. Peffer, *If They Don't Bring Their Women Here*, 33–37; See also: Mark Kanazawa, "Immigration, Exclusion, and Taxation: Anti-Chinese Legislation in Gold Rush California," Journal of Economic History 65, no. 3 (September 2005): 779–805; Daniel Immerwahr, *How to Hide an Empire: A History of the Greater United States* (New York: Farrar, Strauss, and Giroux, 2019), 53; Edward Lillie Pierce, ed., *Memoir and Letters of Charles Sumner:*, Vol. 4, *1860–1874* (Boston: Robert Brothers, 1893), 424–25; Beth Lew-Williams examines the 6.7 percent of Chinese Americans who, in 1900, had managed to be naturalized as American Citizens and become voters, in "Chinese Naturalization, Voting, and Other Impossible Acts" *Journal of the Civil War Era* 13, no. 4 (December 2023): 515–36.

21. Conversations with Li Hung-Chang, June 12–14, 1879, The Papers of Ulysses S. Grant Digital Edition. Charlottesville: University of Virginia Press, Rotunda, 2018. Vol. 29: October 1, 1878–September 30, 1880. http://rotunda.upress.virginia.edu; Matthew Frye Jacobson, *Barbarian Virtues: The United States Encounters Foreign Peoples at Home and Abroad, 1876–1917* (New York: Hill and Wang, 2000), 79–81.

22. Eric Foner noted that when the state of Louisiana paid White, Black, and Chinese laborers the same wage to fix a series of broken levees, the White laborers were angry that they were not making double the wages of the Black laborers. At the same time, the Black laborers were happy that everyone was making equal wages

and the Chinese laborers were excited to be making the same wages as Americans. Eric Foner, *Reconstruction: America's Unfinished Revolution, 1863–1877* (New York: Harper and Row, 1988), 362; *New National Era*, January 19, 1871; May 4, 1871; July 20, 1871; *Weekly Louisianian*, June 8, 1872; Halpern, "Solving the 'Labour Problem,'" 27–29; Mark Wahlgren Summers, *The Ordeal of the Reunion: A New History of Reconstruction* (Chapel Hill: University of North Carolina Press, 2014), 187–91.

23. *New National Era*, April 20, 1871; May 4, 1871; John Roy Lynch, "Political Status of the Colored Race," in Stephen Middleton, ed., *Black Congressmen during Reconstruction: A Documentary Sourcebook* (Westport, CT: Praeger, 2002), 189.

24. Douglass, 318; "Composite Nation" (Lecture in the Parker Fraternity Course), Boston, 1867, Folder 3 of 3, FD papers, LC; In this handwritten draft of the speech Douglass noted that he welcomed Chinese immigrants not only as laborers but as citizens of the United States.

25. *New National Era*, July 27, 1871; February 29, 1872; *Weekly Louisianian*, December 7, 1872; June 26, 1875.

26. For new scholarship on African American settlers on what was once Native American land see Tiya Myles, "Beyond a Boundary: Black Lives and the Settler-Native Divide," *William and Mary Quarterly* 76, no. 3 (July 2019): 417–26; Richardson, *West from Appomattox*, 45–47; *New National Era*, May 25, 1871; Charles J. McClain, *In Search of Equality: The Chinese Struggle Against Discrimination in Nineteenth-Century America* (Berkeley: University of California Press, 1994), 40–42; Tian Xu offers a look at gender and the law during this period and how California courts transformed the lives of Chinese women there, both for good and ill. Tian Xu, "Chinese Women and Habeas Corpus Hearings in California, 1857–1882" *Journal of the Civil War Era* 13, no. 4 (December 2023): 494–514.

27. Wooster, *The Military and United States Indian Policy*, 149–59; Karuka, *Empire's Tracks*, 138.

28. Karuka, *Empire's Tracks*, 138; USG Speech, May 28, 1872, John Y. Simon, ed., *The Papers of Ulysses S. Grant*, Vol. 23, February 1–December 31, 1872 (Carbondale: Southern Illinois University Press, 2000), 144–48.

29. Simon, *The Papers of Ulysses S. Grant*, 159–67; Felix R Brunot to USG, February 14, 1874; William W. Belknap to Columbus Delano, February 21, 1874, *The Papers of Ulysses S. Grant Digital Edition*. Charlottesville: University of Virginia Press, Rotunda, 2018. Vol. 25: 1874. http://rotunda.upress.virginia.edu; Karuka, *Empire's Tracks*, 75–79.

30. Charles, M. Robinson III, *A Good Year to Die: The Story of the Great Sioux War* (New York: Random House, 1995), 21–22; Peters Cozzens, *The Earth is Weeping: The Epic Story of the Indian Wars for the American West* (New York: Alfred A. Knopf, 2016), 218–20; Peter Cozzens, "Ulysses S. Grant Launched an Illegal War Against the Plains Indians, Then Lied About It," *Smithsonian Magazine* (November 2016),

https://www.smithsonianmag.com; Pekka Hämäläinen, *Lakota America: A New History of Indigenous Power* (New Haven, CT: Yale University Press, 2019), 352–54; Charles M. Robinson III, *The Diaries of John Gregory Bourke*, Vol. 1, *November 20, 1872-July 28, 1876* (Denton: University of North Texas Press, 2003), 272–73; Philip Sheridan to Alfred Terry, November 9, 1875, Letter Books, 1874, Dec. 10–1875, Dec. 31, Philip Henry Sheridan papers, LC; November 4–5, 1875, HF Diary, HF papers, LC.

31. Clinton Fisk to USG, January 1, 1876, *The Papers of Ulysses S. Grant Digital Edition*. Charlottesville: University of Virginia Press, Rotunda, 2018. Vol. 27: January 1–October 31, 1876. http://rotunda.upress.virginia.edu.

32. Michael A. Elliott, *Custerology: The Enduring Legacy of the Indian Wars and George Armstrong Custer* (Chicago: University of Chicago Press, 2007), 23–26; Senate Executive Document, July 7, 1876, 44-1-81; William T. Sherman to USG, July 8, 1876, *The Papers of Ulysses S. Grant Digital Edition*. Charlottesville: University of Virginia Press, Rotunda, 2018. Vol. 27: January 1–October 31, 1876. http://rotunda.upress.virginia.edu; USG to Congress, August 11, 1876, *The Papers of Ulysses S. Grant Digital Edition*. Charlottesville: University of Virginia Press, Rotunda, 2018. Vol. 27: January 1–October 31, 1876. https://rotunda.upress.virginia.edu.

Conclusion

1. Eric Foner argued correctly that the Thirteenth, Fourteenth, and Fifteenth Amendments "should be seen not simply as an alteration of an existing structure but as a 'second founding,' a 'constitutional revolution,' in the words of Republican leader Carl Schurz, that created a fundamentally new document with a new definition of both the status of blacks and the rights of all Americans." Eric Foner, *The Second Founding: How the Civil War and Reconstruction Remade the Constitution* (New York: W. W. Norton, 2019), xx.

2. *New National Era*, May 2, 1872.

3. Heather Cox Richardson, *The Death of Reconstruction* (Cambridge, MA: Harvard University Press, 2004), 129; USG to Edwards Pierrepont, September 13, 1875, *The Papers of Ulysses S. Grant Digital Edition*. Charlottesville: University of Virginia Press, Rotunda, 2018. Vol. 26: 1875. https://rotunda.upress.virginia.edu.

4. Simon, ed., *The Papers of Ulysses S. Grant*, Vol. 26, 320–21; This section on Revels is derived from an article published by the author in the *Journal of Mississippi History* cited in an earlier footnote. Semmes, "Hiram R. Revels, Ulysses S. Grant, Party Politics, and the Annexation of Santo Domingo," 62–64.

5. Richardson, *The Death of Reconstruction*, 154; Jenkins, "Black Voices in Reconstruction," 93.

6. *New National Era*, December 22, 1870.

7. See Nell Irvin Painter, *Exodusters: Black Migration to Kansas After Reconstruction* (New York: Alfred A. Knopf, 1977); Barbara Carol Behan, "Forgotten Heritage: African Americans in the Montana Territory, 1864–1869," *Journal of African*

American History 91, no. 1 (Winter 2006): 23–40; Eric Foner, *Forever Free: The Story of Emancipation & Reconstruction* (New York: Vintage Books, 2005), 183–85; Richardson, *The Death of Reconstruction*, 156–82; Dray, *Capitol Men*, 273–99; Blight, *Frederick Douglass*, 601–5; Todd Arrington, "Exodusters," Homestead National Monument of America, https://www.nps.gov.

8. Edwin L. Godkin, "Socialism in South Carolina," *The Nation* 18, no.459 (April 16, 1874): 247–48; Richardson, *The Death of Reconstruction*, 117; Philip M. Katz, *From Appomattox to Montmartre: Americans and the Paris Commune* (Cambridge, MA: Harvard University Press, 1998), 110–113; Charles W. Calhoun, *The Presidency of Ulysses S. Grant* (Lawrence: University Press of Kansas, 2017), 550–51; USG to Daniel H. Chamberlain, July 26, 1876, Simon, Ed., *The Papers of Ulysses S. Grant*, Vol. 27, *January 1-October 31, 1876* (Carbondale: Southern Illinois University, 2005), 200.

9. George Anthony Peffer, *If They Don't Bring Their Women Here: Chinese Female Immigration before Exclusion* (Urbana: University of Illinois Press 1999), 121.

10. Andrew F. Lang, *In the Wake of War: Military Occupation, Emancipation, and Civil War America* (Baton Rouge: Louisiana State University Press, 2017), 234–35; Summers, *Ordeal*, 5; David Blight, *Race and Reunion: The Civil War in American Memory* (Cambridge, MA: Belknap Press, 2001), 3; Caroline E. Janney, *Remembering the Civil War: Reunion and the Limits of Reconciliation* (Chapel Hill: University of North Carolina Press, 2013), 310–11.

11. USG Speech, September 29, 1875, Simon, ed. *The Papers of Ulysses S. Grant*, Vol. 26, *1875* (Carbondale: Southern Illinois University Press, 2003), 342–44.

BIBLIOGRAPHY

Manuscript Collections/Institutions

British Library, London, UK
Lord Ripon papers
William E. Gladstone papers

British Library (online)
The British Newspaper Archive: http://www.britishnewspaperarchive.co.uk/

Duke University, Durham, NC (online)
Broadsides and Ephemera Collection

Huntington Library, Pasadena, CA
Francis Lieber papers, 1815–1888

Library of Congress, Washington, DC
Nathaniel P. Banks papers, 1829–1911
Frederick Douglass papers, 1841–1967 (online), https://www.loc.gov/
Hamilton Fish papers, 1732–1914
Ulysses S. Grant papers, 1819–1974
Benjamin Moran journals, 1851–1875
Philip Henry Sheridan papers, 1853–1896 (online), https://www.loc.gov/
Elihu B. Washburne papers, 1829–1915 (online), https://www.loc.gov/

Mississippi State University, Starkville, MS
Orville E. Babcock papers
Ulysses S. Grant Presidential Library collection
Carl Schurz collection, 1857–2001, FVWCL.2017.050

Newberry Library, Chicago, IL
Orville E. Babcock papers, 1849–1947
Ely Parker papers (online)

University of Rochester, Rochester, NY

Ely Samuel Parker Papers, A.P24

Online Primary Sources

*Burlingame Treaty. July 28, 1868: Additional Article to the Treaty between the United States and the Ta-Tsing Empire of the 18th of June 1858.*https://iowaculture.gov.

Clinton v. Englebrecht. 80 U.S. 434 (1871). https://supreme.justia.com.

Foreign Relations of the United States. http://digital.library.wisc.edu.

Fourteenth Amendment to the United States Constitution. https://www.law.cornell.edu.

House of Commons, United Kingdom Parliament, "Spain—Case of Mary Lowell," Volume 199, March 14, 1870, https://hansard.parliament.uk.

Palner, Beverly, ed. *The Selected Letters of Charles Sumner,* 597–601; "Speech of Gerrit Smith," 3, https://idn.duke.edu.

The Papers of Ulysses S. Grant Digital Edition. Charlottesville: University of Virginia Press, Rotunda, 2018. https://rotunda.upress.virginia.edu.

Republican Party Platform, 1856. The American Presidency Project: UC Santa Barbara. https://www.presidency.ucsb.edu.

Speech of the Honorable Columbus Delano delivered at Raleigh, North Carolina, July 24, 1872, 5. https://archive.org.

Statutes at Large and Proclamations of the United States of America from December 1869 to March 1871 . . . Vol. XVI, 1131–32. Boston: Little Brown and Co, 1871. https://memory.loc.gov.

Sumner, Charles. "Naturalization Laws: No Discrimination on Account of Color. Remarks in Senate, July 2 and 4 1870," in *Charles Sumner: His Complete Works, Vol. XVIII,* edited by George F. Hoar, 144–68. Boston: Lee and Shepherd, 1900. http://www.gutenberg.org.

"Treaty of Guadalupe Hidalgo," Article VIII, National Archives and Records Administration, Milestone Documents, https://www.archives.gov.

Published Primary Sources

An Act concerning the Rights of American Citizen in foreign States, 15th Statutes at Large 223: 40th Congress, 2nd Session, Chapter 249, 1868, 223–24.

Affairs in the Indian Department, U.S. Congress. House. Report No. 39, 41st Congress, 3rd Session, Committee on Appropriations, February 25, 1871.

Alexander, Shawn Leigh, ed., *T. Thomas Fortune the Afro-American Agitator: A Collection of Writings, 1880–1928.* Gainesville: University Press of Florida, 2008.

The Argument at Geneva: Complete Collection of the Forensic Discussions on the Part of the United States and of Great Britain, Before the Tribunal of Arbitration Under the Treaty of Washington. New York: D. Appleton and Company, 1873.

Bancroft, Frederic. *Speeches, correspondence and political papers of Carl Schurz*, Volume II. New York: G. P. Putnam Sons, 1913.

Blassingame, John W. and John R. McKivigan, eds. *The Frederick Douglass Papers, Series One: Speeches, Debates, and Interviews*, Volume 4: 1864–80. New Haven, CT: Yale University Press, 1991.

Carleton, George W. *James Stephens, Chief Organizer of the Irish Republic: Embracing an Account of the Origin and Progress of the Fenian Brotherhood*. New York: Carleton Publisher, 1866.

Chinese Emigration, The Cuba Commission: Report of the Commission Sent by China to Ascertain the Condition of Chinese Coolies in Cuba. Shanghai: Imperial Maritime Customs Press, 1877.

Congressional Globe. Washington, DC: Government Printing Office, 1870.

Congressional Record. Washington, DC: Government Printing Office, 1869–1877.

Cox, Jacob D. "How Judge Hoar Ceased to be Attorney-General," *Atlantic Monthly* 76, August 1895: 162–73.

Cushing, Caleb. *The Treaty of Washington*. New York: Harper and Brothers, 1873.

Douglass, Frederick. *Life and Times of Frederick Douglass*. New York: Pathway Press, 1941.

Fabens, Joseph W. *Resources of Santo Domingo: From a Paper read before the American Geographical and Statistical Society of New York, 1862*. Washington, DC: Gibson Brothers, Printers, 1869.

Fitch, Suzanne Pullon, and Roseann M. Mandziuk, eds., *Sojourner Truth as Orator: Wit, Story, and Song*. Westport, CT: Greenwood Press, 1997.

Foner, Philip S., ed. *The Life and Writings of Frederick Douglass*: Volume IV, *Reconstruction and After*. New York: International Publishers, 1955.

Franklin, John Hope, ed. *Reminiscences of an Active Life: The Autobiography of John Roy Lynch*. Chicago: University of Chicago Press, 1970.

Godkin, Edwin L. "Socialism in South Carolina." *The Nation* 18, no.459 (April 16, 1874): 247–48.

Investigations into Indian Affairs before the Committee on Appropriations of the House of Representatives, Argument of N. P. Chapman on Behalf of Hon. E. S. Parker, Commissioner of Indian Affairs. Washington, DC: Powell, Ginck, and Co., 1871.

Journal of the Senate of the United States of America, Being the second session of the forty-third Congress, December 7, 1874. Washington, DC: Government Printing Office, 1874.

Langston, John Mercer. *From the Virginia Plantation to the National Capitol*. New York: Arno Press, 1969.

Mabee, Carlton and Susan Mabee Newhouse. *Sojourner Truth: Slave, Prophet, Legend*. New York: New York University Press, 1993.

Middleton, Stephen, ed. *Black Congressmen during Reconstruction: A Documentary Sourcebook*. Westport, CT: Praeger, 2002.

Pierce, Edward L. *Memoir and Letters of Charles Sumner*, Volume IV, *1860–1874*. Boston: Roberts Brothers, 1893.

Proceedings of the Fourth National Congress of the Fenian Brotherhood, Held in New York City, January 1866. New York: New York Printing Co., 1866.

Report of the Commission of inquiry to Santo Domingo, with the introductory message of the President, special reports made to the commission, state papers furnished by the Dominican government, and the statements of over seventy witnesses, Washington, DC: Government Printing Office, 1871.

Report of the Secretary of the Interior; being part of the message and documents communicated to the two Houses of Congress at the beginning of the second session of the Forty-third Congress, 1874, Volume 1. Washington, DC: Government Printing Office, 1874.

Report of the Select Committee Appointed to Investigate the Memorial of Davis Hatch, Senate Resolution 234, June 1870.

"Report to the President of the Indian Peace Commission, January 7, 1868," *Annual Report of the Commissioner of Indian Affairs for the Year 1868*. Washington, DC: Government Printing Office, 1868.

Robinson, Charles M., III. *The Diaries of John Gregory Bourke*, Volume 1: *November 20, 1872-July 28, 1876*. Denton: University of North Texas Press, 2003.

Simon, John Y., ed. *Papers of Ulysses S. Grant*. Carbondale: Southern Illinois University Press, 1967–2012.

Slavery in Cuba: A Report of the Proceedings of the Meeting held at Cooper Institute, New York City, December 13, 1872. New York: Powers, MacGowan, and Slipper Printers, 1872.

Sumner, Charles. *The Alabama Claims Speech of the Honourable Charles Sumner, Delivered in Executive Session of the United States Senate, On Tuesday, April 13th, 1869, Against the ratification of the Johnson-Clarendon Treaty for the Settlement of the Alabama and Other Claims*. London: Stevens Brothers, 1869.

Sumner, Charles. *Naboth's Vineyard: Speech of Hon. Charles Sumner, of Massachusetts, on the Proposed Annexation of "The Island of San Domingo," December 21, 1870*. Washington, DC: F. and J. Rives and George A. Bailey, 1870.

United States Statutes at Large, 37th Congress, 2nd Session 501–2.

Williams, Charles Richard, ed. *Diary and Letters of Rutherford B. Hayes: Nineteenth President of the United States*, Volume III, *1865–1881*. Columbus: Ohio State Archaeological and Historical Society, 1924.

Newspapers

United States

Alexandria Gazette and Virginia Advertiser
Daily Chronicle (Knoxville, TN)
Evening Star (Washington, DC)
Harper's Weekly
Nashville Union and American
National Republican (Washington, DC)
New Era (Washington, DC)
New National Era (Washington, DC)
Evening Post (New York)
New York Herald
The (NY) Sun
New York Times
The Republican (Maryville, TN)
Semi-Weekly Louisianian (New Orleans)
Weekly Louisianian (New Orleans)
Yorkville (SC) Enquirer

United Kingdom

Birmingham Daily Post
Gloucester Journal
Grantham Journal
Manchester Courier and Lancashire General Advertiser

Secondary Sources

Ankli, Robert E. "The Reciprocity Treaty of 1854." *The Canadian Journal of Economics* 4, no. 1 (February 1971): 1–20.

Armitage, David, et al., "Interchange: Nationalism and Internationalism in the Era of the Civil War." *The Journal of American History* 98, No. 2 (September 2011): 455–89.

Armstrong, William H. *Warrior in Two Camps: Ely S. Parker Union General and Seneca Chief.* Syracuse, NY: Syracuse University Press, 1978.

Arrington, Todd. "Exodusters." Homestead National Monument of America, website. https://www.nps.gov.

Athearn, Robert G. *In Search of Canaan: Black Migration to Kansas, 1879–80.* Lawrence: Regents Press of Kansas, 1978.

Baker, Bruce E. *What Reconstruction Meant: Historical Memory in the American South.* Charlottesville: University of Virginia Press, 2007.

Baptist, Edward E. *The Half Has Never Been Told: Slavery and the Making of American Capitalism.* New York: Basic Books, 2014.

Bayly, C. A. *The Birth of the Modern World, 1780–1914: Global Connections and Comparisons.* Malden, MA: Blackwell Publishing, 2004.

Behan, Barbara Carol. "Forgotten Heritage: African Americans in the Montana Territory, 1864–1869." *Journal of African American History* 91, no. 1 (Winter 2006): 23–40.

Beisner, Robert L. *From the Old Diplomacy to the New, 1865–1900.* Arlington Heights, IL: Harlan Davidson, 1986.

Bender, Norman J. *"New Hope for the Indians": The Grant Peace Policy and the Navajos in the 1870s.* Albuquerque: University of New Mexico Press, 1989.

Bender, Thomas. *A Nation Among Nations: America's Place in World History.* New York: Hill and Wang, 2006.

Bergad, Laird W. "Toward Puerto Rico's Grito de Lares: Coffee, Social Stratification, and Class Conflicts, 1828–1868." *The Hispanic American Historical Review* 60, no. 4 (November 1980): 617–42.

Billington, Ray Allen, ed. *Allan Nevins on History.* New York: Charles Scribner's Sons, 1975.

Blackbourn, David. *The Long Nineteenth Century: A History of Germany, 1780–1918.* New York: Oxford University Press, 1998.

Blight, David. *Race and Reunion: The Civil War in American Memory.* Cambridge, MA: Belknap Press, 2001.

Blight, David. *Frederick Douglass: Prophet of Freedom.* New York: Simon and Schuster, 2018.

Blight, David W., Gregory P. Downs, and Jim Downs. "Introduction." In *Beyond Freedom: Disrupting the History of Emancipation,* edited by David W. Blight and Jim Downs, 1–4. Athens: University of Georgia Press, 2017.

Bradford, Richard H. *The Virginius Affair.* Boulder: Colorado Associated University Press, 1980.

Brands, H. W. *The Man Who Saved the Union: Ulysses Grant in War and Peace.* New York: Anchor Book, 2012.

Broadhead, Michael J. *Isaac C. Parker: Federal Justice on the Frontier.* Norman: University of Oklahoma Press, 2003.

Brown, Thomas N. *Irish-American Nationalism, 1870–1890.* Philadelphia: J. B. Lippincott Company, 1966.

Burge, Daniel J. *A Failed Empire: The Collapse of Manifest Destiny, 1845–1872.* Lincoln: University of Nebraska Press, 2022.

Calhoun, Charles W. *Conceiving a New Republic: The Republican Party and the Southern Question, 1865–1900.* Lawrence: University Press of Kansas, 2006.

Calhoun, Charles W. *From Bloody Shirt to Full Dinner Pail: The Transformation of Politics and Governance in the Gilded Age.* New York: Hill and Wang, 2010.

Calhoun, Charles W. *The Presidency of Ulysses S. Grant*. Lawrence: University Press of Kansas, 2017.

Campbell, Charles S. *The Transformation of American Foreign Relations, 1865–1900*. New York: Harper and Row Publishers, 1972.

Chernow, Ron. *Grant*. New York: Penguin Press, 2017.

Clayton, Lawrence A. "The Nicaragua Canal in the Nineteenth Century: Prelude to American Empire in the Caribbean." *Journal of Latin American Studies* 19, no. 2 (November 1987): 323–52.

Cook, Adrian. *The Alabama Claims: American Politics and Anglo-American Relations, 1865–1872*. Ithaca, NY: Cornell University Press, 1975.

Corning, A. Elwood. *Hamilton Fish*. New York: The Lanmere Publishing Co., 1918.

Cozzens, Peter. *The Earth is Weeping: The Epic Story of the Indian Wars for the American West*. New York: Alfred A. Knopf, 2016.

Cozzens, Peter. "Ulysses S. Grant Launched an Illegal War Against the Plains Indians, Then Lied About It." *Smithsonian Magazine*, November 2016. https://www.smithsonianmag.com.

Cumberland, Barlow. *The Fenian Raid of 1866 and Events on the Frontier*. Ottawa: Royal Society of Canada, 1911.

Davidson, Christina Cecelia. "Black Protestants in a Catholic Land: The AME Church in the Dominican Republic, 1899–1916." *New West Indian Guide* 89, no. 3/4 (2015): 258–88.

Davidson, Christina Cecelia. "Disruptive Silences: The AME Church and Dominican-Haitian Relations." *Journal of Africana Religions* 5, no. 1 (2017): 1–25.

Davis, J. C. Bancroft. *Mr. Fish and the Alabama Claims: A Chapter in Diplomatic History*. Boston: Houghton, Mifflin and Co., 1893.

Dean, Adam Wesley. *An Agrarian Republic: Farming, Antislavery Politics, and Nature Parks in the Civil War Era*. Chapel Hill: University of North Carolina Press, 2015.

Delaney, Norman C. *John McIntosh Kell of the Raider Alabama*. Tuscaloosa: University of Alabama Press, 1973.

Diamond, Jeff. "African American Attitudes toward United States Immigration Policy." *The International Migration Review* 32, no. 2 (Summer 1998): 451–70.

Dierks, Konstantin, Juan Pablo Scarfi, et al. "Forum: The Monroe Doctrine at 200." *Diplomatic History* 47, no. 5 (November 2023): 731–870.

Donald, David. *Charles Sumner*. New York: De Capo Press, 1996.

Donald, David. *Charles Sumner and the Rights of Man*. New York: Random House, 1970.

Downs, Gregory P. *Declarations of Dependence: The Long Reconstruction of Popular Politics in the South, 1861–1908*. Chapel Hill: University of North Carolina Press, 2011.

Downs, Gregory P., and Kate Masur, eds. *The World the Civil War Made*. Chapel Hill: University of North Carolina Press, 2015.

Downs, Gregory P. *The Second American Revolution: The Civil War-Era Struggle over Cuba and the Rebirth of the American Republic*. Chapel Hill: University of North Carolina Press, 2019.

Doyle, Don H. *The Cause of All Nations: An International History of the American Civil War*. New York: Basic Books, 2015.

Doyle, Don H. *American Civil Wars: The United States, Latin America, Europe, and the Crisis of the 1860s*. Chapel Hill: University of North Carolina Press, 2017.

Dray, Philip. *Capitol Men: The Epic Story of Reconstruction Through the Lives of the First Black Congressmen*. Boston: Houghton Mifflin Company, 2008.

Du Bois, W. E. B. *Black Reconstruction in America, 1860–1880*. New York: The Free Press, 1992.

Dulles, Foster Rhea. *Prelude to World Power: American Diplomatic History, 1860–1900*. New York: The MacMillan Company, 1965.

DuVal, Kathleen. "Debating Identity, Sovereignty, and Civilization: The Arkansas Valley after the Louisiana Purchase." *Journal of the Early Republic* 26 (Spring 2006): 25–58.

Edwards, Laura F. *A Legal History of the Civil War and Reconstruction: A Nation of Rights*. New York: Cambridge University Press, 2015.

Egan, Timothy. *The Immortal Irishman: The Irish Revolutionary who became an American Hero*. Boston: Houghton Mifflin Harcourt, 2016.

Efford, Allison Clark. "The Arms Scandal of 1870–1872: Immigrant Liberal Republicans and America's Place in the World." In *Reconstruction in a Globalizing World*, edited by David Prior, 94–120. New York: Fordham University Press, 2018.

Eller, Anne. *We Dream Together: Dominican Independence, Haiti, and the Fight for Caribbean Freedom*. Durham, NC: Duke University Press, 2016.

Elliott, Michael A. *Custerology: The Enduring Legacy of the Indian Wars and George Armstrong Custer*. Chicago: University of Chicago Press, 2007.

Emberton, Carole. *Beyond Redemption: Race, Violence, and the American South after the Civil War*. Chicago: University of Chicago Press, 2013.

Embry, Jessie L., and Lois Kelley. "Polygamous and Monogamous Mormon Women: A Comparison." In *Women in Utah History: Paradigm or Paradox?*, edited by Patricia Lyn Scott, Linda Thatcher, Susan Allred Whetstone, 1–36. Logan: Utah State University Press, 2005.

Epps, Garrett. *Democracy Reborn: The Fourteenth Amendment and the Fight for Equal Rights in Post-Civil War America*. New York: Henry Holt and Company, 2006.

Ertman, Martha M. "Race Treason: The Untold Story of America's Ban on Polygamy." *Columbia Journal of Gender and Law* 19 (2010): 287–366.

Ferrer, Ada. *Cuba: An American History.* New York: Scribner, 2022.

Ferrer, Ada. *Insurgent Cuba: Race, Nation, and Revolution, 1868–1898.* Chapel Hill: The University of North Carolina, 1999.

Fitzgerald, Michael W. "Reconstruction Politics and the Politics of Reconstruction." In *Reconstructions: New Perspectives on the Postbellum United States*, edited by Thomas J. Brown, 91–116. New York: Oxford University Press, 2006.

Fitzgerald, Michael W. *Splendid Failure: Postwar Reconstruction in the American South.* Chicago: Ivan R. Dee, 2007.

Fleche, Andre. "The Last Filibuster: The Ten Years' War in Cuba and the Legacy of the American Civil War." In *Reconstruction and Empire: The Legacies of Abolition and Union Victory for an Imperial Age*, edited by David Prior, 27–53. New York: Fordham University Press, 2022.

Fluhman, J. Spencer. *"A Peculiar People": Anti-Mormonism and the Making of Religion in Nineteenth-Century America.* Chapel Hill: University of North Carolina Press, 2012.

Foner, Eric. *Forever Free: The Story of Emancipation & Reconstruction.* New York: Vintage Books, 2005.

Foner, Eric. *Free Soil, Free Labor, Free Men: The Ideology of the Republican Party Before the Civil War.* New York: Oxford University Press, 1995.

Foner, Eric. *Nothing but Freedom: Emancipation and Its Legacy.* Baton Rouge: Louisiana State University Press, 1983.

Foner, Eric. *Reconstruction: America's Unfinished Revolution, 1863–1877.* New York: Harper and Row, 1988.

Foner, Eric. *The Second Founding: How the Civil War and Reconstruction Remade the Constitution.* New York: W. W. Norton and Company, 2019.

Foreman, Amanda. *A World on Fire: Britain's Crucial Role in the American Civil War.* New York: Random House, 2012.

Fowler, Will. *Santa Anna of Mexico.* Lincoln: University of Nebraska Press, 2009.

Fox, Stephen. *Wolf of the Deep: Raphael Semmes and the Notorious Confederate Raider CSS* Alabama. New York: Alfred A. Knopf, 2007.

Franklin, John Hope. *George Washington Williams: A Biography.* Chicago: University of Chicago Press, 1985.

Franklin, John Hope. *Reconstruction after the Civil War*, 3rd. ed. Chicago: University of Chicago Press 2012.

French, Gregg. "Domestic Stability and Imperial Continuities: U.S.-Spanish Relations in the Reconstruction Era." In *Reconstruction and Empire: The Legacies of Abolition and Union Victory for an Imperial Age*, edited by David Prior, 79–104. New York: Fordham University Press, 2022.

Garvin, Tom. *Nationalist Revolutionaries in Ireland, 1858–1928.* Dublin, Ireland: Gill and Macmillan, 1987.

Genetin-Pilawa, C. Joseph. *Crooked Paths of Allotment: The Fight over Federal Indian Policy after the Civil War.* Chapel Hill: University of North Carolina Press, 2012.

Genetin-Pilawa, C. Joseph. "Ely Parker and the Contentious Peace Policy." *Western Historical Quarterly* 41, no. 2 (Summer 2010): 196–217.

Genetin-Pilawa, C. Joseph. "Ely S. Parker and the Paradox of Reconstruction Politics in Indian Country." In *The World the Civil War Made,* edited by Gregory P. Downs and Kate Masur, 183–205. Chapel Hill: University of North Carolina Press, 2015.

Geyer, Martin H., and Johannes Paulmann, eds. *The Mechanics of Internationalism: Culture Society, and Politics from the 1840s to the First World War.* London: Oxford University Press, 2001.

Gillette, William. *Retreat from Reconstruction, 1869–1879.* Baton Rouge: Louisiana State University Press, 1979.

Glade, William. "Latin America and the International Economy." In *The Cambridge History of Latin America,* Volume IV, *1870 to 1930,* edited by Leslie Bethell, 1–56. New York: Cambridge University Press, 1986.

Gleeson, David T. *The Irish in the South, 1815–1877.* Chapel Hill: University of North Carolina Press, 2001.

Gleeson, David T. *The Green and the Grey: The Irish in the Confederate States of America.* Chapel Hill: The University of North Carolina Press, 2015.

Gleeson, David T., and Simon Lewis, eds. *The Civil War as Global Conflict: Transnational Meanings of the American Civil War.* Columbia: University of South Carolina Press, 2014.

Godkin, Edwin L. "Socialism in South Carolina." *The Nation* 18, no.459 (April 16, 1874): 247–48.

Gott, Richard. *Cuba: A New History.* New Haven, CT: Yale University Press, 2004.

Graber, Jennifer. "'If a War it May Be Called': The Peace Policy with American Indians." *Religion and American Culture: A Journal of Interpretation* 24, no. 1 (Winter 2014): 36–69.

Green, Hilary. *Educational Reconstruction: African American Schools in the Urban South, 1865–1890.* New York: Fordham University Press, 2016.

Greenberg, Amy S. *Manifest Manhood and the Antebellum American Empire.* New York: Cambridge University Press, 2005.

Guelzo, Allen C. *Reconstruction: A Concise History.* New York: Oxford University Press, 2018.

Guyatt, Nicholas. "America's Conservatory: Race, Reconstruction, and the Santo Domingo Debate." *Journal of American History* 97, no. 4 (March 2011): 974–1000.

Gyory, Andrew. *Closing the Gate: Race, Politics, and the Chinese Exclusion Act.* Chapel Hill: University of North Carolina, 1998.

Hadad, John R. *America's First Adventure in China: Trade, Treaties, Opium, and Salvation*. Philadelphia: Temple University Press, 2013.

Hahn, Steven. *A Nation without Borders: The United States and Its World in an Age of Civil Wars, 1830–1910*. New York: Viking, 2016.

Hahn, Steven. "Slave Emancipation, Indian Peoples, and the Projects of a New American Nation-State." *Journal of the Civil War Era* 3, no. 3 (September 2013): 307–30.

Halpern, Rick. "Solving the 'Labour Problem': Race, Work and the State in the Sugar Industries of Louisiana and Natal, 1870–1910." *Journal of Southern African Studies* 30, no. 1 (March 2004): 19–40.

Hämäläinen, Peka. *Lakota America: A New History of Indigenous Power*. New Haven, CT: Yale University Press, 2019.

Hämäläinen, Peka. "Reconstructing the Great Plains: The Long Struggle for Sovereignty and Dominance in the Heart of the Continent." *Journal of the Civil War Era* 6, no. 4 (December 2016): 481–509.

Haskin, James. *Pinckney Benton Stewart Pinchback*. New York: Macmillan Publishing, 1973.

Hietala, Thomas R. *Manifest Design: American Exceptionalism and Empire*. Ithaca, NY: Cornell University Press, 2002.

Hixson, Walter L. *The Myth of American Diplomacy: National Identity and U.S. Foreign Policy*. New Haven, CT: Yale University Press, 2008.

Hogan, Michael J., and Thomas G. Paterson, eds. *Explaining the History of American Foreign Relations*. Cambridge: Cambridge University Press, 2004.

Hoganson, Kristin L. *Fighting for American Manhood: How Gender Politics Provoked the Spanish-American and Philippine-American Wars*. New Haven, CT: Yale University Press, 1998.

Horne, Gerald. *Race to Revolution: The United States and Cuba during Slavery and Jim Crow*. New York: Monthly Review Press, 2014.

Hudson, Linda S. *Mistress of Manifest Destiny: A Biography of Jane McManus Storm Cazneau, 1807–1878*. Austin: Texas State Historical Commission, 2001.

Ignatiev, Noel. *How the Irish Became White*. New York: Routledge, 1995.

Immerwahr, Daniel. *How to Hide an Empire: A History of the Greater United States*. New York: Farrar, Strauss, and Giroux, 2019.

Jacobson, Matthew Frye. *Barbarian Virtues: The United States Encounters Foreign Peoples at Home and Abroad, 1876–1917*. New York: Hill and Wang, 2000.

Jacobson, Matthew Frye. *Whiteness of a Different Color: European Immigrants and the Alchemy of Race*. Cambridge, MA: Harvard University Press, 1998.

Janney, Caroline E. *Remembering the Civil War: Reunion and the Limits of Reconciliation*. Chapel Hill: University of North Carolina Press, 2013.

Jenkins, Robert L. "Black Voices in Reconstruction: The Senate Careers of Hiram R. Revels and Blanche K. Bruce." PhD diss., Mississippi State University, 1975.

Jones, Howard. *Blue and Gray Diplomacy: A History of Union and Confederate Foreign Relations*. Chapel Hill: University of North Carolina Press, 2010.

Jones, Howard. *Union in Peril: The Crisis over British Intervention in the Civil War*. Chapel Hill: University of North Carolina Press, 1992.

Jones, Howard. *To the Webster-Ashburton Treaty: A Study in Anglo-American Relations, 1783–1843*. Chapel Hill: University of North Carolina Press, 1977.

Jones, Martha S. *Birthright Citizens: A History of Race and Rights in Antebellum America*. New York: Cambridge University Press, 2018.

Junco, José Alvarez, and Adrian Shubert, eds. *Spanish History Since 1808*. London: Arnold Publishers, 2000.

Jung, Moon-Ho. *Coolies and Cane: Race, Labor, and Sugar in the Age of Emancipation*. Baltimore, MD: Johns Hopkins University Press, 2006.

Kanazawa, Mark. "Immigration, Exclusion, and Taxation: Anti-Chinese Legislation in Gold Rush California." *Journal of Economic History* 65, no. 3 (September 2005): 779–805.

Kantrowitz, Stephen. "'Not Quite Constitutionalized:' The Meanings of 'Civilization' and the Limits of Native American Citizenship." In *The World the Civil War Made*, edited by Gregory P. Downs and Kate Masur, 75–105. Chapel Hill: University of North Carolina Press, 2015.

Karuka, Manu. *Empire's Tracks: Indigenous Nations, Chinese Workers, and the Transcontinental Railroad*. Berkeley: University of California Press, 2019.

Katz, Philip M. *From Appomattox to Montmartre: Americans and the Paris Commune*. Cambridge, MA: Harvard University Press, 1998.

Keller, Robert H., Jr. *American Protestantism and United States Indian Policy, 1869–1882*. Lincoln: University of Nebraska Press, 1983.

Kelly, Patrick J. "The European Revolutions of 1848 and the Transnational Turn in Civil War History." *Journal of the Civil War Era* 4, no. 3 (September 2014): 431–43.

Keneally, Thomas. *American Scoundrel: The Life of the Notorious Civil War General Dan Sickles*. New York: Random House, 2002.

Kester, Matthew. "Race, Religion, and Citizenship in Mormon Country: Native Hawaiians in Salt Lake City, 1869–1889." *Western Historical Quarterly* 40 (Spring 2009): 51–76.

Knight, Franklin W. *Slave Society in Cuba during the Nineteenth Century*. Madison: University of Wisconsin Press, 1970.

Knight, Melvin M. *The Americans in Santo Domingo*. New York: Vanguard Press, 1928.

LaFeber, Walter. *The Cambridge History of American Foreign Relations*, Volume II: *The American Search for Opportunity, 1865–1913*. New York: Cambridge University Press, 1993.

LaFeber, Walter. *The New Empire: An Interpretation of American Expansion, 1860–1898*. Ithaca, NY: Cornell University Press, 1998.

Lang, Andrew F. *In the Wake of War: Military Occupation, Emancipation, and Civil War America*. Baton Rouge: Louisiana State University Press, 2017.

Lang, Andrew F. *A Contest of Civilizations: Exposing the Crisis of American Exceptionalism in the Civil War Era*. Chapel Hill: University of North Carolina Press, 2021.

Lanza, Michael L. *Agrarianism and Reconstruction Politics: The Southern Homestead Act*. Baton Rouge: Louisiana State University Press, 1990.

Launius, Roger D. *Joseph Smith III: Pragmatic Prophet*. Urbana: University of Illinois Press, 1988.

Lawson, Elizabeth. *The Gentleman from Mississippi: Our First Negro Congressman, Hiram R. Revels*. New York: Elizabeth Lawson, 1960.

Lee, Susanna Michele. *Claiming the Union: Citizenship in the Post-Civil War South*. New York: Cambridge University Press, 2014.

Lew-Williams, Beth. *The Chinese Must Go: Violence, Exclusion, and the Making of the Alien in America*. Cambridge, MA: Harvard University Press, 2018.

Lew-Williams, Beth. "Chinese Naturalization, Voting, and Other Impossible Acts." *Journal of the Civil War Era* 13, no. 4 (December 2023): 515–36.

Link, William A., David Brown, Brian Ward, and Martyn Bone, eds. *Creating Citizenship in the Nineteenth-Century South*. Gainesville: University Press of Florida, 2013.

Love, Eric T. L. *Race over Empire: Racism and U.S. Imperialism, 1865–1900*. Chapel Hill: University of North Carolina Press, 2004.

Loveman, Brian. *No Higher Law: American Foreign Policy and the Western Hemisphere Since 1776*. Chapel Hill: University of North Carolina Press, 2010.

MacDonald, Cheryl. *Canada under Attack: Irish-American Veterans of the Civil War and their Fenian Campaign to Conquer Canada*. Toronto: James Lorimer, 2015.

Manning, Chandra. *Troubled Refuge: Struggling for Freedom in the Civil War*. New York: Vintage Books, 2016.

Mardock, Robert Winston. *The Reformers and the American Indian*. Columbia: University of Missouri Press, 1971.

Marquese, Rafael. "The Civil War in the United States and the Crisis of Slavery in Brazil." In *American Civil Wars: The United States, Latin America, Europe, and the Crisis of the 1860s*, edited by Don H. Doyle, 222–45. Chapel Hill: The University of North Carolina Press, 2017.

Marquese, Rafael. "The Legacies of the Second Slavery: The Cotton and Coffee Economies of the United States and Brazil during the Reconstruction Era, 1865–1904." In *United States Reconstruction across the Americas*, edited by William A. Link, 11–46. Gainesville: University Press of Florida, 2019.

Marszalek, John F. *Sherman: A Soldier's Passion for Order.* Carbondale: Southern Illinois University Press, 1993.

Marszalek, John F., David S. Nolen, and Louie P. Gallo, eds. *The Personal Memoirs of Ulysses S. Grant: The Complete Annotated Edition.* Cambridge, MA: The Belknap Press of the Harvard University Press, 2017.

May, Robert E. *The Southern Dream of a Caribbean Empire, 1854–1861.* Athens: University of Georgia Press, 1989.

McClain, Charles J. *In Search of Equality: The Chinese Struggle Against Discrimination in Nineteenth-Century America.* Berkeley: University of California Press, 1994.

McCullough, Stephen. *The Caribbean Policy of the Ulysses S. Grant Administration: Foreshadowing an Informal Empire.* Lanham, MD: Lexington Books, 2018.

McFeely, William S. *Frederick Douglass.* New York: W. W. Norton and Company, 1991.

McFeely, William S. *Grant.* New York: W. W. Norton and Company, 2002.

McKivigan, John R. "Stalwart Douglass: *Life and Times* as Political Manifesto." *Journal of African American History* 99, no. 1–2 (Winter-Spring 2014): 46–55.

McLaurin, Melton Alonza. *The Knights of Labor in the South.* Westport, CT: Greenwood Press, 1978.

McLean, Edith M. "Treaty of Washington, 1871." *Women's Canadian Historical Society of Ottawa* VI (1915). *Nineteenth Century Collections Online.* Web. Document URL: http://tinyurl.galegroup.com/tinyurl/RksN9.

Merli, Frank J. *The Alabama, British Neutrality, and the American Civil War.* Bloomington: Indiana University Press, 2004.

Merrill, Dennis, and Thomas G. Paterson, eds. *Major Problems in American Foreign Relations.* New York: Houghton Mifflin Company, 2006.

Merritt, Keri Leigh. *Masterless Men: Poor Whites and Slavery in the Antebellum South.* New York: Cambridge University Press, 2017.

Miller, Edward A., Jr. *Gullah Statesman: Robert Smalls from Slavery to Congress, 1839–1915.* Columbia: University of South Carolina Press, 1995.

Miller, Kerby A. *Emigrants and Exiles: Ireland and the Irish Exodus to North America.* New York: Oxford University Press, 1985.

Miller, Nathan. *The U.S. Navy: A History*, 3rd ed. Annapolis, MD: Naval Institute Press, 1997.

Morton, W. L. *The Critical Years: The Union of British North America, 1857–1873.* London: Oxford University Press, 1964.

Myers, Phillip E. *Dissolving Tensions: Rapprochement and Resolution in British-American-Canadian Relations in the Treaty of Washington Era, 1865–1914*. Kent, OH: Kent State University Press, 2015.

Myles, Tiya. "Beyond a Boundary: Black Lives and the Settler-Native Divide." *The William and Mary Quarterly* 76, no. 3 (July 2019): 417–26.

Nabors, Forrest A. *From Oligarchy to Republicanism: The Great Task of Reconstruction*. Columbia: University of Missouri Press, 2017.

Nelson, Megan Kate. *Saving Yellowstone: Exploration and Preservation in Reconstruction America*. New York: Scribner, 2022.

Nelson, William Javier. *Almost a Territory: America's Attempt to Annex the Dominican Republic*. Newark: University of Delaware Press, 1990.

Nevins, Allan. *Hamilton Fish: The Inner History of the Grant Administration*. New York: Dodd, Mead and Company, 1937.

Nye, Joseph S., Jr. *The Future of Power*. New York: Public Affairs, 2011.

Ofari, Earl. *"Let Your Motto Be Resistance": The Life and Thought of Henry Highland Garnet*. Boston: Beacon Press, 1972.

Ottens, Allen. *General John A. Rawlins: No Ordinary Man*. Bloomington: Indiana University Press, 2021.

Paddison, Joshua. *American Heathens: Religion, Race, and Reconstruction in California*. San Marino, CA: Huntington Library Press & University of California Press, 2012.

Painter, Nell Irvin. *Exodusters: Black Migration to Kansas after Reconstruction*. New York: Alfred A. Knopf, 1977.

Painter, Nell Irvin. *Sojourner Truth: A Life, A Symbol*. New York: W. W. Norton and Co., 1996.

Parry, Jonathan. *The Rise and Fall of Liberal Government in Victorian Britain*. New Haven, CT: Yale University Press, 1993.

Parsons, Elaine Frantz. *Ku-Klux: The Birth of the Klan during Reconstruction*. Chapel Hill: University of North Carolina Press, 2015.

Pearson, Lisa Madsen, and Carol Cornwall Madsen. "Innovation and Accommodation: The Legal Status of Women in Territorial Utah, 1850–1896." In *Women in Utah History: Paradigm or Paradox?* edited by Patricia Lyn Scott, Linda Thatcher, and Susan Allred Whetstone, 36–81. Logan: Utah State University Press, 2005.

Peffer, George Anthony. *If They Don't Bring Their Women Here: Chinese Female Immigration before Exclusion*. Urbana: University of Illinois Press 1999.

Pérez, Lisandro. *Sugar, Cigars, and Revolution: The Making of Cuban New York*. New York: New York University Press, 2018.

Pérez, Louis A., Jr. *Cuba and the United States: Ties of Singular Intimacy*. Athens: University of Georgia Press, 1997.

Perret, Geoffrey. *Ulysses S. Grant: Soldier and President*. New York: Random House, 1997.

Pinkett, Harold T. "Efforts to Annex Santo Domingo to the United States, 1866–1871." *Journal of Negro History* 26 (January 1941): 12–45.

Pitre, Merline. "Frederick Douglass and the Annexation of Santo Domingo." *The Journal of Negro History* 62, no. 4 (October 1977): 390–400.

Pitre, Merline. "Frederick Douglass and American Diplomacy in the Caribbean." *Journal of Black Studies* 13, no. 4 (June 1983): 457–75.

Plesur, Milton. *America's Outward Thrust: Approaches to Foreign Affairs, 1865–1890.* DeKalb, IL: Northern Illinois University Press, 1971.

Pons, Frank Moya. *The Dominican Republic: A National History.* Princeton, NJ: Markus Wiener Publishers, 1995.

Priest, Andrew. "Thinking about Empire: The Administration of Ulysses S. Grant, Spanish Colonialism and the Ten Years' War in Cuba." *Journal of American Studies* 48, no. 2 (May 2014): 541–58.

Priest, Loring Benson. *Uncle Sam's Stepchildren: The Reformation of United States Indian Policy, 1865–1887.* New York: Octagon Books, 1969.

Prior, David. *Between Freedom and Progress: The Lost World of Reconstruction Politics.* Baton Rouge: Louisiana State University Press, 2019.

Prior, David. "Civilization, Republic, Nation: Contested Keywords, Northern Republicans, and the Forgotten Reconstruction of Mormon Utah." *Civil War History* 56, no. 3 (September 2010): 283–310.

Prior, David, ed. *Reconstruction in a Globalizing World.* New York: Fordham University Press, 2018.

Prucha, Francis Paul. *American Indian Policy in Crisis: Christian Reformers and the Indian, 1865–1900.* Norman: University of Oklahoma Press, 1976.

Prucha, Francis Paul. *American Indian Treaties: The History of a Political Anomaly.* Berkeley: University of California Press, 1994.

Rable, George C. *But There Was No Peace: The Role of Violence in the Politics of Reconstruction.* Athens: University of Georgia Press, 1984.

Reeve, W. Paul. *Religion of a Different Color: Race and the Mormon Struggle for Whiteness.* New York: Oxford University Press, 2015.

Richardson, Caleb. "'The Failure of the Men to Come Up:' The Reinvention of Irish-American Nationalism." In *Reconstruction in a Globalizing World*, edited by David Prior, 121–44. New York: Fordham University Press, 2018.

Richardson, Heather Cox. *The Death of Reconstruction: Race, Labor, and Politics in the Post-Civil War North, 1865–1901.* Cambridge, MA: Harvard University Press, 2004.

Richardson, Heather Cox. "North and West of Reconstruction: Studies in Political Economy." In *Reconstructions: New Perspectives on the Postbellum United States*, edited by Thomas J. Brown, 66–90. New York: Oxford University Press, 2006.

Richardson, Heather Cox. *West from Appomattox: The Reconstruction of America after the Civil War.* New Haven, CT: Yale University Press, 2007.

Richardson, Heather Cox. *To Make Men Free: A History of the Republican Party.* New York: Basic Books, 2014.

Roediger, David R. *The Wages of Whiteness: Race and the Making of the American Working Class.* London: Verso, 2007.

Roediger, David R. *Working Toward Whiteness: How America's Immigrants Became White: The Strange Journey from Ellis Island to the Suburbs.* New York: Basic Books, 2018.

Roberts, Alaina E. *I've Been Here All the While: Black Freedom on Native Land.* Philadelphia: University of Pennsylvania Press, 2021.

Roberts, Timothy Mason. "Republican Citizenship in the post-Civil War South and French Algeria, 1865–1900." *American Nineteenth Century History* 19, no. 1 (March 2018): 81–104.

Robinson, Charles M., III. *A Good Year to Die: The Story of the Great Sioux War.* New York: Random House, 1995.

Rothera, Evan. *Civil Wars and Reconstructions in the Americas: The United States, Mexico, and Argentina, 1860–1880.* Baton Rouge: Louisiana State University Press, 2022.

Rudolph, Frederick. "Chinamen in Yankeedom: Anti-Unionism in Massachusetts in 1870." *The American Historical Review* 53, no. 1 (October 1947): 1–29.

Salyer, Lucy E. "Reconstructing the Immigrant: The Naturalization Act of 1870 in Global Perspective." *Journal of the Civil War Era* 11, no. 3 (September 2021): 388–95.

Salyer, Lucy E. *Under the Starry Flag: How a Band of Irish Americans Joined the Fenian Revolt and Sparked a Crisis over Citizenship.* Cambridge, MA: Belknap Press, 2018.

Samito, Christian G. *Becoming American Under Fire: Irish Americans, African Americans, and the Politics of Citizenship during the Civil War Era.* Ithaca, NY: Cornell University Press, 2009.

Schor, Joel. *Henry Highland Garnet: A Voice of Black Radicalism in the Nineteenth Century.* Westport, CT: Greenwood Press, 1977.

Scott, Rebecca J. *Degrees of Freedom: Louisiana and Cuba after Slavery.* Cambridge, MA: Harvard University Press, 2005.

Scott, Rebecca J. "Gradual Abolition and the Dynamics of Slave Emancipation in Cuba, 1868–86." *The Hispanic American Historical Review* 63, no. 3 (August 1983): 449–77.

Scott, Rebecca J. *Slave Emancipation in Cuba: The Transition to Free Labor, 1860–1899.* Pittsburgh, PA: University of Pittsburgh Press, 2000.

Sears, Stephen W. *George B. McClellan: The Young Napoleon.* New York: De Capo Press, 1988.

Semmes, Ryan P. "Hiram R. Revels, Ulysses S. Grant, Party Politics, and the Annexation of Santo Domingo." *Journal of Mississippi History* 80, no. 1 and 2 (Spring/Summer 2018): 49–65.

Semmes, Ryan P. "Counselor not Savior: Hamilton Fish and Foreign Policy Decision-Making during the Grant Administration." *American Nineteenth Century History* (December 2022): 255–70.

Senior, Hereward. *The Last Invasion of Canada: The Fenian Raids, 1866–1870.* Toronto: Dundurn Press, 1991.

Sexton, Jay. *Debtor Diplomacy: Finance and American Foreign Relations in the Civil War Era, 1837–1873.* New York: Oxford University Press, 2005.

Sexton, Jay. *The Monroe Doctrine: Empire and Nation in Nineteenth-Century America.* New York: Hill and Wang, 2011.

Sexton, Jay. "Steam Transport, Sovereignty, and Empire in North America, circa 1850–1854," *Journal of the Civil War Era* 7, no. 4, Crises of Sovereignty in the 1860s: A Special Issue (December 2017): 620–47.

Sexton, Jay. "Toward a Synthesis of Foreign Relations in the Civil War Era, 1848–77." *American Nineteenth Century History* 5, no. 3 (Fall 2004): 50–73.

Sexton, Jay. "The United States, the Cuban Rebellion, and the Multilateral Initiative of 1875." *Diplomatic History* 30, no. 3 (June 2006): 335–65.

Sexton, Jay. "William H. Seward in the World." *Journal of the Civil War Era* 4, no. 3 (September 2014): 398–430.

Shannon, Richard. *The Crisis of Imperialism, 1865–1915.* London: Hart-Davis, MacGibbon, 1974.

Sheehan-Dean, Aaron. *The Calculus of Violence: How Americans Fought the Civil War.* Cambridge, MA: Harvard University Press, 2018.

Shippee, Lester Burrell. *Canadian American Relations, 1849–1874.* New Haven, CT: Yale University Press, 1939.

Simpson, Brooks D. *The Reconstruction Presidents.* Lawrence: University Press of Kansas, 1998.

Sinha, Manisha. *The Slave's Cause: A History of Abolition.* New Haven, CT: Yale University Press, 2016.

Slap, Andrew L. *The Doom of Reconstruction: The Liberal Republicans in the Civil War Era.* New York: Fordham University Press, 2006.

Smith, Jean Edward. *Grant.* New York: Simon and Schuster, 2001.

Smith, Mark M. "The Past as a Foreign Country: Reconstruction, Inside and Out." In *Reconstructions: New Perspectives on the Postbellum United States,* edited by Thomas J. Brown, 117–40. New York: Oxford University Press, 2006.

Smith, Mark M. *How Race Is Made: Slavery, Segregation, and the Senses.* Chapel Hill: University of North Carolina Press, 2006.

Smith, Stacey L. "Emancipating Peons, Excluding Coolies: Reconstructing Coercion in the American West." In *The World the Civil War Made,* edited by Gregory P. Downs and Kate Masur, 46–74. Chapel Hill: University of North Carolina, 2015.

Smith, Stacey L. "Beyond North and South: Putting the West in the Civil War and Reconstruction." *Journal of the Civil War Era* 6, no. 4 (December 2016): 566–91.

Smith, Theodore Clarke. "Expansion After the Civil War, 1865–1871." *Political Science Quarterly* 16 (September 1901): 412–36.

Snay, Mitchell. *Fenians, Freedmen, and Southern Whites: Race and Nationality in the Era of Reconstruction*. Baton Rouge: Louisiana State University Press, 2007.

Spencer, Warren F. *The Confederate Navy in Europe*. Tuscaloosa: University of Alabama Press, 1983.

Spencer, Warren F. *Raphael Semmes: The Philosophical Mariner*. Tuscaloosa: University of Alabama Press, 1997.

Stahr, Walter. *Seward: Lincoln's Indispensable Man*. New York: Simon and Schuster, 2012.

Stolberg, Maty M. "Politician, Populist, Reformer: A Reexamination of 'Hanging Judge' Isaac C. Parker." *The Arkansas Historical Quarterly* 47, no. 1 (Spring 1988): 3–28.

Stampp, Kenneth. *The Era of Reconstruction, 1865–1877*. New York: Alfred A. Knopf, 1966.

Stephanson, Anders. *Manifest Destiny: American Expansion and the Empire of Right*. New York: Hill and Wang, 1995.

Stockwell, Mary. *Interrupted Odyssey: Ulysses S. Grant and the American Indians*. Carbondale: Southern Illinois University Press, 2018.

Stokes, Eric. "Rural Revolt in the Great Rebellion of 1857 in India: A Study of the Saharanpur and Muzaffarnagar Districts." *Historical Journal* 12 (December 1969): 606–27.

Stuart, Reginald C. *United States Expansionism and British North America, 1775–1871*. Chapel Hill: University of North Carolina Press, 1988.

Summers, Mark Wahlgren. *A Dangerous Stir: Fear, Paranoia, and the Making of Reconstruction*. Chapel Hill: University of North Carolina Press, 2009.

Summers, Mark Wahlgren. *The Era of Good Stealings*. New York: Oxford University Press, 1993.

Summers, Mark Wahlgren. *The Ordeal of the Reunion: A New History of Reconstruction*. Chapel Hill: University of North Carolina Press, 2014.

Summers, Mark Wahlgren. *The Press Gang: Newspapers and Politics, 1865–1878*. Chapel Hill: University of North Carolina Press, 1994.

Tansill, Charles Callan. *The United States and Santo Domingo, 1798–1873*. Baltimore, MD: Johns Hopkins University Press, 1938.

Thompson, Julius E. "Hiram Rhodes Revels, 1827–1901: A Reappraisal." *The Journal of Negro History* 79, no. 3 (Summer 1994): 297–303.

Treudley, Mary. "The United States and Santo Domingo." *Journal of Race Development* 7 (July 1916): 83–145.

Tunnell, Ted. *Crucible of Reconstruction: War, Radicalism and Race in Louisiana, 1862–1877.* Baton Rouge: Louisiana State University Press, 1984.

Turner, John G. *Brigham Young: Pioneer Prophet.* Cambridge, MA: Belknap Press, 2012.

Ulrich, Laurel Thatcher. *A House Full of Females: Plural Marriage and Women's Rights in Early Mormonism, 1835–1870.* New York: Alfred A. Knopf, 2017.

Wang, Xi. *The Trial of Democracy: Black Suffrage and Northern Republicans, 1860–1910.* Athens: University of Georgia Press, 1997.

Waugh, Joan. *U. S. Grant: American Hero, American Myth.* Chapel Hill: University of North Carolina Press, 2009.

Welles, Sumner. *Naboth's Vineyard: The Dominican Republic, 1844–1924.* New York: Payson and Clarke, 1928.

Wessling, H. L. *The European Colonial Empires, 1815–1919.* Translated by Diane Webb. Harlow, England: Pearson Longman, 2004.

West, Elliott. *The Last Indian War: The Nez Pearce Story.* New York: Oxford University Press, 2009.

West, Elliott. "Reconstructing Race." *Western Historical Quarterly* 34 (Spring 2003): 7–26.

Weston, Rubin Francis. *Racism in U.S. Imperialism: The Influence of Racial Assumptions on American Foreign Policy, 1893–1946.* Columbia: University of South Carolina Press, 1972.

White, Richard. *The Republic for Which It Stands: The United States during Reconstruction and the Gilded Age, 1865–1896.* New York: Oxford University Press, 2017.

White, Ronald C. *American Ulysses: A Life of Ulysses S. Grant.* New York: Random House, 2016.

Whitner, Robert L. "Grant's Peace Policy on the Yakima Reservation, 1870–1882." In *The Western American Indian: Case Studies in Tribal History,* edited by Richard N. Ellis, 50–62. Lincoln: University of Nebraska Press, 1972.

Wilkerson, Isabel. "The Great Migration, 1914–1919." In *Four Hundred Souls: A Community History of African America, 1619–2019,* edited by Ibram X. Kendi and Keisha N. Blain, 278–82. New York: One World, 2021.

Wilkins, Christopher. "'They had heard of emancipation and the enfranchisement of their race': The African American Colonists of Samana, Reconstruction, and the State of Santo Domingo." In *The Civil War as Global Conflict: Transnational Meanings of the American Civil War,* edited by David T. Gleeson and Simon Lewis, 211–34. Columbia: University of South Carolina Press, 2014.

Williams, William Appleman. *The Tragedy of American Diplomacy.* New York: W. W. Norton and Company, 1982.

Wooster, Robert. *The Military and United States Indian Policy, 1865–1903*. New Haven, CT: Yale University Press, 1988.

Wynne, William H. *State Insolvency and Foreign Bond Holders: Selected Case Histories of Governmental Foreign Bond Defaults and Debt Readjustments*, Volume II. Washington, DC: Beard Books, 2000.

Xu, Tian. "Chinese Women and Habeas Corpus Hearings in California, 1857–1882." *Journal of the Civil War Era* 13, no. 4 (December 2023): 494–514.

Yingling, Charlton W. *Siblings of Soil: Dominicans and Haitians in the Age of Revolutions*. Austin: University of Texas Press, 2022.

Zakaria, Fareed. *From Wealth to Power: The Unusual Origins of America's World Role*. Princeton, NJ: Princeton University Press, 1998.

INDEX

abolitionism, 1, 4, 27, 40, 41, 59, 67, 75–76, 82, 85, 91–92, 95, 173n29
Adams, Charles Francis, 1, 32
Adams, Henry, 69
Adams, John, 69
Adams, John Quincy, 69
African Americans: 8, 25, 27, 31, 103, 108, 124, 153; antislavery activism, 75, 76; Chinese immigrant relations, 10–11, 13, 73–74, 133–34, 136–40; Christianity, 138, 139, 149; citizenship, 2, 3, 8, 9, 17, 31, 37, 50–51, 68, 104, 107, 121, 147; Grant Caribbean policy criticism, 10, 11; labor issues, 10, 54, 68, 73, 136–37, 150, 180–81n22; Native American relations, 74, 138, 139; political participation, 27, 50, 83, 84, 107; proposed Dominican Republic emigration, 30, 36, 51, 54–55, 59, 89, 95, 104, 136, 160n23, 166n7, 167–68n18; Republican Party support, 10, 11, 86–87, 147–49, 151; social equality, 27, 50; support for Grant, 86, 90, 91, 92, 147–48, 151–52; violence against, 68, 121, 128, 134, 139–40, 150; voting rights, 19, 84, 86, 107, 121, 147, 151; Westward migration, 17, 73–74, 97, 136, 139, 167n10; white racism, 67, 68, 104, 119, 149; *see also* Dominican Republic annexation proposal: African American criticism
Akerman, Amos T., 134
Alabama (Confederate cruiser) claims, 1, 18, 38–39, 42, 44, 45, 49, 56, 62, 65–67, 71, 74–75, 77, 94, 96, 97
Alaska, 26, 66
American Colonization Society, 55
American exceptionalism, 28
American idealism, 31, 68
American nationalism, 19, 90, 151
American republicanism: 68, 161n9, 161–62n10; African Americans, 32, 84, 104; Christianity, 54, 102; citizenship, 2, 31; civic virtue/civilizing virtue, 2, 97, 102, 110, 152; expansionism, 2, 8–9, 17, 20, 26, 35, 39, 46, 67, 83–84, 86, 97, 104, 147; immigrants, 132, 150–51; Native Americans, 7, 104, 107, 110, 113, 120, 147, 153; natural rights protection, 2, 32, 39, 51, 152
Ames, Adelbert, 148, 149
annexation: 18, 32, 37, 38, 66, 75, 88; *see also* Dominican Republic annexation proposal
Anti-Ku Klux Klan Acts. *See* Enforcement Acts
Arthur, Chester A., 136

Babcock, Orville E., 12, 87; Dominican Republic annexation proposal, 12, 33–35, 47–48, 54, 77–78, 85, 88, 95–96, 162n16; Hatch case, 78–79, 96; Senate investigation, 48, 78–79, 83–85, 91, 117; Sumner attacks, 83–84, 88, 94, 117, 173n21

Badeau, Adam, 69, 83
Baez, Buenaventura, 34–35, 36, 47–48, 54, 78–79, 96, 162n16
Bahamas, 62
Banks, Nathaniel, 27, 30
Bassett, Ebenezer Don Carlos, 107
Battle of Little Bighorn, 144
Beck, James, 115
Beecher, Henry Ward, 42
Belknap, William, 141, 142
Bendell, Herman, 107
biological racism, 82, 92
Black Hills, 122, 141–44
Blasdel, Henry G., 133
Bosler, James, 116, 117
Bourke, John G., 143
Boutwell, George S., 25, 69, 81, 94
Brazil, 20, 50, 58, 64
Brooks, Preston S., 94
Bureau of Indian Affairs (BIA), 102–3, 104, 107, 114, 117, 118, 127, 140
Burlingame Treaty (1868), 131–32, 133, 135–36, 140, 145
Burton, Allan, 87

Cabral, José María, 47, 79
Calhoun, Charles W., 95, 159n18
Cameron, J. Donald, 145
Canada, 6, 38, 52, 57, 65–66, 74–75
Carpenter, Matthew, 82
Catholicism, 37, 53–54, 89, 129, 152
Cazneau, William, 48, 78, 79, 96, 163n18
Chandler, Zachariah, 142, 144
Chase, Salmon P., 5
Checote, Samuel, 112
Cherokee Nation, 101, 110, 125
Cheyenne tribe, 141, 144–45
Chickasaw Nation, 101, 125
Chinese Exclusion Act (1882), 19, 21, 136
Chinese immigrants: 13, 139–40, 150, 181n26; alleged lack of civilization, 15, 74, 134, 152; citizenship, 73, 131, 134, 135, 138, 181n24; forced labor, 13, 133, 136, 179n13; free labor, 10, 150–51, 180–81n22; labor conflicts, 10–11, 73–74, 138–39; racism against, 121, 133–34, 135–36, 137–38; rights activism, 19, 132; sexual slavery, 18, 131, 132, 134–36, 151
Chipman, Norton, 115–16, 177n24
Chippewa tribe, 122
Choctaw Nation, 101, 125
Christianity: 58, 116, 131, 150; civilization, 7, 101, 102, 104, 114, 119, 138, 151; republicanism, 7, 102, 104, 121; *see also* African Americans: Christianity; American republicanism: Christianity; Native Americans: Christianity; Peace Policy: Christianity
citizenship: conceptions of, 3; naturalization, 6, 10, 11–12, 30, 38, 39, 45; Reconstruction, 13, 18; whiteness, 2, 3, 19–20; *see also* African Americans: citizenship; Fourteenth Amendment; Native Americans: citizenship
Civil Rights Act (1866), 3
Civil Rights Act (1874), 149
Clark, Peter H., 92
coffee, 41, 52, 58
Colfax massacre, 128
Colfax, Schuyler, 4, 128
Columbus, Christopher, 29
Comanche tribe, 141
Congressional Board of Indian Commissioners (BIC), 102, 113–18, 119, 140, 141
Conkling, Roscoe, 72
Converse, Harriet Maxwell, 119
Cowen, Benjamin R., 142
Cox, Jacob, 35, 106, 116

Creek Nation: 101, 110, 112; *see also* Checote, Samuel

Crook, George, 142, 143

Cuba: African American support for rebellion against Spain, 76, 86; annexation discussions, 37, 40–41, 43; economic/military significance of, 55–56, 58, 62; immigrants to US, 39, 40, 45, 53, 150; racism against, 37, 41; rebellion against Spain, 29, 39, 40, 41–42, 45–46, 65, 66, 67, 74; slavery, 1, 16, 19, 20, 29, 42, 50, 58, 62, 64, 65, 67, 71, 75–76, 133; US citizenship, 15, 16, 40, 44, 45, 74; US diplomatic relations, 16, 41–42, 43–45; US policy on rebellion against Spain, 18, 25–26, 28–29, 39–40, 42–45, 52, 66, 69–72, 75–77, 86, 151

Cuban Junta, 44, 45, 70, 71, 74–75, 171–72n10

Custer, George Armstrong, 142, 144–45

Dana, Charles A., 42

Davis, Garrett, 85

Davis, J. C. B., 44, 45

Davis, Noah, 72

Declaration of Independence, 8, 10

Delano, Columbus: Native Americans, 12–13, 112, 113, 114–15, 118, 122–30, 178n2; racism, 124, 126–27

Democratic Party: African Americans, 87, 89, 90, 148, 149; Chinese immigrants, 72, 73, 121, 132, 134–35, 139, 150; Dominican Republic annexation proposal, 83, 90, 92–93; European immigrants, 13, 72; citizenship expansion, 13, 30; racism, 30, 33, 85, 87, 89, 90, 121, 149, 153; violence/terror tactics, 148, 149, 150

Dominican nationalism, 37–38, 90

Dominican Republic annexation proposal: African American perspectives, 32, 86, 92–93, 97; racial makeup of DR, 33, 47; economic/military significance of, 55–58, 59, 61–65, 80; national debt, 29, 33, 47, 48, 63, 64; Samaná Bay lease, 36, 37, 48–49, 53, 60, 80, 87, 89, 91–92, 163n18; slavery, 29, 57–59, 82; US Senate ratification battle, 49, 59–60, 61, 65, 72, 77, 79–82, 83–85; 2, 8, 10, 12, 15–16, 20–21, 25–28, 30–38, 40–42, 45, 47–54, 69, 70–72, 77–97, 104, 109, 122, 149, 151, 156n11, 160n23, 160–61n3, 162n16, 166n7, 168–69n18; *see also* Babcock, Orville E.: Dominican Republic annexation proposal; Democratic Party: Dominican Republic annexation proposal; Douglass, Frederick: Dominican Republic annexation proposal; Fish, Hamilton: Dominican Republic annexation proposal; Orth, Goodlove: Dominican Republican annexation proposal; Republican Party: Dominican Republic annexation proposal; Schurz, Carl: Dominican Republic annexation proposal; Sumner, Charles: Dominican Republic annexation proposal

Douglass, Frederick, Jr., 87

Douglass, Frederick: 76, 86, 138; African American political participation, 84, 87, 88, 90, 173n29; Chinese immigration, 73, 138, 181n24; Cuban insurgency, 76, 86; Dominican Republic annexation proposal, 88–89, 91, 92, 97; *New National Era* ownership, 84, 87, 89; Republican Party support, 11, 86, 87, 147–48; support for Grant, 11, 76, 86, 87, 90–91

Douglass, Lewis, 87
Downs, Gregory P., 14
DuVal, Kathleen, 3

Edmund-Tucker Act (1887), 131
European colonialism, 16, 32, 36, 39, 41, 43
Expatriation Act (1868), 72

Fabens, Joseph W., 25–26, 29, 30, 48, 78, 96
Fifteenth Amendment, 9–10, 19, 31, 51, 90, 93, 104, 140, 147, 182n1
Fish, Hamilton: 1, 12, 16, 66, 144, 165n4, 170n1; *Alabama* claims, 39, 67, 71, 74, 77, 96; Cuban rebellion, 16, 37, 39–45, 67, 69–71, 74–77, 86, 91; Dominican Republic annexation proposal, 12, 25–26, 33–38, 47, 49, 52, 59, 60, 61, 65, 69, 77–78, 79–80, 83, 91–93, 168–69n18; Great Britain relations, 1, 38, 25, 38, 52, 66; Hatch case, 79; immigration, 72, 74, 179n13; no-transfer principle, 16, 160n22; racism, 27, 37, 41–42, 165n5; relations with Spain, 25, 43–44, 52; Sumner friendship, 80–82, 84–85, 94–95, 172n17
Fisk, Clinton, 144
Foner, Eric, 35, 180–81n22, 182n1
forced labor, 13, 58, 132, 151
Fort Laramie Treaty (1868), 141, 142
Fourteenth Amendment, 3, 8, 10, 19, 31, 51, 93, 104–105, 106, 108, 121–23, 140, 147, 182n1
France, 28, 29, 67, 68, 161n5
free labor: 17, 52, 58; African Americans, 2–3, 17, 28, 51; Chinese immigrants, 10–11, 132, 133, 150–51; Grant support for, 2, 9, 16, 19, 31, 39, 50, 54, 59, 61–62, 90, 138; Native Americans, 102, 120; Republican support for, 90, 124, 128
free soil-ism, 28, 124

Garnet, Henry Highland, 75, 76
Gautier, Don Manuel, 47, 48, 91–92
German immigrants, 13, 72
Germany, 60, 67
Gerolt, Friedrich von (Baron), 37
gold, 102, 142, 143, 144, 145
Grant, Hannah Simpson, 4
Grant, Jesse, 4
Grant, Julia, 49
Grant, Ulysses S.: 156–57n12, 160n22, 170n1; African American policies, 2, 6, 9–10, 11, 13, 14, 27, 30–31, 37, 54–55, 68, 76, 82, 86–89, 128, 136, 149–50, 151–52, 160n23; *Alabama* claims, 74–75, 96; Caribbean policy, 10, 11, 12, 14, 15–16, 21, 26, 39–46, 52, 53, 67–71, 74–75, 138, 165n4, 166n8; Chinese immigrants, 10–11, 15, 73, 132–36, 150–51, 179n13; Christianization push, 7, 53–54, 102, 121, 139; citizenship policy, 2, 3, 7–8, 11, 12–13, 15, 19, 31, 37, 72, 86, 101, 103–106, 118–20, 121–22, 127–28, 138–39, 151, 152–53; constitutional changes, 1, 9–10, 51, 152; diplomatic relations with Great Britain, 1, 18, 38–39, 46, 52, 56, 66, 74–75, 96; diplomatic relations with Spain, 39, 40, 44, 46, 52, 67, 70–71; Dominican Republic annexation proposal, 8–9, 15–17, 20, 25–27, 30–36, 47–64, 77–96, 104, 149, 151, 156n11, 160n23, 160–61n3, 166n7, 168–69n18; early life, 4, 5; immigration policy, 40; Native American policies, 3, 6–8, 9, 12–13, 21, 97, 101–20, 122–25, 127–31, 138–39, 140–45, 151; Reconstruction

policy, 10, 11, 13, 17–18, 20, 25, 35–36, 50–51, 54, 68, 86–87, 95, 97, 101–102, 147–49, 159n18; republicanism, 2, 7, 9, 16, 19, 26, 51, 65, 68, 84, 101, 138, 147; slavery opposition, 16, 19, 31–32, 41, 49, 50, 59, 76; Sumner relations, 29, 56–57, 59–60, 65, 77–78, 80–82, 85, 90–91, 93–95; US Army service, 5, 64, 105, 108; US citizens abroad, 8, 40, 71; westward expansionism, 15, 97, 104, 139; *see also* African Americans: support for Grant; Parker, Ely S.: Grant friendship; Peace Policy; Republican Party: relations with Grant; Sumner, Charles: Grant criticism

Grant Doctrine: 67, 68, 138; Caribbean expansionism, 9, 12, 15–16, 27, 30, 35, 50, 52, 65, 81, 86, 95, 97, 104, 122, 153; civilization, 9, 97; citizenship, 16–17, 19, 151; emancipation, 9, 16, 19, 64, 75–76, 131, 132; free labor, 19, 132; relationship to Reconstruction, 11, 51, 101, 152–53; republicanism, 9, 17, 35, 51, 64, 86, 104, 133, 147; US as freedom/democracy arbiter, 8, 10, 17, 50, 51, 95

Great Britain: 35, 39, 60, 46; influence in Caribbean, 39, 55, 56, 65–66; US diplomatic relations, 1, 6, 26, 38, 46, 52, 56–57, 62, 65–66, 93; see also *Alabama* (Confederate cruiser) claims; Fish, Hamilton: Great Britain relations

Great Migration, 17, 55, 150, 167n10
Great Sioux War, 142, 144
Greater Reconstruction, 14, 15
Greely, Horace, 87

Hale, John P., 25
Hamburg massacre (SC), 128, 150
Hatch, Davis, 78–79, 84, 96

Hayes, Rutherford B., 79, 117, 159n18
Hoar, Ebenezer R., 69, 70, 106
Homestead Act (1862), 124
homesteads/homesteading: 101, 122, 124–26, 129, 130; *see also* Homestead Act (1862); Southern Homestead Act (1866)
Howe, Gridley, 87
Howe, Timothy, 94
Hung-Chang, Li, 136

imperialism, 2, 16, 20, 26–27, 39, 41, 61, 86
Indian agencies, 103, 114
Indian Aid Association, 119
Indian Intercourse Act (1834), 126
Indian Peace Commission/Policy, 14, 108, 120, 151
Indian Rights Association, 119
Irish-Fenian raids/riots, 66, 69, 74, 75
Irish immigrants, 13, 38, 39, 40, 134

Jenkins, Robert, 149
Johnson, Andrew, 1, 4, 5, 38, 78
Johnson, Reverdy, 1, 25, 38–39
Johnson-Clarendon Convention, 38–39, 56, 57
Jones, Martha S., 3, 17

Kiowa tribe, 141
Know-Nothing party, 28, 54, 72, 134
Ku Klux Klan, 84, 85, 87, 134, 140, 150

Lakota Sioux Nation, 141, 142–43, 144–45
Lang, Andrew F., 2, 3, 161n5
Lawrence, William, 115
Lee, Robert E., 5
Lemus, José Morales, 44
Liberal Republicans, 32, 36–37, 87, 90, 148

Lieber, Francis, 72
Lincoln, Abraham, 1, 5, 159n18
L'Ouverture, Toussaint, 29
Love, Eric T. L., 80, 166n7, 168–69n18
Lynch, James, 84
Lynch, John R., 11, 84, 96–97, 137–38

Manifest Destiny, 59, 92
Mary Lowell (US ship), 25
Masur, Kate, 14
McKinley, William, 20, 96
Mexican American War, 4, 41, 64, 129
Mission tribe, 129
Modoc tribe, 141
Monroe Doctrine, 16, 32, 36, 49, 51–52, 58, 60, 63–64, 160–61n3
Monroe, James, 16, 32
Moran, Benjamin, 1
Mormonism: 128, 131, 152; *see also* polygamy; Young, Brigham
Morrill, Justice Smith, 170n1
Morrill, Lot M., 80
Morton, Oliver P., 85
Motley, John L., 93

Napoleon III, 28, 161n5
Native Americans: 19, 127, 139, 141, 143, 144, 152, 179n11; access to food & goods, 103, 141, 142, 143; and African Americans, 138–39; attempted "civilizing" of, 3, 7–8, 15, 21, 97, 102–104, 105, 110, 114, 120, 127–30, 151; Christianity, 101, 102, 104, 114, 119, 120; citizenship, 3, 6–8, 10, 13, 18, 101, 104–7, 110, 113, 118–25, 128–30, 139–40, 147, 151; cultures, 3–4, 8, 102–3, 105, 111–13, 114–15, 119; forced removals, 7, 17, 74, 102, 108, 125–26; Indian agencies, 103, 108, 109, 114, 117 ; land ownership, 101, 113, 121, 124, 125–26, 127, 129–30, 142–43; racism against, 3, 90, 113, 128, 138; reservations/territories, 9, 101, 104, 107, 111, 112, 113, 119, 120, 142, 151; sovereignty of, 7, 107, 110–12; taxation, 3, 106, 110, 122, 123; tribal governance, 111, 112, 119; violence against, 7, 13, 97, 103, 105, 108–109, 121, 126, 127–28, 140–41, 144–45; *see also* Bureau of Indian Affairs (BIA); Cheyenne tribe; Colfax massacre; Comanche tribe; Congressional Board of Indian Commissioners (BIC); Fort Laramie Treaty (1868); Great Sioux War; homesteads/homesteading: Native Americans; Indian Aid Association; Indian Intercourse Act (1834); Indian Rights Association; Kiowa tribe; Lakota Sioux Nation; Mission tribe; Modoc tribe; Office of Indian Affairs; Ottawa tribe; Peace Policy; Pueblo tribe; Red Cloud; Spotted Tail
Naturalization Act, 72
Nevins, Allan, 34–35, 156–57n12
Niblack, William Ellis, 30, 33
Nicaragua, 53, 166n8
Nye, James, 4, 94

Office of Indian Affairs (OIA), 114, 116
Okmulgee territory, 111–14, 117
Orth, Godlove, 27, 28, 29, 30
Ottawa tribe, 122

Page Act (1875): 19, 132, 135–36; *see also* Chinese Exclusion Acts
Page, Horace F., 135, 136
Panama, 5, 53
Panic of 1873, 142
Parker, Ely S.: assimilationism, 103, 106, 107, 110, 113; Bureau of Indian Affairs Commissioner, 7, 12, 102, 105–7, 108,

118, 119; Bureau of Indian Affairs transfer to War Department, 102, 103, 108–9; credibility, 12, 105–106; embrace of Western civilization, 12, 104, 110–11, 129; fraud allegations, 114, 115–19, 177n24; Grant friendship, 5, 12, 90, 104, 117, 118; Native citizenship, 13, 106, 113, 119–20, 122; Native cultures, 105, 110–11, 114, 120; Native governance, 107, 110, 111–12, 117, 119; potential Oklahoma statehood, 9, 179n11; racism against, 113, 116, 119

Parker, Isaac, 130

paternalism, 112, 126

patriotism, 51, 152

Peace Policy: 109, 121, 138, 147; assimilationism, 9, 19, 21, 120, 123; Christianity, 102, 114, 119, 120, 139; citizenship, 2, 3, 10, 12, 18, 102, 103, 104, 106, 120, 122–24, 139, 144, 145, 151, 153; civilizing notions, 12, 102, 104–5, 106, 107, 108, 109, 120, 139, 141, 145; land ownership, 101, 121; Native resistance to, 120, 121, 145; Oklahoma statehood, 9, 12, 104

Perry, Matthew, 47, 48

Perry, Raymond, 79, 83

Pierrepont, Edwards, 43

Pinchback, P. B. S., 11, 75, 76, 92

Polk, James K., 64

polygamy, 128, 130–31, 179n12

Prim, Juan, 41, 43

Protestantism: 43, 54, 89, 152; *see also* Catholicism; Christianity

Pueblo tribe, 129

Puerto Rico, 16, 20, 41, 43, 50, 65, 76, 133

racial reconciliation, 27, 68, 149

racism: 29–30, 68, 77, 82–83, 90, 92, 121; *see also* African Americans: white racism; biological racism; Chinese immigrants: racism against; Cuba: racism against; Delano, Columbus: racism; Democratic Party: racism; Fish, Hamilton: racism; Republican Party: racism; Schurz, Carl: racism; Sumner, Charles: racism

Radical Republicans, 30

railroads, 74, 102, 105, 137, 140, 150

Rawlins, John, 5, 44

Reconstruction Amendments. *See* Fifteenth Amendment; Fourteenth Amendment; Thirteenth Amendment

Reconstruction: citizenship, 10, 11, 13, 17, 18, 50, 103, 138, 147; contrasting scholarly views, 13, 14, 156–57n12; economic stability, 53, 63; exportation of, 15–16, 26–27, 32, 35–37, 49, 51, 55, 64, 82, 95, 97, 156n11; failures of, 11, 31, 68, 153, 159n18, 166n7; immigration, 13, 73, 133, 134, 138–40, 151; national reconciliation, 9, 13, 15, 83; Native Americans, 101–102, 123, 153; slavery, 13, 50, 58, 95, 125, 152; Southern white backlash against, 9, 33, 93, 148–49, 152, 153; stabilization of Union, 27, 37, 50, 53, 63, 90, 103; violence, 10, 84, 134, 149; voting rights, 50, 128; *see also* Greater Reconstruction

Red Cloud, 141, 142, 143

Republican Party: 1, 65, 66, 124; African Americans, 10–11, 15, 31, 33, 37, 51, 68, 86–87, 89, 107, 147–49, 151–52; Chinese immigrants, 121, 132, 133, 134, 135, 139, 150–51; Cuban immigrants, 39, 42, 71, 75–76, 150; Dominican Republic annexation proposal, 27, 31–32, 34–36, 79, 81–83, 89; European immigrants, 72, 131, 150; Native

Republican Party (*continued*)
Americans, 103, 105, 112, 129; racism, 9, 18, 30, 32, 33, 36, 49, 50, 68, 77, 105, 121, 139; Reconstruction, 2, 49, 60, 63, 83, 87, 90, 93, 138, 151–52, 182n1; relations with Grant, 2, 5, 8–9, 13, 60, 71, 78, 81–83, 85, 91–92; westward expansion, 35, 102, 112; *see also* Liberal Republicans
Revels, Hiram R., 11, 84–86, 91, 92, 148–49
Richardson, Heather Cox, 15, 18
Roberts, Alaina E., 125, 126
Roberts, Don M. Lopez, 25
Robeson, George M., 69, 70
Roosevelt, Theodore, 20, 96

Sackett, Delos B., 47, 48
Santana, Pedro, 36
Sargent, Aaron A., 115, 116
Schurz, Carl, 32, 36, 72, 79–80, 82–83, 87, 94, 182n1
Scottron, Samuel Raymond, 76
Seminole Nation, 101
Seneca tribe: 5, 7, 12, 102, 104, 105, 119; *see also* Parker, Ely S.
settler colonialism, 105, 108, 130
Seward, William Henry, 26, 38, 39
Sexton, Jay, 16, 160–61n3
Seymour, Horatio, 5
Sheridan, Phillip, 109, 141, 142–43
Sherman, John, 42
Sherman, William T., 37, 109, 141, 145
Sickles, Daniel, 40, 43
Siegel, Franz, 87, 90
slavery: eradication as US foreign policy, 9, 16, 18–19, 39–42, 49–52, 58–60, 62, 64–65, 95, 131–33, 136, 147, 151; in US South, 32, 37, 39, 64, 75, 108, 125; *see also* Chinese immigrants: sexual slavery

Smith, Edward P., 142
Smith, Gerrit, 47, 92
Smith, Somers, 47
Smith, Stacey L., 13
socialism, 32, 68
Southern Homestead Act (1866), 124
Spain: 26, 35; Cuban insurgency, 39, 40, 41–42, 43–46, 65, 67, 70–71; slavery, 39, 40, 41, 71, 76; US diplomatic relations, 52, 70
Spotted Tail, 141
Stanton, Edward, 49
sugar, 32, 41, 52, 58
Summers, Mark Wahlgreen, 13
Sumner, Charles: 8, 87, 97, 117; *Alabama* claims, 1, 39, 56–57, 66, 93–94; Babcock attacks, 88, 117, 173n21; Chinese immigration, 73, 135; Dominican Republic annexation proposal, 47, 59–60, 65, 77, 79–86, 88, 93, 96; Fish friendship, 79–80, 82, 94; Grant criticism, 65, 77–78, 81, 84–85, 89, 90–91, 93–95, 172n17; Haiti, 29, 86; naturalization process views, 73, 135; racism, 80, 82, 90, 92, 93; Senate Foreign Relations Committee chairmanship loss, 94–95, 96–97
Surratt, Mary, 1

Taylor, Nathaniel, 106
Taylor, Zachary, 4
Ten Years' War, 67
Terry, Alfred H., 143
Texas, 25, 37, 114, 141
Thayer, John M., 106
Thirteenth Amendment, 8, 10, 19, 51, 93, 108, 182n1
Thornton, Edward, 25, 66
tobacco, 58, 63
Treaty of Guadalupe Hildalgo (1848), 129

Treaty of Washington (1871), 93, 96
Trumbull, Lyman, 32
Truth, Sojourner, 11

US Army, 5, 7, 17, 33, 102–3, 108, 126, 140, 144
US Department of State, 37, 40, 44–45, 74, 78, 79, 96, 121; *see also* Fish, Hamilton
US Department of the Interior: 102, 103, 108–9, 113, 121, 122, 127, 129–30; *see also* Chandler, Zachariah; Cox, Jacob; Delano, Columbus; Parker, Ely S.
US Department of War, 102, 103, 108–9, 140, 144
US economic power, 18, 28–29
US Merchant Marine, 61–62, 64
US Navy: 43, 56; *see also* Robeson, George M.

Villiers, George William Frederick (Earl of Clarendon), 1, 38

Wade, Benjamin, 87
Washburne, Elihu B., 5
Welsh, William, 114, 115–16, 118, 119
West, Elliot, 14
white labor, 13, 132, 134
white supremacism: violence, 9, 11, 13, 17, 140, 156–57n12
White, Andrew, 87

xenophobia, 54, 72–73, 137

Young, Brigham, 131
Young, John Russell, 95